How to Do *Everything* with Your

Zune™

Rick Broida

New York   Chicago   San Francisco   Lisbon
London   Madrid   Mexico City   Milan   New Delhi
San Juan   Seoul   Singapore   Sydney   Toronto

The **McGraw·Hill** Companies

Cataloging-in-Publication Data is on file with the Library of Congress

McGraw-Hill books are available at special quantity discounts to use as premiums and sales promotions, or for use in corporate training programs. For more information, please write to the Director of Special Sales, Professional Publishing, McGraw-Hill, Two Penn Plaza, New York, NY 10121-2298. Or contact your local bookstore.

How to Do Everything with Your Zune™

234567890 DOC DOC 0198

ISBN-13: 978-0-07-149070-2
ISBN-10:   0-07-149070-1

Sponsoring Editor
Megg Morin

Editorial Supervisor
Jody McKenzie

Project Manager
Vasundhara Sawhney,
   International Typesetting
   and Composition

Acquisitions Coordinator
Carly Stapleton

Technical Editor
Jasmine France

Copy Editor
Lisa McCoy

Proofreader
Megha Ghai

Indexer
Broccoli Information
   Management

Production Supervisor
George Anderson

Composition
International Typesetting
   and Composition

Illustration
International Typesetting
   and Composition

Art Director, Cover
Jeff Weeks

Cover Designer
Pattie Lee

For James Kim

About the Author

Rick Broida has written about computers and technology for more than 15 years. A contributor to *Computer Shopper, Popular Science, Wired,* and numerous other publications, he specializes in mobile technology. In 1997, recognizing the unparalleled popularity of the Palm PDA and the need for a printed resource covering the platform, Rick founded *Handheld Computing.* He has written more than a dozen books, including *How to Do Everything with Your GPS* and six editions of the bestselling *How to Do Everything with Your Palm Handheld.* He writes the "Tech Savvy" column for Michigan's *Observer & Eccentric* newspapers and lives in Michigan with his wife and two children.

About the Technical Editor

Jasmine France is currently a full-time associate editor at CNET, an Internet-based media company that provides information on all things tech. Over the past four years, she has focused mainly on digital audio products, ranging from MP3 players to headphones to music software and services. Along with managing and editing contributions from other writers, Jasmine writes a variety of stories for the Web site. She currently lives in San Francisco, where she's a dedicated foodie.

Contents

Acknowledgments x
Introduction xi

PART I   **Get to Know Your Zune**

CHAPTER 1   **Introduction to Zune** **3**
              A Brief History of Portable Music Players 5
              What Zunes Do—And Don't Do 8
                   Music 8
                   Video 10
                   Photos 11
                   Radio 11
                   Podcasts 12
                   Audiobooks 13
                   File Storage 13
                   Sharing Music 14
              Zune vs. iPod 16
                   Zune, 1; iPod, 0 16
                   Zune, 0; iPod, 1 16
              Make Sure Your PC Meets the Zune Requirements 18
                   Operating System 18
                   Processor 18
                   RAM 18
                   Hard Drive 19
                   USB Port 19
              Unpacking and Charging Your Zune 21
                   Charging the Zune 21
              Identifying the Zune's Controls 24
                   Using the Control Pad 25
              Start Using Your Zune Right Away 28
                   Choose a Background Image 29
              Zune Resources 32

CHAPTER 2   **Set Up Your Zune** **35**

Installing the Zune Software 36

      Understanding Firmware 37

      Adding Media to the Zune Software 38

      Sign Up for a Zune Account 44

Connecting the Zune to Your PC 53

      Synchronize the Zune Automatically 53

      Synchronize the Zune Manually 55

      Work with "Guest" Synchronization 56

      Disconnecting Your Zune 57

CHAPTER 3   **Using the Zune** **59**

Use Your Zune 60

      Use Zune Controls 61

      Use the Music Menu 63

      Use the Videos Menu 74

      Use the Pictures Menu 75

      Use the Radio Menu 79

      Use the Community Menu 80

      Use the Settings Menu 80

CHAPTER 4   **Use the Zune Software** **85**

Use the Zune Software Interface 86

      Use the Navigation Pane 88

      Use the Details Pane 103

      Use the Search Bar 107

      Use the List Pane and Task Selectors 111

      Modify the Interface 114

Playing Music on Your PC 117

      Playing Local Music 118

      Playing Zune Marketplace Music 119

      Rating Songs 121

Stream Music from Your PC to Your Xbox 360 123

Burn CDs 125

      Burn an MP3 CD 128

PART II   **Pack Your Player**

CHAPTER 5   **Music** **131**

Get Music from Zune Marketplace 132

      Download Subscription Music 133

      Buy Songs from Zune Marketplace 137

Convert Songs from Other Online Services 143
    Wait a Second, I Thought the Zune Could Play
        AAC Files! 144
    Are There Any DRM-Free Alternatives? 145
Rip Songs from CDs 147
    Choose Where to Store Ripped Songs 147
    Choose an Audio Format 149
    Choose a Bit Rate 151
    Rip Your First CD 152
Rip Songs from Cassette Tapes 155
    Why Bother? 156
    What You Need 156
    Getting Started 157
Understanding Playlists 158
    Create a New Playlist 159
Use Song Tags and Album Art 166

CHAPTER 6   **Video** **167**
Understanding Video Formats 168
Copy DVDs to Your Zune 169
    Comparing Commercial Software 169
    Using a Free Solution 174
Watch TV Shows on Your Zune 178
    The Ultimate Source for TV Shows: Media Center PCs ... 178
Watch Other Videos on Your Zune 183
    Internet Downloads, Home Movies, and More 183
    Add Video Podcasts to Your Zune 185
    Download YouTube Videos 190
    Where to Find It 192

CHAPTER 7   **Pictures** **193**
Add Pictures to Your Zune 194
    Add Pictures from Outside the Zune Software 197
    Adjust Zune Photo Sizes and Resolutions 198
    Use the Zune Photo Library 199
View Pictures on Your Zune 200
    Use Picture Playback Options 201
    Play Music During a Slideshow 202
    Where to Find It 202

PART III	**Get More From Your Zune**	
CHAPTER 8	**FM Radio**	**205**
	Tune in FM Stations	207
	Add or Remove Station Presets	208
	Tune to Station Presets	208
	Use Radio Playback Controls	209
	Understand RBDS	209
	Use Your Zune with Your Car Stereo	210
CHAPTER 9	**Podcasts and Audiobooks**	**211**
	What's a Podcast?	212
	Find Podcasts	213
	Install iTunes	214
	Run iTunes	216
	Load Podcasts on Your Zune	217
	Play Podcasts on Your Zune	222
	Find Audiobooks for Your Zune	223
	Download Audiobooks from Audible.com	226
	Rip Audiobooks from CDs and Tapes	230
	Where to Find It	230
CHAPTER 10	**Share Music and More with Other Zunes**	**231**
	Enable Wireless Communication	233
	Set Your Online Status	234
	Find Other Zunes	234
	Share Songs and Pictures	236
	Sharing Limitations	238
	Receive and Play Songs and Photos	240
	Synchronize Received Media with Your PC	241
CHAPTER 11	**Zune Accessories**	**245**
	Choose a Case	246
	Apply a Skin	250
	Protect the Zune Screen	252
	Use Your Zune in Your Car	252
	Use Car Mounts for Zunes	253
	Connect the Zune to Your Stereo	254
	Connect the Zune to Your TV	255
	Choose Zune Speakers	258
	Choose Replacement Headphones	260
	Watch Video on a Virtual Screen	262
	Recharge Your Zune While Traveling	263
	Where to Find It	266

CHAPTER 12   **Hack and Upgrade Your Zune** **267**
    Read Books and Magazines on Your Zune 268
        Read Magazines with Perooz 269
        Read E-books 269
    Install a Larger Hard Drive 274
    Replace Your Zune's Battery 276
    Use Your Zune as an External Hard Drive 277
        Copy Files from Your Zune to Your PC 282
    Convert Recorded TV Shows for Zune Viewing 285
    Watch Divx Videos on Your Zune 285
    Find Other Zune Hacks 286
        Where to Find It. 288

CHAPTER 13   **Zune Problems and Solutions**. **289**
    Get Help Online 290
    Reset Your Zune. 295
    Update Your Zune's Firmware 295
    Maximize Battery Life 296
    Repair a Broken Zune 297
    Fix Your Songs 298
        Fix Volume Levels. 298
        Fix Metadata 301
        Fix Album Art 303
    Frequently Asked Questions. 306
        Where to Find It. 308

    Index **309**

Acknowledgments

This book had a tragic beginning. In November 2006, CNET Editor James Kim approached me to serve as technical editor for a book he was writing about the Zune. Because I'd worked with James for several years prior and was intimately familiar with the *How to Do Everything* series of which the book was to be a part, I readily agreed.

Just over a month later, I learned that James and his family were missing, having failed to arrive at a friend's house during a vacation road-trip. Over the course of a surreal, terrifying week, the story attracted national attention as search parties attempted to locate the Kims in the vast Oregon woods where they were last seen. Thankfully, James's wife and two daughters were found in good health. But James himself made the ultimate sacrifice in attempting to find rescue for his family.

Needless to say, it was with a heavy heart that I agreed to take over the writing of this book. I'd like to think James would approve, and I was particularly heartened when Jasmine France, one of his colleagues at CNET, agreed to come aboard as technical editor. Her fast and incisive work was absolutely indispensable in getting this book done.

I'd also like to thank everyone at McGraw-Hill who helped me along the way: Lisa McCoy, Carly Stapleton, Vasundhara Sawhney, and especially Megg Morin, who was faced with the painful task of replacing James as the lead writer.

Additional shout-outs to the vendors who supplied review samples, software, photos, and other helpful stuff: 22Moo's Jason Chan, Altec Lansing's Shana Meganck, Applian's Leslie Bee, Belkin's Jackie Romulo, Coding Workshop's Andy, DecalGirl's Amanda Peters, DLO's Sally Comollo, M2Solutions' Rob Weiss, PQDVD.com's Frank, Xilisoft's Irene Fuller, and everyone else.

Thanks also to the Microsoft folks who pitched in: Matt Jubelirer, Scott Erickson, James Boldman, Nabil Pike, Anne Paschal, and Sara Ball.

Finally, endless thanks to my wife and family for their support during the always-grueling book-writing process. I couldn't have done this without you.

Introduction

Easy is in the eye of the beholder. The Microsoft Zune may have one of the easiest interfaces of any portable media player on the market (Apple's iPod included), but there's a lot more to using it than just navigating the interface. You need to know how to get music off your CDs and onto the device. You need to discover other sources of music, like Zune Marketplace. You'll definitely want to learn how to copy DVDs and other videos to the device to take advantage of its big, beautiful screen. And don't forget all those hacks and accessories that can take the Zune experience to the next level.

And, lo, a book was born.

The Zune, of course, is Microsoft's answer to the Apple iPod—and a good answer at that. The device plays music and videos, displays photos, tunes in FM radio, and shares files wirelessly with other Zunes and via USB with Xbox 360s. The Zune software allows users to manage files on the player, rip audio CDs, and buy songs at the online Zune Marketplace. Subscribe to a Zune Pass, and gain unlimited access to Zune Marketplace's staggering library of songs, which, as of this writing, includes more than 3 million titles.

This book is all about getting the most from your Zune, whether it's using playlists to organize music or tricking the Zune software into converting the TV shows you recorded on your PC. (Watching TV on your Zune rocks, trust me.) In Part I, "Get to Know Your Zune," you'll learn the basics: setting up the player, connecting it to your PC, and getting started with the Zune software. Part II, "Pack Your Player," delves into music, videos, and photos, and how you'll move them from your PC to your Zune. Part III, "Get More From Your Zune," tackles everything from FM radio and podcasts to wireless music sharing and Zune accessories (some of which are truly outstanding—head to Chapter 11 if you can't wait).

It's worth noting that as I put the finishing touches on this book, rumors were swirling about new Zune models, changes to the Zune Marketplace, and the like. Have no fear: Virtually all the information in these pages will still apply when Microsoft inevitably unveils new Zunes and adds more content to Zune Marketplace. Of course, this is the Internet Age, which is why I've created a special blog (http://zunebook.wordpress.com) that will provide updates, corrections, and other Zune-related information. After all, you paid good money for this book (which I appreciate, by the way!), so it's only fair that you get the latest and greatest material. Check the blog from time to time for *How to Do Everything with Your Zune* updates.

In the meantime, I hope you enjoy the book! Go forth, learn a lot, and have fun. And feel free to contact me with any questions or comments you may have. I'll do my best to reply to everyone who writes, though I apologize in advance if I'm a bit slow (you wouldn't believe how much mail I get). Send your thoughts to zunebook@gmail.com.

Part I

Get to Know Your Zune

Chapter 1

Introduction to Zune

How to . . .

- Understand what a Zune can and can't do
- Compare Zune vs. iPod
- Make sure your PC meets the Zune requirements
- Unpack and charge your Zune
- Identify your Zune's controls
- Start using your Zune right away
- Use Zune resources

It's amazing what you can fit in your pocket nowadays.

Here's what I have in mine: 2,900 songs, 150 photos, several dozen podcasts, four feature-length movies, an entire season of *The Shield,* and an FM radio.

No, I'm not walking around in freakishly oversized pants (I gave those up in the '80s after my "MC Hammer" phase). Thanks to remarkable strides in consumer electronics, every item I just mentioned can be stored in a single pocket-size device: the Microsoft Zune. This amazing gadget plays music, movies, photos, and more. It also shares music like no other portable player, enabling you to wirelessly beam songs to other Zune owners and receive songs. It's more than just a jukebox in your pocket: It's a personal entertainment center.

In the pages and chapters to come, you'll learn the history of portable devices like the Zune; what separates the Zune from Apple's venerable iPod; and, of course, everything you need to know about using your Zune to the fullest.

A Brief History of Portable Music Players

Remember the Sony Walkman? It's hard to believe that the device that kicked off the portable-music revolution made its debut nearly 30 years ago. The almost-pocketable Walkman, which first went on sale in Japan in 1979, let listeners plug in their headphones and play cassette tapes anytime, anywhere. What a concept!

Throughout the '80s and into the '90s, portable cassette players like the Walkman grew smaller, more affordable, and downright ubiquitous. Needless to say, people loved the convenience of on-the-go music. But there were limitations, of course: A cassette tape could hold only about 90 minutes' worth of music, and if you wanted to bring along your tape collection, you needed a bulky, inconvenient tape case. Worst of all, if you wanted to play a certain song, you had to search for it by manually rewinding or fast-forwarding the tape.

Of course, the compact disc solved that problem, and it wasn't long before portable CD players hit the scene. But they were necessarily bigger than cassette players, and they still required you to travel with media. In fact, a CD could hold a maximum of 70 minutes of music—even less than a tape. That was progress?

Things really started to change in 1998 with the arrival of the Diamond Multimedia PMP300 (see Figure 1-1), the first mass-market digital audio player. The PMP300 had no mechanical parts to wear out or break down, and it relied entirely on digital media rather than on magnetic tape or digital disc. So where were the songs stored? In the device's internal "flash" memory. How did they get there? They were "ripped" from CDs, turned into digital bits and bytes—not much different from those used to store documents on your PC—and copied to the player.

The advantages of the digital audio player quickly became clear. Because they initially required no moving parts, they could be made much smaller than a cassette or CD player. Indeed, the PMP300 was barely larger than a stack of credit cards, and it could slip easily into a pocket. What's more, because the songs were

FIGURE 1-1   The Diamond Multimedia PMP300 was the first mass-market MP3 player. It paved the way for players like the Zune.

digital, you could skip to any one almost instantly. And perhaps best of all, you didn't have to bring along anything but the player: no tapes, no CDs, no media of any kind—just MP3s, the songs ripped from CDs and made digital.

The digital music revolution was underway. Just one problem: The first players had fairly limited storage capacity, meaning they lacked the memory to hold more than one or two albums' worth of music. In those days, flash memory was expensive, and the technology topped out at around 128 megabytes (MB).

Too bad they couldn't cram a hard drive in there.

Flash forward three short years to 2001, when the Apple iPod (among a handful of other players) did exactly that. Suddenly, you could carry not just a few dozen songs, but a thousand. In your pocket. Not bad.

Just What Is an MP3, Anyway?

You've probably heard the term "MP3" before, and many people describe the Zune generically as an "MP3 player" (even though it's much more than that). Just what does "MP3" mean? First things first: The "M" doesn't stand for music. The "P" doesn't stand for power or platinum or anything cool like that. And the "3" has nothing to do with triangles or Three Dog Night. MP3 is a simple, albeit catchy, abbreviation for a kind of compression technology, one that has become universally popular for sharing, downloading, and transporting songs. (Think of someone zapping a 45-rpm record and turning it into zeroes and ones.)

If you're really interested in the technical description, MP3 stands for MPEG audio layer 3. So what the heck is MPEG? It stands for Moving Picture Experts Group, a consortium of companies and organizations that develops compression, decompression, and processing standards for audio and video. So, all spelled out, those innocuous three characters become Moving Picture Experts Group audio layer 3.

Whew—glad that's out of the way. That's just about the most complicated aspect of MP3, and it's not even important that you remember it. Here's a more real-world explanation: an MP3 file is a song, usually taken from a CD, that's converted into an electronic format and compressed to become very small. It can then be played on your PC or portable music player, like, say, the Zune.

Of course, MP3 isn't the only digital audio format. Others include AAC and WMA, both of which can be played on the Zune. We'll talk more about these formats and how they're significant in later chapters.

Needless to say, the iPod took the world by storm, evolving over the years and spawning countless imitators. The Zune, let's face it, is one of those imitators, but it's a darn good one, and it deserves a place in the pantheon of portable digital players.

When you look at the Zune, it's easy to see the Walkman's legacy. The device shares its predecessor's rectangular shape, simple controls, and, of course, headphone jack. But this is not your father's Walkman. Let's learn more about it.

What Zunes Do—And Don't Do

You probably already have a pretty good idea what your Zune can do; otherwise, you wouldn't have bought it. Ah, but did you know that if you press the play button three times, turn in a circle, and yell "Mumba Wumba!", your Zune will dispense Pez candies? Okay, not really, but it can do more than you think. Let's take a closer look at the Zune's capabilities, both obvious and hidden.

Music

Music is not only the Zune's *raison d'etre*, but also its forté. It possesses a certain *je ne sais quoi*, music-wise. Okay, I've used up all my high-school French. But it goes without saying that most folks buy a Zune so they can listen to music, and it definitely excels in that department.

1

Where does this music come from, and how do you load it on your Zune? You'll find out in the chapters to come, but here's a quick overview:

■ Music comes from two primary sources: CDs and music-download services. You can "rip" songs from your CDs to a digital format that's compatible with the Zune, and you can download songs to your PC (and then to your Zune) from services like Zune Marketplace.

■ Microsoft's Zune software makes it possible to load songs (and other media) onto your player.

Once you've packed your Zune with tunes, you have total control over how you listen. You can shuffle-play every song in your library. You can listen to all the songs by a specific artist or in a specific genre. And you can use playlists to listen to whatever customized selection of songs you want. Find out more about these playback options in Chapter 3.

While you're listening to music, you can view the album art for each song. It's not quite the same as flipping through big ol' LP album covers and reading liner notes (you have to be at least 35 to remember that), but it's still pretty cool. Find out more in Chapter 5.

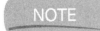

It may come as surprise—and a disappointment—to learn that the Zune doesn't work with the vast majority of online music services, including Apple iTunes, Napster, Rhapsody, and Yahoo! Music. If you want music downloads for your Zune, you'll have to get them from Zune Marketplace or one of the handful of services (like www.eMusic.com) that sells MP3-formatted files. More on that in Chapter 2.

Video

You didn't think the Zune's 3 inch color screen was just for showing off album art, did you? Silly reader. The Zune can also play video: TV shows, movies, music videos, YouTube clips, your home movies, and so on. However, you can't just copy a DVD to your Zune or use its wireless capabilities (see Chapter 9) to download music videos at the local Starbucks. Getting video onto your Zune requires some time and effort. It's not nearly as easy or convenient as it should be. That may change if Microsoft adds video downloads to Zune Marketplace, but as of this writing, video requires a fair amount of hoop-jumping. Find out all about it in Chapter 6.

In the meantime, let's talk about some different sources for Zune video and what's involved in working with them:

- **DVDs** Yep, you can "rip" movies from DVDs in much the same way that you rip music from CDs, but you'll need some third-party software and a fair amount of patience: The process can take hours.

- **Recorded TV shows** If you have a TiVo or Media Center PC, you can convert recorded TV shows to a Zune-compatible format. As with DVDs, there's some work involved, but for my money, there's nothing better than kicking back with a few episodes of *The Shield* while you're on a coast-to-coast flight. (I'd even go so far as to argue that TV shows are a better fit than movies for the Zune's relatively small screen.)

- **YouTube** Can't get enough Mentos-powered pop bottles and other YouTube clips? With the right software, you can "record" YouTube videos to your PC and then convert them for viewing on the Zune. The same process can work for other Internet video services, too, like Google Video and iFilm.

- **Home movies** Want to watch the kids' birthday party on your Zune? How about that goofy *Star Wars* fan movie you made? Pretty much anything you've recorded with your camcorder can be viewed on your Zune. It's just a matter of copying it to your PC and/or converting it to the proper format.

- **Video podcasts** Podcasts are audio programs distributed in MP3 format. Video podcasts are video programs distributed in, well, various video formats, most of which can sync straight to your Zune. There's some great stuff out there, from original cartoons to shows about technology to *NBC Nightly News*. Find out more in Chapter 8.

- **Most video files** Just about any video clips you have on your PC, regardless of where they came from, can be converted for viewing on the Zune.

Photos

Hey, is that a photo album in your pocket? It is if you're carrying a Zune. You can add digital photos to the Zune software just as easily as you can music and then sync those photos to your device for on-the-go viewing. And not just boring old one-at-a-time viewing: The Zune can run a slideshow, complete with your music playing in the background as a soundtrack. Find out everything you need to know about photos in Chapter 7.

Radio

One of the Zune's chief advantages over an iPod is its built-in FM radio tuner. (As of press time, not a single iPod model offered this feature.) Radio may sound a bit boring compared with your massive library of songs, but it's really a great extra. You can tune into NPR for news, local stations for your favorite morning programs, and so on. I find it particularly useful at the local gym, which broadcasts TV audio on FM frequencies.

The Zune supports the Radio Data System, meaning that for some stations, it can display station ID, artist, song name, and other info. This cool feature is a rare find in a standalone MP3 player. Find out more about Zune radio in Chapter 8.

Podcasts

Podcasts are audio programs distributed in MP3 format. What kinds of programs? I'll give you an idea by listing some of my favorites:

- *This American Life*
- *Battlestar Galactica* (in which show creator Ronald Moore discusses episodes of the series)
- NPR's *All Songs Considered*
- NPR's *Story of the Day*
- *60 Minutes*

Needless to say, you can get some pretty killer content in podcast form. Better still, most podcasts are free. Find out more in Chapter 9.

Audiobooks

It stands to reason that if you can listen to podcasts (most of which are spoken-word programs) on your Zune, you should be able to listen to audiobooks as well. (In the old days, we called them "books on tape," but obviously there's no tape involved with digital files.) Unfortunately, the Zune doesn't support the Audible.com service, which I consider to be the Web's best source for audiobook downloads. However, you can download compatible audiobooks from other sites. Find all the details in Chapter 9.

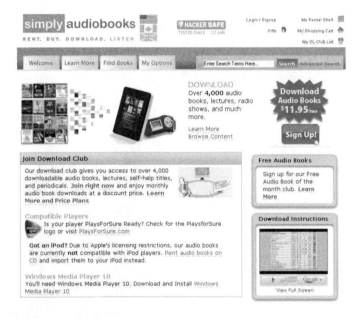

File Storage

How does your Zune manage to store such copious amounts of music, videos, photos, and the like? Simple: It has a miniature hard drive inside. The drive can hold 30 gigabytes' (GB) worth of data, which is mighty impressive when you consider that just a few years ago that was considered a normal amount of storage for an entire PC.

So if the Zune has a hard drive inside, shouldn't it be able to function like a portable hard drive? Shouldn't you be able to use it to move files from one PC to another or even to make quick backups of important data? Well, yes, you should—but you can't. At least, not without a little hacking. Find out how to enable this capability in Chapter 12.

Need more than 30 GB? At press time, Microsoft had yet to announce any Zune models with larger hard drives, though I'd say it's inevitable that they will. In the meantime, if you're willing to void your Zune's warranty, you can "hack" the device and install a larger drive—up to 120 GB, believe it or not. Read all about it in Chapter 12.

Sharing Music

Finally, we come to a Zune feature that is truly unique: music sharing. Your Zune can communicate wirelessly with other nearby Zunes (see Figure 1-2) to send and receive songs (photos, too). In other words, suppose you just discovered this great new band and want to share it with a friend: Just link your two Zunes and "squirt" the songs to him. (*Squirt* is the term Microsoft coined to describe the process of wirelessly transmitting a song from one Zune to another. What, was something

FIGURE 1-2 Zunes can wirelessly transmit songs to each other, but only when they're in close proximity.

wrong with beam? Or zap? Or even Zune-Zune? "Hey, check out this cool new Brendan Benson track—I'll Zune-Zune it to ya!")

There are a couple of catches associated with squirting. First, you have to be in relatively close proximity to other Zunes in order to share songs. Although the Zune itself includes the same kind of Wi-Fi radio used by computers to access the Internet, you can't share songs across a network. Maybe someday, but not yet. Second, any songs you receive on your Zune can be played just three times, after which they "time out." The idea behind squirting is to let you sample new music, not to actually give you songs to keep forever. If you like what you hear, you'll have to buy it or download it using your Zune Marketplace subscription (see Chapter 2). To find out more about sharing songs, see Chapter 10.

NOTE   *Yeah, the way Microsoft implemented song sharing is kind of weak. Hey, I never said the Zune was perfect. With any luck, future updates to the device will expand its wireless capabilities and make sharing more practical. In the meantime, don't expect to be doing a lot of squirting unless you know a bunch of other Zune owners and see them often.*

Sharing with an Xbox 360

The Zune is capable of another kind of sharing. If you own an Xbox 360 game console, you can connect your Zune and play your media library—music, photos, and videos—through the Xbox dashboard. In other words, you can enjoy hearing your music through your fancy home-theater speakers and seeing your photos on your big-screen TV. As for videos, well, they play at the Zune's relatively low resolution of 320 × 240 pixels, so they don't look great on TV, but it's still pretty neat.

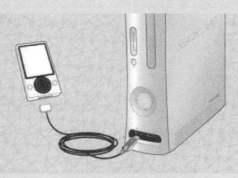

Zune vs. iPod

In the portable media player universe, iPod is king. For all its merits, the Zune received a relatively lukewarm reception from the press and users alike upon its launch in November 2006. The general consensus: "It's no iPod-killer." Even so, the Zune surpasses the iPod in several key areas. Let's take a look at some (as well as a few of its shortcomings) so you can wipe the smile off those smarmy iPod users' faces.

Zune, 1; iPod, 0

How does the Zune beat the iPod? Let me count the ways:

- **A bigger screen**   The Zune's 3 inch screen fairly well dwarfs the iPod's, making it a much better choice for viewing videos, photos, and even album art.

- **FM radio**   iPod users have long clamored for a built-in FM tuner, but Apple has yet to provide one. The Zune lets you listen to your favorite stations and even provides information like song and artist name.

- **Music subscription**   By subscribing to Zune Marketplace, you gain access to millions of songs for a nominal monthly fee. iPod users have no such option; they have to pay 99 cents per track. Once you've tried subscription downloads, you'll wonder how you lived without them. Find out more in Chapter 2.

- **Twist interface**   Although this is a highly subjective point, I'd argue that the Zune's interface beats the iPod's. It's prettier, for one thing, but it also enables faster selection of music-sorting options, like artist, album, and genre. The iPod retains the edge when it comes to sifting through long song lists, but overall, I find the Zune's interface to be superior.

- **Wi-Fi**   As discussed in the section "Sharing Music," Zune users can wirelessly beam songs and photos to each other. In fact, it's one of the only players in the world with this capability. Take that, iPod!

Zune, 0; iPod, 1

Okay, the Zune isn't perfect. Here are some areas that need improvement:

- **Games, Outlook synchronization, and other extras**   At present, the Zune doesn't venture beyond music, videos, and photos. With an iPod, you can play games, view your contacts and calendar, and plenty more. With any luck, it won't be long before the Zune catches up.

■ **Podcast support**   The Zune is perfectly capable of playing podcasts, but as of press time, the Zune software doesn't provide any way for you to access them (unlike Apple's iTunes software, which does a beautiful job of it). This is almost certain to change, but for now, you have to rely on third-party software. See Chapter 9 for details.

■ **Wi-Fi**   The Zune has built-in Wi-Fi, but all it can do is swap songs. How about wireless access to Zune Marketplace so we can buy or download songs on the run? How about Internet connectivity so we can swap songs with other Zune users around the world? And while you're at it, we wouldn't mind pulling down Really Simple Syndication (RSS) feeds, either. Of course, the iPod doesn't have Wi-Fi at all, nor any other wireless capabilities.

■ **Zune Marketplace**   Hey, Microsoft, where are the TV shows? Where are the movies? The music videos? The video podcasts? iTunes totally has you whipped in the video department. This, too, is sure to change, but for now, Zune Marketplace visitors have access to music and only music.

The Future of Zune

As I gaze into my crystal ball, I see big things in the Zune's future. Of course, they're all merely speculation on my part, as Microsoft won't say much about what's coming next. Still, I suspect that by the time this book reaches your hands (or shortly thereafter), you'll see at least some of these advances:

■ **Games**   Actually, Microsoft has already committed to producing games for the Zune, though not until 2008. And why not? The big screen and four-way controller make the Zune a natural for Bejeweled, Soduku, Ms. Pac Man, and other classic handheld games. Anyone for Pocket Halo?

■ **Movie downloads**   Microsoft has already partnered with movie-download service Vongo to bring movies to the Xbox 360, so it's a natural next step to add them to Zune Marketplace. And Vongo's all-you-can-eat subscription plan would give the Zune a huge advantage over iTunes, which charges $10 to $15 *per movie*.

■ **More models**   Microsoft will undoubtedly release a Zune with a larger hard drive, as 30 GB just doesn't cut it for some people. Also likely: a smaller, flash-memory–based Zune to challenge Apple's iPod nano.

Make Sure Your PC Meets the Zune Requirements

Hopefully, you didn't run out and buy a Zune without reviewing the system requirements first. Your PC needs a certain amount of horsepower to run the Zune software and establish a connection with the Zune itself. Most PCs manufactured within the last couple of years should be fine, but let's review the requirements and look at some upgrades you might need to consider.

Operating System

The Zune software requires one of the following operating systems:

■ Windows XP Home, Professional, or Tablet PC Edition and Service Pack 2 (www.microsoft.com/windowsxp/sp2/default.mspx)

■ Windows XP Media Center Edition 2005 with Update Rollup 2 (www .microsoft.com/windowsxp/mediacenter/upgrade/rollup2.mspx)

■ Windows Vista

If your computer has an older operating system, like Windows 98 or Windows 2000, you're out of luck—the software won't run. Can you upgrade to XP or Vista? Technically, yes, but your PC probably lacks sufficient processing power and memory to run either operating system at a reasonable speed. To really make the most of the Zune, you should have a computer with XP or Vista preloaded.

Processor

Microsoft says you need at least a 500-megahertz (MHz) processor for the Zune software or a 1.5-gigahertz (GHz) processor if you want to play video. However, you need more than 500 MHz to run Windows XP or Vista, so the 1.5-GHz requirement is really more accurate for most users. I wouldn't want to run the Zune software with anything slower.

RAM

Your PC should have at least 512 MB of random access memory (RAM). If it has only 256 MB (or less), you can usually upgrade by installing more memory modules. Jumping from, say, 256 MB to 512 MB shouldn't cost more than around $75, but make sure you get the right kind of memory for your computer. Visit sites like www.crucial.com and www.kingston.com to find compatible RAM based on your make and model.

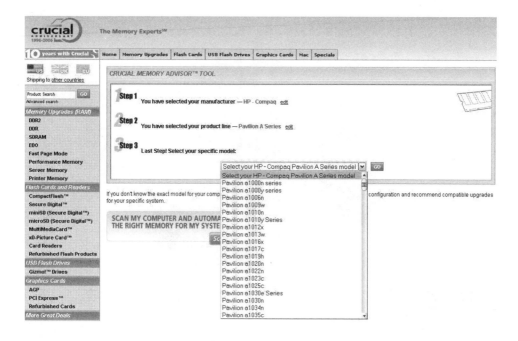

Hard Drive

Although the Zune software itself requires only 200 MB of space on your hard drive, chances are good that your music collection will occupy a lot more than that. My library of 2,900 songs, for instance, consumes about 12 GB. And if you take advantage of a Zune Marketplace subscription to download thousands of songs, you might need even more space than that. Of course, in these days, when 200-GB hard drives are considered average, even a 20-GB song collection is a drop in the bucket. And if you're running low on space, it's simple and relatively inexpensive to plug an external hard drive into your PC (see Figure 1-3) and add significantly more storage.

We'll talk about the Zune's hard drive in the upcoming section "Identifying the Zune's Controls."

USB Port

A Universal Serial Bus (USB) 2.0 port is mandatory for connecting your Zune to your PC. Okay, how do you know if your PC has USB 2.0 ports? If it was built within the last couple of years, you're probably in good shape. If it's older than that, check the manual. The Zune *will* work with older, slower USB 1.1 ports, but you won't be happy with the performance. Copying even a few gigabytes' worth of songs can take hours.

FIGURE 1-3 An external hard drive plugs into a USB port and adds extra storage space for your music library.

NOTE *Unfortunately, you can't identify the speed of a USB port just by looking at it. USB 1.1 and USB 2.0 ports look identical.*

So if your PC does have USB 1.1 ports, do you have to chuck it and buy a new computer just to use the Zune? Nope. It's easy and inexpensive to add USB 2.0 ports. Desktop owners can install a PCI card, like the Belkin Hi-Speed USB 2.0 five-port PCI card, while notebook owners need only plug in an expansion card, like the Belkin Hi-Speed USB 2.0 PC Card.

FIGURE 1-4   The Zune sync cable connects the player to your PC. It can also connect
to an Xbox 360 and various charger accessories.

The Zune relies on its included sync cable (see Figure 1-4) to connect to
your PC. This cable also charges your Zune's battery, so it's arguably the most
important accessory in the box. Don't lose it!

Unpacking and Charging Your Zune

I have to assume that your Zune is at least out of the box by now, if not already
connected to your PC. And, of course, I'm sure you followed the quick-start guide
to the letter. If not, well, have a look: It provides all the basic setup info you'll
need. However, let me run through a few points about charging the Zune.

 *Before you do anything else, you should charge your Zune. That means
connecting it to your PC* before *installing or running the Zune software.
Give the Zune four full hours for its initial charge.*

Charging the Zune

There are several ways to charge your Zune's battery, most of them involving the
sync cable:

- **Connect it to your PC** Your PC's USB port not only establishes a data
  connection with the Zune, it also charges the battery. Note, however, that

your PC must be on for this to work. If it's off (or in suspend mode, in the case of a notebook), it's not supplying any power to its USB ports.

- **Connect it to the optional AC adapter** Microsoft's Zune AC adapter is available alone or as part of the Zune Home A/V Pack.

- **Connect it to the car kit** Microsoft's Zune Car Pack includes a charger that plugs into the cigarette lighter.

- **Connect it to an Xbox 360** Just like a PC, the Xbox 360 charges the Zune when it's connected via USB. (The Xbox can also be used to play the stuff stored on your Zune. More on that in Chapter 4.) As with a PC, the Xbox must be on for this to work.

■ **Connect a third-party power source**   Products like the Belkin TunePower provide supplemental power for the Zune while charging its battery at the same time.

So how long does it take to fully charge the Zune's battery? Assuming the battery is fully drained, plan on waiting about 3 hours, assuming you're charging it via USB.

You can charge the battery faster by using an AC adapter. A USB port provides only a trickle of current, so it takes longer.

Want to find out how to maximize your Zune's battery life (that is, to make it play longer between charges)? Skip ahead to Chapter 12. Just be sure to come back, because there's lots of good stuff between here and there!

Identifying the Zune's Controls

There's not much to the Zune—and I mean that in a good way. The device has few controls and a simple interface, so you should have no trouble learning to use it. Let's take a peek at the hardware and talk about what everything does.

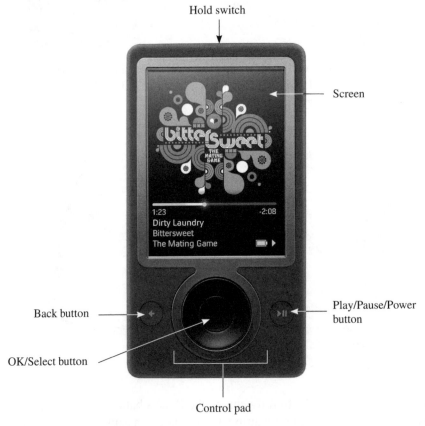

A few of these items might not be self-explanatory, so let's look a little closer:

■ **Hold switch** No, it's not for putting calls (or music) on hold. Instead, sliding the hold switch locks all the Zune's controls. Use this when the

Zune is off to keep it from accidentally turning on (like when it's riding in a pocket or bag) and draining the battery. Use it when the Zune is playing so you don't accidentally nudge the control pad and skip a track or crank up the volume.

■ **Headphone/AV jack** The same jack where you plug in your headphones is also used to output video. That's right: With an optional audio-video kit (see Chapter 10), you can connect the Zune to a TV or stereo and watch videos or play music.

■ **Back button** Press the Back button to return to the previous screen. Hold it down for 2 seconds to return to the main Zune menu (also known as the "top" menu).

■ **Play/Pause/Power button** Hold this button for 3 seconds to turn the Zune on or off. Otherwise, it serves as a play/pause toggle when you're listening to music, watching videos, etc.

The control pad requires a bit more explanation, which is why it gets its very own section—right after this one.

Using the Control Pad

Now let's take a closer look at the control pad, which can be pressed in four directions, and the button at its center. The pad and button actually take on different functions, depending on what you're doing with your Zune. For example, if you're listening to music, here's what the control pad does:

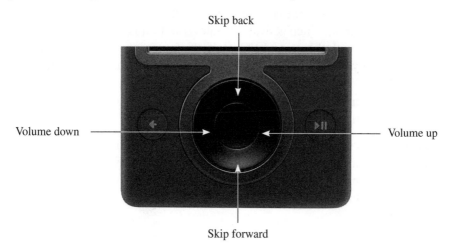

Skip back

Volume down

Volume up

Skip forward

Pretty straightforward, right? But if you're navigating the Zune's menus, the control pad is used for, well, navigation:

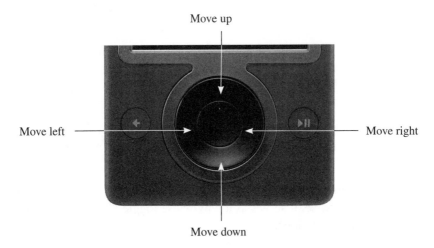

Move up

Move left —————— —————— Move right

Move down

If you've ever touched an iPod, which relies on a scroll wheel for navigation, your natural inclination will be to run your finger around the control pad—which, of course, will accomplish nothing. Think of it as a four-way clicker.

 *If you hold down the control pad in any direction, it will repeat the selected command. For instance, while scrolling through your song list, hold down the control pad up or down to quickly scroll through the list.*

There's a fifth element to the control pad: the button at its center. This is the "OK" or "Select" button, which activates whatever option is highlighted on the screen. However, as with the control pad itself, the button's function can change depending on what you're doing. Here are some OK/Select button scenarios:

- **Navigating menus** While navigating menus, pressing the button selects whatever option is highlighted.

- **Listening to music** While listening to music, pressing the button brings up a secondary screen, where you can rate the currently playing song, enable options like shuffle and repeat, and more. Find out more about these options in Chapter 3.

- **Watching videos**   While watching videos, pressing the button displays an information screen including the name of the video, the total run time, and a description (if available). Press it again to return to the video.

- **Viewing photos**   As with music, pressing the OK/Select button while viewing photos displays a secondary screen with various options—including one to set the current image as the background for the Zune interface. See "Choose a Background Image" later in this chapter for more information on that option; see Chapter 3 for more about the photo sub-menu.

- **Listening to radio**   The OK/Select button plays a major role in radio: Pressing it displays the station preset screen, where you can add, remove, or select a preset.

It's worth noting that in most of these scenarios, if you do nothing for a few seconds after pressing the OK/Select button, the Zune will return to the previous screen. Alternately, pressing the Back button will accomplish the same thing.

Believe it or not, that's just about everything you need to know about operating your Zune. I'll cover a few other aspects in greater detail in later chapters, but for now, you should have no trouble navigating the menus and performing basic operations.

 *Actually, there's one other important thing you should know about the control pad. See "Hey, What Happened to My Screen and Control Pad?" later in the chapter.*

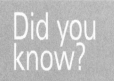 **The Zune's Secret Radio Antenna**

The Zune's earbud headphones do more than just pipe music to your ears: They also serve as an antenna for the FM radio. Without them, the device wouldn't be able to tune in any stations. Of course, you wouldn't be able to hear proof of that without the earbuds, but you'll just have to trust me on this.

Start Using Your Zune Right Away

Right out of the box, your Zune comes ready to rock and roll (both literally and figuratively). It has music to play, videos to watch, and even a few photos to view. In this section, you'll get a chance to dive into these areas and have some fun. Don't worry if you get a bit lost along the way; you'll learn the finer points of navigating the interface in Chapter 3.

Start by making sure your Zune is charged. Plug in the earphones, and then perform the following steps:

1. Turn on the Zune by pressing the Play/Pause button. It may take a few seconds for the device to start up.

2. Using the control pad to press up or down as needed, highlight Music, and press the OK/Select button.

3. Press left or right (your choice) on the control pad until Songs is highlighted. (What you're experiencing here is the Zune's "twist" interface, which navigates left and right in addition to up and down. Pretty cool, eh? More to come in Chapter 3.)

4. You can then press down on the control pad to select an individual song. However, choose the first highlighted option—Shuffle All—and press OK/Select. The music begins!

5. Too loud? Press the control pad down a few times; you'll notice an onscreen volume gauge appears temporarily. Not loud enough? I'm sure you can guess what to do: Press the control pad up.

6. Don't like the song that's playing? Press the control pad to the right to skip to the next one.

That's all there is to it! To return to the top-level menu and try something else, press the Back button several times or just hold it down for a few seconds.

Before you delve into photos and videos, read the sidebar, "Hey, What Happened to My Screen and Control Pad?" Because something *truly shocking* is about to happen!

Choose a Background Image

One of the other fun things you can do right away with your Zune is change the background image for the interface, much like selecting wallpaper for your PC. You can use any photo as your background, though for the purposes of this tutorial, let's work with one of the preloaded images. Here's how:

1. From the top menu, select Pictures.

2. Scroll down to Graffiti, and select it.

3. Scroll through the thumbnails until you reach the last photo, and then select it.

4. The photo appears in full-screen size. Press the OK/Select button, and then choose Apply As Background.

Hey, What Happened to My Screen and Control Pad?

Before you get started with photos and videos, you need to be aware of a rather unique Zune feature: The screen rotates when you view these items. It makes sense when you think about it. Movies and photos are traditional "wide" media, but the Zune's screen is taller than it is wide. Turn the device on its side, however, and the reverse becomes true.

Yes, I'm sure you could have figured this out on your own, but there's one aspect that might not be so obvious: the controls rotate, too. Specifically, when you turn the Zune on its side to view photos and videos, the control pad's functions change accordingly. Left/right becomes up/down, and up/down becomes left/right. Everything else stays the same.

5. Use the Back button to return to the interface. Presto! The selected image is now your background.

Find Custom Backgrounds on the Web

You don't have to rely on your own photos for Zune background images. You can also find countless options on the Web. Start with some home-brewed backgrounds created especially for the Zune—head to Zune Wallpapers (http://tinyurl.com/yf5h68), located in the forum section of the Zunerama fan site. Check out the sports-themed examples in the following illustration.

When you find a Zune-specific image you like, just right-click it, choose Save Image, and save the image in your My Pictures folder. It'll get copied to your Zune the next time you synchronize (see Chapter 2 to learn all about that).

Make Your Own Backgrounds

Want to create your own Zune background image? Using your favorite image-editing software (I recommend IrfanView, an excellent freeware program), simply resize or crop a digital image to 240 × 320 pixels. Then save it in your My Pictures folder as described in the previous section, making sure to save it in the JPEG format.

Zune Resources

Although the Zune was only about a month old when I started this book, dozens of fan sites had already sprung up to support it. What can you find on these sites? Here's a sampling:

- News
- Product reviews
- Tips and tricks
- Message boards (a.k.a. forums)

Message boards are a particularly valuable resource, as that's where the experts tend to hang out. If you have a problem, forums are a great place to find a solution. I'll talk more about this in Chapter 12. In the meantime, check out these great Zune sites:

- **Zunerama (www.zunerama.com)**   Tons of Zune info, including reviews, a buyer's guide, Zune documentation, and active forums (see Figure 1-5).

- **Zune Thoughts (www.zunethoughts.com)**   Similar to Zunerama, this blog-style site serves up news, links, forums, and more.

- **Zunester (www.zunester.com)**   A Zune blog authored by David Caulton, who works on Microsoft's Zune team.

■ **Zune.net (www.zune.net)**   Zune central, courtesy of Microsoft. Here's
the official source for Zune information, accessories, support, and so on.

Chapter 2

Set Up Your Zune

How to...

- Install the Zune software

- Add media to the Zune software

- Sign up for a Zune account

- Connect the Zune to your PC

- Synchronize the Zune automatically

- Synchronize the Zune manually

- Work with "guest" synchronization

- Disconnect your Zune

Okay, it's time to dive in. You already spent some time fiddling with your Zune in Chapter 1; now we're going to focus on the PC side of the equation. That means installing the Zune software, synchronizing your device, getting to know Zune Marketplace, and possibly signing up for a Zune Pass—far and away the best method for packing your Zune with tunes.

This chapter also covers connecting your Zune to devices other than your PC, like your Xbox. Why would you want to do that? Well, in a nutshell, you can turn your Xbox—and, by proxy, your entertainment center—into a Zune player. Pretty cool stuff. Read on to learn more.

Installing the Zune Software

There's not much to installing the Zune software that came in the box: Just insert the CD and follow the setup instructions (see Figure 2-1). But be prepared to wait awhile: In my experience, the Zune software takes time to install, especially if it has to download an updated version (which is a distinct possibility, as Microsoft has already released newer Zune software than what came on the CD). If you have any trouble, refer to the quick-start guide or visit Microsoft's software setup page online: http://tinyurl.com/y8hy9w.

If you haven't already installed the software, consider downloading it directly from the Zune.net Web site. That way, you will get the latest version, which will save you having to download it later.

2

FIGURE 2-1   Your first step is to install the Zune software on your PC.

I'm not going to rehash the step-by-step process of installing the software, but am I going to identify a few of the steps along the way and explain what they mean—starting with firmware.

As noted in Chapter 1, the Zune software won't work with older versions of Windows—specifically, any version prior to Windows XP. Check the Zune.net Web site (and Chapter 1) for more information on Zune system requirements.

Understanding Firmware

During the software-installation process, you may be informed that your Zune's *firmware* is being updated. (Likewise, as time passes, the Zune software may notify you that additional firmware updates are available.) Just what is firmware, and why should you care?

Put simply, firmware is the core software that operates your Zune. Microsoft periodically releases updates that add new features, fix problems, and/or improve performance. For example, as I'm writing this book, the Zune lacks support for podcasts (see Chapter 8). You can play them on the device, but there's no special menu devoted to them (as there is for, say, music). When Microsoft gets around to adding this inevitable podcast menu, it'll be part of a firmware update for the Zune.

Thankfully, the Zune software manages firmware updates automatically—you shouldn't have to do anything except click OK once or twice.

Adding Media to the Zune Software

The Zune software serves as the gateway between the songs, videos, and photos stored on your PC and your Zune device. When you first install the software, it will scan your hard drive in search of any such media. However, before it does that, it will ask if you want to include photos and videos in the search. Your best bet is to skip this stuff for now, depending on just how much of this media you have stored on your hard drive (and whether you even want it copied to your Zune). This isn't a permanent decision: You can always choose to add these items later (see "Automatic Synchronization" later in this chapter).

Let's start with music. By default, the Zune software will scan the My Music folder (usually located at *C:\Documents and Settings\Username\My Documents\ My Music*) on your hard drive in search of any music files that might already be there. (Don't worry if you keep your songs somewhere else: You can tell it to search specific folders later on.) Basically, there are two possible scenarios here:

■ You already have some MP3s and/or other kinds of music files on your hard drive.

■ You have no music whatsoever on your hard drive.

If you fall into the latter category, don't worry—you'll learn how to add music in Chapter 4. But if you're like most users, you probably have at least a few music files sitting around, if not a whole library. The Zune software will find them and add them to its own library, where you can play them and, of course, copy them to your Zune. You can even burn CDs if you want—find out more in Chapter 3.

Adding items to your Zune software library isn't the same thing as queuing them up to sync with your Zune. For example, you can have hundreds of photos in the library, but choose to sync only a handful of them. See "Connecting the Zune to Your PC" later in this chapter for more details.

Supported Music File Formats

When most people think of digital music, they think of MP3s (see Chapter 1 if you're not sure what an MP3 is). But an MP3 is just one of many digital music *formats*. Think of it this way: There are many different kinds of apples (Gala, Red Delicious, etc.), but they're all apples. Same goes for music formats: AAC, MP3, WMA, and all the rest are more or less the same thing, just different containers for the music.

The Zune software and player support the following music formats:

- **Advanced Audio Coding (AAC)**   This format is used primarily by Apple's iTunes software. If you used that program to rip songs from your CDs, they probably wound up in AAC format. Fortunately, the Zune can play them! (It cannot, however, play "protected" AACs, the kind you purchase from the iTunes store.)

- **MP3**   The world's most popular format for digital music. MP3 files are almost universally compatible.

- **Windows Media Audio (WMA)**   This is Microsoft's format for digital music, so it stands to reason that the Zune would support it. However, there are two primary types of WMA files: protected and unprotected. The Zune can play both, but only certain kinds of protected WMAs.

You'll learn more about these formats, and why they're significant, in Chapter 4. In the meantime, be aware that you can populate the Zune software (and, subsequently, your Zune) with only these kinds of music files.

Migrate from iTunes or Another Digital Music "Ecosystem"

The Zune and Zune Marketplace are by no means the first portable media player and online music store to hit the scene. If you were already using another device and/or service—another "ecosystem"—before you bought your Zune, you might be wondering if you can migrate everything to your new player. Well, I've got good news and bad news.

The bad news is that the Zune hardware works only with the Zune software. You can't connect it to, say, Apple's iTunes software (see Figure 2-2) and load it with

FIGURE 2-2   Songs purchased from iTunes and other online music stores aren't directly compatible with the Zune—but there's a way around this.

content from there. The other bad news is that the Zune can't play songs purchased from most other online services, including iTunes, Rhapsody, Napster, and Yahoo. That's because these songs employ a form of copy protection that's incompatible with the Zune. (For the record, Zune Marketplace imposes a similar kind of protection—see the sidebar "DRM, PlaysForSure, and Other Copy-Protection Nonsense.")

At press time, music label EMI had just announced plans to distribute music without copy protection. That means some songs purchased from iTunes will *play on your Zune. Find out more in Chapter 5.*

The good news is that it is possible to migrate a copy-protected music collection to your Zune. It takes a bit of work, but it's possible. Find out how in Chapter 4.

The better news is that you might not need to bother. If you subscribe to Zune Pass (see "What Is a Zune Pass?" later in this chapter), you can simply re-download all the songs you purchased with the other service(s).

Sharing Media with an Xbox 360

Another question you'll be asked during the software-installation process is whether you want to share your media library with an Xbox. Specifically, if you own an Xbox 360 and it's connected to your home network (assuming you *have* a home network), the Zune software can *stream* music, photos, and videos from your PC to the Xbox. You can answer no, of course, if you don't have an Xbox 360.

 *This isn't the same thing as connecting your Zune directly to your Xbox, which you can also do. The end result is the same—your Xbox plays your Zune media through your TV or stereo—but the source is your PC, not your Zune. I know, it's a little confusing. But it's worth it, because the whole Zune/Xbox connection is really cool.*

Adding Media Folders Manually

As noted previously, the Zune software automatically searches your My Music folder for songs to add to the library. But what if you store all your music in, say, a folder called "MP3s" that's located somewhere else on your hard drive? No problem: You just need to tell the Zune software where to look. Here's how:

1. Click the Options button, and then choose Add Folder To Library. (You can accomplish the same thing by pressing the F3 key.) See Figure 2-3 for an example of this setup screen.

2. In the box that appears, click the Add Folder button. Navigate to the folder on your hard drive that contains your music files (making sure they're in one of the formats mentioned in the "Supported Music File Formats" section). Click the main folder itself (for example, *C:\MP3s*), not any of the subfolders within it. By default, the Zune software will include any subfolders and the music files therein, so always choose the top-level folder.

3. Click OK, and you're good to go. The Zune software will add the contents of that folder and monitor it in case you add more music later on (see "Understanding Folder Monitoring").

TIP   *You can apply this same process to adding video and/or picture folders. But if your Zune isn't set up to sync videos and photos, you'll need to modify its settings. Microsoft has a great support page that shows you how: http://tinyurl.com/25f25j.*

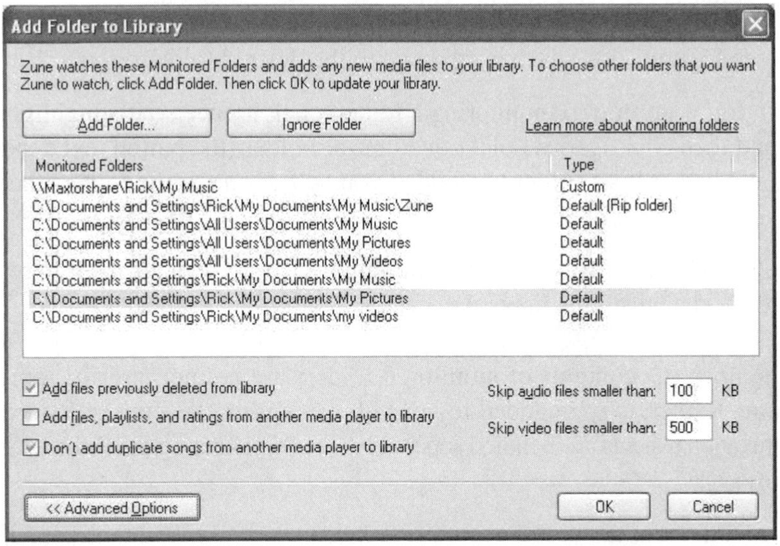

FIGURE 2-3   Folder monitoring is one of the Zune software's best features, as it tracks changes made to various media folders.

Another way to add music to the Zune software is by dragging it. Just open a window in Windows (or a file-management tool like Windows Explorer), find the music you want (either individual files or an entire folder), and then drag it to the Zune software window. You can drop it in any pane.

Understanding Folder Monitoring

It's important to understand that the Zune software isn't simply importing music from these folders or performing a one-time scan. Instead, it's monitoring these folders (see Figure 2-3), the idea being that if you add music to them, the software will automatically find the new songs (or remove them if you delete stuff). That sure beats having to import songs manually (as you do with, ahem, Apple's iTunes).

You may want to change the folders that the Zune software monitors. For example, if you have a giant library of digital photos on your PC and don't plan to add more than the occasional few to your Zune, there's no point in monitoring the Photos folder; it just takes extra time and bogs down the software. Conversely, if you're using a podcast program to download your favorite shows, you may want the Zune software to monitor that folder so the podcasts automatically end up on your Zune. Here's how to make changes to folder monitoring:

1. Press the F3 key.

2. If you want to add a folder to be monitored, click the Add Folder button (see Figure 2-3), and then navigate to the desired folder on your hard drive.

3. If you want to stop monitoring a folder, click it once so it's highlighted, and then click Ignore Folder or Remove Folder (the button text depends on whether it's a folder you added yourself or one of the folders that the software monitors by default).

4. Click OK and then wait while the Zune software updates itself to reflect these changes. This may take a while.

Remember, the contents of monitored folders are not necessarily copied to your Zune. Rather, they're added to your library within the Zune software. The synchronization aspects are handled separately (see "Connecting the Zune to Your PC" to learn more).

Sign Up for a Zune Account

Another thing you'll be asked to do during the Zune software installation is to create a Zune account. This is optional, but you'll need one if you want to buy songs from Zune Marketplace or sign up for a Zune Pass. You can also sign up for one and not buy anything at all, though you'll still need to provide a credit card number. This makes some people nervous, but I think it's entirely safe. Again, you don't need a Zune account to use your Zune, but you'll be missing out on a world of cool stuff if you skip it.

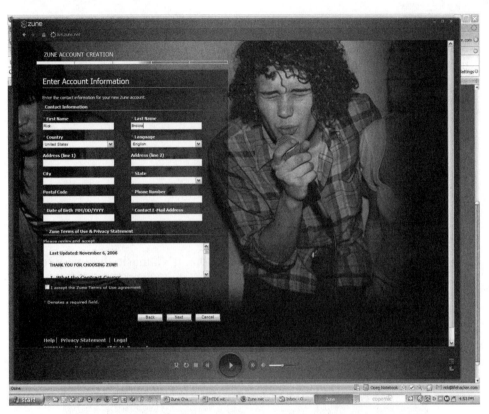

 *If you already have a Windows Live ID from an Xbox Live account, MSN account, or any other Microsoft service, you can use that in lieu of creating a new account. Just type in your ID and password when prompted.*

Family Settings and Child Accounts

Want to set up a Zune account for a youngster in the house? You can do so, but you'll need to provide a credit card number to prove you're an adult. (Some people I know, that's no proof whatsoever.) From there, you can establish "family settings" that determine whether the child is allowed to purchase premium and/or explicit content.

Microsoft provides perfectly good instructions on this, so I'm not going to rehash them here. Find what you need online: http://tinyurl.com/2zg74y.

Did you know?

What's a Download?

You'll notice I use the term *download* quite a bit when talking about Zune Marketplace. If you're unfamiliar with the term, it refers to the process of transferring a file—in this case, a song file—from an online service to your PC. Thus, when I talk about downloading songs, I mean copying them from Zune Marketplace to your computer's hard drive. How long does this take? It depends on how many songs you're downloading and the speed of your Internet connection. Here's hoping you have a cable or DSL modem (that is, a broadband connection), in which case you download a song in just a few seconds. If you're still using a dial-up modem, however, each song can take several minutes. Time for an upgrade!

What Is Zune Marketplace?

Zune Marketplace is many things. It's a music store. It's a music-discovery service. It's a music-delivery service. And, at some point, in the future (I *hope*—Microsoft has yet to confirm it), it'll be a video store and service, too. The only way to access Zune Marketplace is from within the Zune software.

Let's take a closer look at the Zune Marketplace and what you can do with it:

■ **Browse a massive music library**   As of this writing, Microsoft reported that Zune Marketplace contained over 2.5 million songs. You can browse all of them, reading notes about the artists and albums along the way. Zune Marketplace also shows you related artists and genres to help you discover other music you might like.

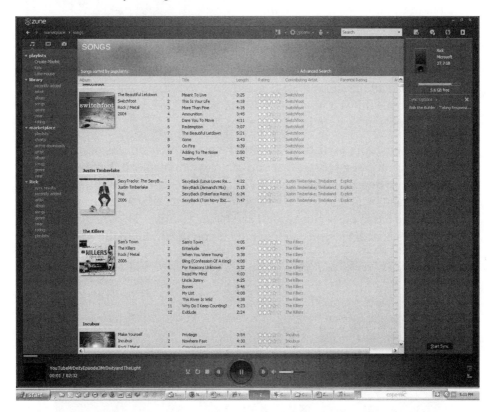

■ **Listen to a sample of each song**   While browsing the library, you can listen to a 30-second sample of any song. Subscribe to Zune Pass, however, and you'll be able to listen to all the songs in their entirety. (You'll be able to download them, too.)

■ **Buy songs and albums**   Because Zune Marketplace is, at heart, a music store, it should come as no surprise that it *sells* music. You can buy individual songs or entire albums, and then play them on your Zune and PC. You can also burn them to CDs using the Zune software (more on that in Chapter 4).

However, Zune Marketplace relies on a *point system* for these transactions: You buy points and then exchange them for music. Why does Microsoft employ this crazy system? Your guess is as good as mine. Anyway, find out more about Zune Pass in the following sections.

- **Download unlimited songs**   With a Zune Pass subscription, you gain unlimited access to the Zune Marketplace library. Specifically, you can download all the songs you want and stuff your Zune with as many as it'll hold. To me this is a no-brainer: If you own a Zune, you'll want a Zune Pass. Find out more in the next section.

- **Access custom playlists**   Zune Marketplace offers dozens of *playlists*—theme-centric song lists—that you can play or download. For example, the Girl Rock Bands playlist contains songs from over a dozen different artists, all of them, well, girl rock bands. These playlists let you discover and listen to music based on genres, styles, and bands you like. They're not terribly well-organized, but you can find gold if you're willing to dig a bit.

- **Videos? Podcasts?** As of this writing, Zune Marketplace carried only music. Hopefully, by the time you read this, the store will stock podcasts, TV shows, and movies. For now, however, you'll have to rely on other methods to stock your Zune with these items. See Chapter 8 for podcast information and Chapter 5 to learn about copying movies and TV shows.

By far, the best way to access Zune Marketplace is with a Zune Pass. Read on to learn more about it.

What Is a Zune Pass?

Do you buy at least one new CD per month? If so, you're a perfect candidate for a *Zune Pass*—arguably the greatest thing to happen to music fans since, well, The Beatles. Zune Pass is a subscription service that gives you the proverbial keys to the Zune Marketplace library and the 2.5 million songs therein, all for $14.99 per month (as of this writing).

Here's what you get with your subscription:

- **Unlimited downloads** You can download each and every song in the Zune Marketplace library—assuming you have enough space on your computer to hold them all. You wouldn't be able to fit them all on your Zune, of course, but you could play them via the Zune software.

- **Unlimited streaming** You can also *stream* songs from Zune Marketplace, which is kind of like tuning into a radio station: The songs play on your PC, but aren't actually downloaded.

- **Unlimited copying to your Zune** All the songs you download can be copied to your Zune. Two Zunes, actually, so go ahead and buy another one for your spouse, child, or significant other.

The only "catch" is that you can't burn downloaded songs to CDs; that requires you to buy them outright. Zune Pass is really a kind of music-rental service, and if you decide to cancel at any time, your downloads expire. Keeping your subscription paid up keeps the copy-protected audio files unlocked; stop making the monthly payment, and eventually they'll stop playing.

The idea of yet another monthly bill can be hard to swallow, especially for anyone accustomed to buying music on CDs. Plunk down your $15 and that disc is yours forever, and you can copy and rip it to your heart's content (for personal use only, of course). But consider this: If you typically buy just one new CD per month (or 15 songs), you could put that same money into a Zune Pass—and access *tens of thousands* of CDs instead. True, you can't burn your own copies, but the Zune more or less obviates the need for CDs anyway. If you simply must have physical media, you can always purchase the tracks you want and burn them to a disc (using the Zune software—see Chapter 4). But you won't spend one extra penny on songs you don't like, because you'll have had the chance to sample the album in its entirety, over and over again, and not just in 30-second snippets.

If nothing else, take advantage of the Zune Pass trial that you received with your Zune. It'll give you a chance to check out the service and see why I'm so jazzed about the idea of unlimited downloads. I think once you've had the chance to experience music this way, you'll never go back to buying music the old-fashioned way.

DRM, PlaysForSure, and Other Copy-Protection Nonsense

Remember Napster, the file-sharing service that enabled people to swap MP3s free of charge? Understandably, artists and record labels didn't like that very much. Lawsuits ensued, Napster shut down (but was later reborn as a commercial music service), and the days of the free music lunch were over. Well, not exactly—other file-sharing software arose to take Napster's place.

In the meantime, several legitimate music services were born, most of them selling songs for the reasonable price of 99 cents each. However, the recording industry would agree to this only if the songs themselves were copy-protected, meaning users couldn't just trade them over the Internet. Instead, the songs would be licensed to the individual user and his or her PC. If someone else tried to play them, they simply wouldn't work. This copy protection—this Digital Rights Management (DRM) technology—was, and is, a necessary evil.

DRM takes on many forms. Apple's version is called FairPlay; it restricts songs purchased from iTunes so that they play only on the user's PC or an iPod. Other services, including Napster and Yahoo Music Unlimited, rely on something called PlaysForSure, which was actually developed by Microsoft.

You would think, then, that the Zune and Zune Marketplace would use the same system. Wrong! Instead, Microsoft opted to create a new DRM system akin to Apple's: the songs you purchase or download from Zune Marketplace can be played only within the Zune software or on a Zune player. That means if you already have a bunch of songs you purchased from, say, Napster, you're out of luck: they won't play on the Zune. Fortunately, there's a fairly easy way around that, as mentioned in the section "Migrate from iTunes or Another Digital Music 'Ecosystem.'" Even so, it's annoying and frustrating that all these different DRM schemes are incompatible, but that's the way it is.

2

What Are Microsoft Points?

Speaking of buying music, there may be times when you want to do exactly that. Maybe there are songs and albums you consider good enough to own forever, or perhaps you want to burn a CD that you can play in the car or give as a gift. Whatever the reason, Zune Marketplace does let you buy music outright rather than just "renting" it with a Zune Pass.

Unfortunately, you can't just pay 99 cents per song or $9.99 per album and be done with it, as you can with virtually every other online music store on the planet. Instead, Microsoft forces you to buy *points*, which you then exchange for music. In my opinion, it's an annoying, pointless scheme, but you're stuck with it. At least it's not complicated.

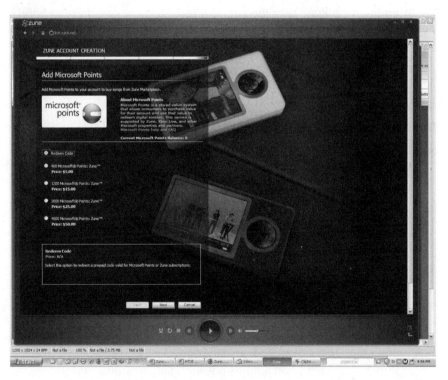

Here's how it works: You buy a predetermined number of points that stay in your account. Then you "spend" those points when you buy music. As of this writing, here's what Microsoft charges for various points packages:

- $5: 400 points

- $15: 1,200 points

- $25: 2,000 points

- $50: 4,000 points

Now it's time for a little math. A typical song "costs" 79 points, meaning that if you bought 400 points (the $5 package), you'd be able to buy 5 songs and have 5 points left over. What can you do with those 5 points? Well, nothing. Songs cost 79 points, remember? At some point, you might have enough leftover points to nab another song, but you can see why this is just an absurd system. (What, me bitter?)

As you can see, there's no advantage in buying larger blocks of points up front, so you might as well buy small blocks of points as you need them.

Want to give a Zune user the gift of points? You can buy prepaid points cards. Look for them wherever you can buy other kinds of gift cards, such as Best Buy and Circuit City.

Zune, Zune Marketplace, Zune Pass, and Other Zune Terms Defined

Zune this, Zune that… How about if we pause for a moment and define a few of the different "Zune" terms floating around? Sometimes even *I* get confused:

- **Zune**   The Zune device itself.

- **Zune firmware**   The software that's built into the Zune and provides the interface, menus, etc.

- **Zune software**   The Windows program that runs on your PC and provides access to your media library and Zune Marketplace. It also enables you to "rip" CDs, a topic we'll discuss more in Chapter 3.

- **Zune Marketplace**   An online music store that you access from within the Zune software. You can discover new music, play song samples, buy songs and albums outright, and download a ton of music (if you have a Zune Pass).

- **Zune Pass**   The Holy Grail for Zune users, a Zune Pass entitles you to download all the songs you want from Microsoft's music library, which currently consists of 2.5 million tunes.

- **Zune Points**   You buy points and then exchange them for songs.

Connecting the Zune to Your PC

As noted in Chapter 1, there's only one way to connect your Zune to your PC: the sync cable, which plugs into the bottom of your Zune at one end and into one of your PC's Universal Serial Bus (USB) ports at the other. This connection is necessary, not only for charging the battery, but also for *synchronizing* your Zune with your music, video, and photo libraries (all of which reside in the Zune desktop software, as described earlier).

What does it mean to synchronize your Zune? In a nutshell, it means that your Zune absorbs copies of some or all of the media in your PC—the songs, videos, and photos you've imported or downloaded into the Zune software. This is a one-way process—even if someone has squirted songs to your Zune (see Chapter 1), they don't wind up back on your PC.

 *Actually, the sync process isn't entirely one-way. If you rate a song on your Zune, that rating will appear in your library after you synchronize. Find out more in Chapter 4.*

Your first synchronization will probably take some time, though how much depends on how many songs, videos, and photos you've loaded into the Zune software (and whether you've configured videos and photos to auto-sync). Just be prepared: Even if you're just synchronizing a library of a few thousand songs, the first time out, it can take a couple hours. Subsequent syncs should go much faster (completing in a matter of minutes).

Let's take a closer look at your synchronization options, which include automatic, manual, and "guest."

Synchronize the Zune Automatically

The Zune software was designed with the Zune player in mind, so it stands to reason that the two would communicate efficiently. They do, thanks to automatic synchronization. Put simply, whenever you connect your Zune, the Zune software automatically copies over any newly added media and playlists. That saves you having to manually queue up any new songs you've downloaded, playlists you've created, photos you've added, and so on.

However, it's possible to disable automatic synchronization if you prefer to keep a tighter grip on what gets copied to the Zune. For example, suppose you have a library of several dozen videos on your PC—videos that the Zune software pulled into its library by way of a monitored folder (see "Understanding Folder

Monitoring" earlier in this chapter). You probably wouldn't want to copy them all to your Zune (there might not be enough space to hold them all!), but you do want to keep them at the ready so you can add new videos after you've watched the old ones.

In a situation like that, you'd disable automatic synchronization for videos. That doesn't mean you can't add videos to your Zune; it just means you'll add them selectively, using the drag-and-drop method described in the next section.

In fact, it's likely that when you first installed the Zune software, you elected to leave photos and videos for manual synchronization. If you change your mind, you can auto-sync the photo and/or video folders the Zune software is monitoring.

1. Start the Zune software, connect your Zune, and wait for the initial synchronization to finish (or click Stop Sync if you want to interrupt it).

2. Find your Zune's name (the one you chose during the initial setup process) in the left pane, right-click it, and choose Set Up Sync.

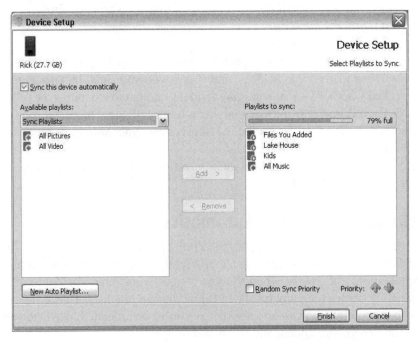

3. Click the drop-down menu under Available Playlists, and choose Sync Playlists. You'll see All Pictures and All Video appear in the box below.

2

4. Choose one of these items, and then click the Add button in the center of the window. You'll see the playlist move to the right pane under Playlists To Sync. Repeat this step with the other item, if desired.

5. Click Finish and you're done. Now be prepared to wait while your Zune syncs all the newly added media.

Photos and videos may have to be converted to a Zune-compatible format before they can be copied to the Zune itself. Fortunately, the Zune software can perform this conversion, but it can add extra time to the sync process. Find out more about video and photo formats in Chapter 5 and Chapter 6, respectively.

Synchronize the Zune Manually

As you might expect, manual synchronization deals with items you add to your Zune…manually. Think of it as drag-and-drop synchronization, as that's usually how you add items to the sync queue. Let's look at a typical example: Your Zune is set up to automatically sync all music, but not videos. However, you have a bunch of videos in your Zune software library. How do you get one onto your Zune?

Simple: you drag it to the sync pane on the right side of the screen. (This presumes your Zune is already connected, of course.) No sync pane? Click the Sync button in the upper-right corner of the screen. (See Chapter 3 for a more detailed description of the Zune software's interface, buttons, etc.) Then just click Start Sync, and you're good to go.

You can also manually synchronize items from outside the Zune software. Suppose you just received some photos in an e-mail and want to add them to your Zune. Save them to a folder on your hard drive, open the folder, select the photos, and then drag them to the Zune software window. (You can drop them directly in the sync pane.) The same method works with song files and videos.

Work with "Guest" Synchronization

Your Zune doesn't have to stick with the same PC its whole life. If you want to sync it with another computer, for example, the one in your office, you can do that quite easily. Just install the Zune software, and then plug in your Zune. You'll see the following dialog box.

As you can see, the first option is Connect This Zune As A Guest. What exactly does that mean? Precisely that: Your Zune connects to the other PC, but with a few limitations. For example:

- Any songs and playlists stored on the Zune won't be transferred to the other PC.

- Songs, playlists, and other media located on the other PC *will* be transferred to the Zune (unless they're already present on it).

- Any ratings you've applied to songs stored on your Zune won't be applied to songs stored on the other PC.

Confused yet? That's understandable—this is a somewhat confusing topic. All you really need to know is that it's possible to sync your Zune with more than one PC. Find out more about this topic at the blog site for this book: http://zunebook .wordpress.com.

Some users have reported that their PC treats their Zune like a guest even though it's brand new and has never been synced elsewhere. What causes this glitch? As of this writing, there's no answer, but you can go ahead and choose the second option, Sync With The Library On This PC." Doing so will erase the preloaded music from your Zune, but you can replace it with the Zune Pre-loads playlist that's available from Zune Marketplace.

Disconnecting Your Zune

One final item before we head off to Chapter 3 and learn how to navigate the Zune and the Zune software: how to disconnect your Zune from your PC. Nothing too complicated, here. You just need to remember never to unplug it while it's in the process of synchronizing. Doing so could foul up your Zune library and even the Zune itself.

The best practice is to wait until synchronization is complete (you'll know because the Zune's screen says "Connected" rather than "Synchronizing"), shut down the Zune software, and then disconnect your Zune. It's not mandatory that you exit the software, but I think it's better to be safe than sorry. Disconnecting your Zune while it's communicating with the PC is a potential source of problems.

It's absolutely fine to leave your Zune connected if it's not in the process of synchronizing. In fact, that's how you charge the battery!

Chapter 3

Using the Zune

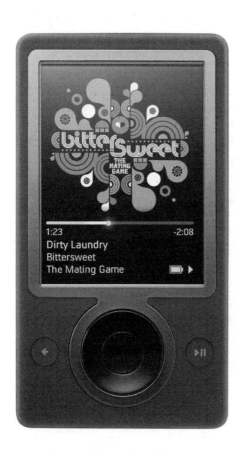

How to...

- Use your Zune
- Use Zune controls
- Use the Music menu
- Use the Videos menu
- Use the Pictures menu
- Use the Radio menu
- Navigate the Community menu
- Use the Settings menu

As you learned in Chapter 1 (or just from fiddling around), the Zune isn't hard to use. In fact, if you've mastered the control pad and Back button, you've probably already visited all the major areas of the device's menus by now. Pretty easy, right? Well, just in case you're having trouble, or if you think there might be areas of the interface you haven't explored but should, this chapter teaches you the finer points of Zune operation.

Use Your Zune

In Chapter 1 you learned about the Zune's controls. Now it's time to put them to use. Let's start by discussing the Zune's interface in general terms and then dive into the nitty-gritty.

The best way to master the interface is to think about it as a hierarchy. There's a main menu, which you can think of as "home base," and a bunch of sub-menus that branch off from there. Here's a diagram that should help illustrate this idea:

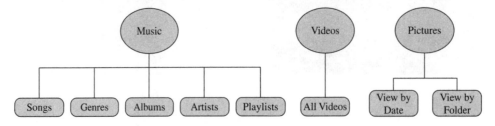

NOTE *Depending on what source(s) you use for video, you may see more than just an "all videos" sub-menu in the videos menu. See chapter 6 for details.*

Keep in mind that within each of these main sections, you may not find much in the way of actual content if you haven't loaded any using Zune Marketplace. As discussed in Chapter 1, the Zune comes preloaded with some sample music, videos, and photos, but ultimately, it's up to you to fill it with stuff. See Chapter 2 if you missed the discussion on how to do that.

Use Zune Controls

In Chapter 1 you learned to identify the various Zune controls. Now let's learn how they actually work within the context of the Zune menus. For example, what happens if you press the Back button while viewing the main menu? Is there anywhere to go "back" to? Will your Zune suddenly flip over and show you its back side? Could you accidentally go back in *time*? No, of course not, that's just silly. Or *is* it?

Yes, it is.

Or *is* it?

Yes, it is.

Sorry. Writing a book can really take a toll on your brain.

Or *can* it?

Anyway, let's take a look at a few control-related issues you'll encounter while navigating the Zune's menus.

The Back Button

As mentioned in Chapter 1, each press of the Back button takes you back one screen. Holding down the Back button for a few seconds returns you to the main menu, regardless of what menu you're viewing or what activity you're performing (such as watching a video or listening to music).

Interestingly, the Back button has a kind of memory. In other words, even after returning to the main menu, you can press Back again and return to the screen you were viewing previously. Press it again, and you'll go back to the screen before that. It's like a Zune breadcrumb trail. The best way to learn the "intricacies" of the Back button is just to fiddle with it.

Doing Nothing

Easy on those buttons, there, pardner. There are times when you can just do nothing and the Zune will go about its business. For example:

- While viewing a playback options menu (see the upcoming sections on music and picture menus), the Zune will return to the now-playing screen after a few seconds of inactivity.

- While viewing the main menu, the Zune will return to the now-playing screen after 10 seconds of inactivity (but only if there's music playing).

- If there's no music playing, the Zune will retreat to standby mode after a designated period of inactivity. When that happens, just press the Play/ Pause button to reactivate the Zune.

- If music is playing, the Zune will turn off the screen's backlight (but keep the music playing) after a designated period of inactivity (see "Use the Settings Menu" later in this chapter to learn how to set that period of time).

The Play/Pause Button

The Play/Pause button is context-sensitive, meaning it functions a bit differently, depending on what you're doing. For example, suppose you're looking at your list of playlists. You scroll down to the one you want to hear. Pressing Play/Pause can have two different results:

- **If no music is playing** Pressing Play/Pause will immediately start playing the highlighted playlist (or song, album, artist, etc.). That's a bit quicker than pressing OK/Select, which, in most cases, will take you to a sub-menu, where you'll have to press OK/Select at least once more.

- **If music is already playing** Pressing Play/Pause will pause the music. If you subsequently press the button again, it will start playing whatever item is highlighted—*not* the song you just paused. To get back to that song, you'll need to press the Back button.

I know this is a bit confusing, but after you try these options a few times, it should all make sense.

Need a quick way to pause your Zune without fumbling for the Play/ Pause button? Just pull out the headphones (carefully, of course). This automatically pauses playback.

Quick-Scrolling

If you have a lot of music stored on your Zune, you may find it daunting to search for a particular song or album. The quick-scroll feature aims to make this a bit easier. When viewing your song list, for example, you can hold down the control pad in the up or down direction to quickly scroll through the list. When you do this, quick-scrolling starts a bit slowly at first and then accelerates. When that happens, you'll see large letters appear on the screen, cycling through in alphabetical order. This helps you pinpoint just where you are in the list.

For example, if you're looking for a song that begins with the letter R, just start quick-scrolling until the R appears, and then release the control pad. You won't land exactly on your song, of course, but you'll have quickly reached the R's. From there, you can more easily zero in on the desired song.

Use the Music Menu

It's a pretty safe bet that you'll be spending most of your time in the Music menu, so you'll want to get intimately familiar with it. It's also a pretty safe bet that you've never encountered anything quite like the Zune's Music menu; it's fairly unique. But that's a good thing, as I think you'll find it easy and intuitive.

Specifically, the Music menu relies on what Microsoft calls a "twist" interface. That's a fancy way of saying the interface is two-dimensional: It moves not only up and down, but also left and right. Let's take a closer look at what happens when you select Music from the main menu:

1. From the main menu, press the control pad up or down until Music is highlighted.

2. Press OK/Select.

3. Welcome to the twist interface! Press the control pad left or right and see what happens.

The menu cycles between five different categories of music organization (see Figure 3-1):

- **Songs**   An alphabetical list of all the songs on your Zune

- **Genres**   An alphabetical list of all the song genres on your Zune

- **Albums**   An alphabetical list of all the albums on your Zune.

- **Artists**   An alphabetical list of all the artists on your Zune.

- **Playlists**   An alphabetical list of all the playlists on your Zune.

FIGURE 3-1   The Music menu reveals five different categories of music organization, which you access by scrolling left and right.

From any of these main headings, you can scroll down (or up, if you want to hop directly to the bottom of the list) and select a desired item. But let's look at the big picture. Your Zune contains whatever songs you loaded via the Zune software (in addition to the handful of tunes that came preloaded). These five categories provide different ways of accessing your music. A few are self-explanatory. The Songs category, for instance, simply lists all your songs in alphabetical order. You use the control pad to scroll up or down, find the song you want, and play it.

The Albums category works similarly, except that you're sorting your songs at a higher organizational level: by album. It's akin to the difference between flipping through a big box of 45-rpm records and flipping through a box of LPs. If you wanted to listen to the Billy Joel song "My Life," for instance, you could scroll through the Songs list until you found it. Or, you could hit the Albums list and look for *52nd Street*. Select that album, and you'll see all the songs therein, including "My Life."

The Artists category works one level higher than that: you start with the artist, choose the desired album, and finally the song. Of course, all this presumes that you're looking for an individual song. With the Zune, you can select music any number of ways. You can play "My Life," *52nd Street*, or Billy Joel's entire catalog.

Genres and playlists are a bit different, as they require some input on your part. Let's take a closer look at each of the Music menu options and how you interact with them.

> **NOTE** *For these five menu options to work properly, your songs must have accurate metadata, also known as ID3 tags. Find out more about this in Chapter 5.*

Songs

The Songs sub-menu, as seen in Figure 3-1, couldn't be simpler to use. The first option, Shuffle All, plays every song loaded on your Zune. If you're anything like me, you'll end up using this one a lot.

> **NOTE** *Technically, the Shuffle All option plays every audio file loaded on your Zune. If that includes podcasts or other spoken-word programs, don't be surprised if those pop up in the mix. That's one reason to rely on playlists, as discussed in Chapter 5: you can create a playlist consisting of only music, and then play that playlist in shuffled order.*

Alternately, you can scroll through the song list to find an individual song, press OK/Select, and perform any of the following tasks:

- Play the song.

- Send the song to another Zune user via the Zune's Wi-Fi radio (see Chapter 10).

- Add it to your Quick List (see the section "The Quick List: The Fastest Way to Find a Song" later in this chapter).

Actually, there's a fourth option: you can select a different song. You might think this would require pressing the Back button to return to the song list, but you can leverage the Zune's twist interface and scroll left or right instead. As you do so, you'll see song names slide left and right at the top of the screen. Try it!

This isn't a terribly practical method of song selection. You'll find that left/right item selection comes in handier when you're dealing with much shorter lists, like playlists and top-level menus.

When your Zune finishes playing whatever song you selected from the list, it will automatically go on to the next song and keep going in alphabetical order from wherever you started. The exception is if you've enabled shuffle mode, in which case, the next song will be whatever random selection the Zune makes. See "Music Playback Options" later in this chapter for more details.

If you're looking for a song that starts with "The" (such as Billy Joel's "The Ballad of Billy the Kid"), don't bother scrolling down to the T's. Zune filters out "the" when it appears at the beginning of a song title, instead alphabetizing the second word. Thus, Billy's song would actually be listed in the B's.

Albums

As noted previously, the Albums sub-menu lists your songs by album (see Figure 3-1). Again, the first option you see is Shuffle All. This works exactly like the Songs version, meaning your Zune instantly plays all your songs in a shuffled order. And, as with Songs, you can scroll up or down until you find a desired album. Press OK/Select, and you can perform any of the following tasks:

- ■ Play the album.

- ■ Send the album to another Zune user via the Zune's Wi-Fi radio (see Chapter 10).

- ■ Add it to your Quick List (see the "The Quick List: The Fastest Way to Find a Song" later in this chapter).

- ■ View a list of all the songs in the album and select any of them individually. From there, the same menu options apply as with the Songs menu (Play, Send, and Add To Quick List). However, after the first song plays, the Zune will continue playing songs from only that album.

Don't forget that the twist menu applies here as well. After you press OK/ Select from the main Albums list, you can scroll left or right to select a different album. As you do, the aforementioned four options appear for each album in turn.

NOTE
As with songs, Zune filters out "the" from the beginning of an album title and alphabetizes by the second word. So, if you're looking for an album that starts with "The" (such as Brendan Benson's The Alternative to Love*), don't bother scrolling down to the T's: Brendan's album would actually be listed in the A's.*

Artists

You know the drill by now: The first item in the Artists list (see Figure 3-1), Shuffle All, randomly plays all your songs. From there, you get an alphabetical list of all the artists on your Zune. Press OK/Select on any of them, and you'll see the albums for that artist. You can select one of them or choose one of these two options:

- Play all albums for that artist.

- Add all of that artist's albums to the Quick List.

If you select an individual album, you end up with same options outlined in the previous section, "Albums."

Once again, you can take advantage of the twist menu and scroll left or right to select a different album.

Genres

Now we come to a tricky spot. As with the previous three Music sub-menus, the first item that appears under Genres (see Figure 3-1) is Shuffle All. Press OK/Select to randomly play all of your songs. However, that's where the similarities end. The Genres menu offers a wholly different way to access your music: by genre!

A genre, of course, is a category of music. Some examples:

- Alternative

- Bluegrass

- Blues

- Classic rock

- Comedy

- Film soundtrack

- Latin jazz

- Power pop

- Swing revival

The list goes on and on; there are dozens upon dozens of music genres. As you can see, they can range from broad (blues, rock, etc.) to fairly narrow (Latin jazz, swing revival, etc.) Although the categories themselves are pretty self-explanatory, what makes this complicated is the way genres are defined and assigned.

Let's start with the way songs and albums are assigned to a specific genre. This ties in directly to the discussion of metadata (also known as ID3 tags) we'll have in Chapter 5. Suffice it to say that each song on your Zune carries with it various pieces of information, one of which is the genre. How does a song inherit this information? There are several possibilities:

- You manually assign the genre for each and every song or album in your library (a fairly time-consuming process).

- The genre information is retrieved from an Internet database when you rip songs from a CD.

- The genre information is already included in songs you download from an online service (such as eMusic or Zune Marketplace).

- There simply is no genre information included with the song, either because you didn't supply it or it wasn't included with one of the aforementioned methods.

Needless to say, this can lead to some inconsistencies. For example, suppose I want to find all the movie soundtracks I have on my Zune. Looking through the Genres menu, I find the following categories: Film Soundtrack, Scores/ Soundtracks, Sound Track, and Soundtrack. That's the result of my having a large, eclectic music collection. Who knows which of those four categories will lead me to the soundtrack for *American Graffiti*? It might be none of them: the album might be tagged "oldies," or it might not have genre information at all.

There's also the problem of genre definitions. Take Simon and Garfunkel: How would you classify them? Easy listening? Folk rock? Soft rock? Pop? Heck, oldies? You could easily assign them to any of a dozen genres. Or you could burrow even further and assign each individual Simon and Garfunkel song to a seemingly appropriate genre. That's fine, but what happens when you start doing this for all your songs? Unless you're really, really careful and consistent, you end up with a mish-mash of genres that ultimately does little good in helping you find the music you desire.

3

Did you know?

What's a Playlist?

A playlist is nothing more than a list of songs. It's also an essential tool for organizing music libraries. You'll get the full scoop in Chapter 5; in the meantime, let's look at a few examples of how staggeringly useful playlists can be.

Suppose your music library consists of both mainstream stuff (The Police, Green Day, Lily Allen, etc.) and classical music (Beethoven, Handel, etc.). If you use the Zune's Shuffle All feature, you're likely to hear "Roxanne" one moment and "Symphony No. 5" the next. Personally, I don't like to mix such disparate genres—when I'm in the mood for classical, all I want to hear is classical, and so on.

That's where playlists come in. For the scenario just described, I'd create two of them: one titled "mainstream music" and the other "classical," each one containing the appropriate kind of music. It's easy to build a playlist, and you're not limited in any way: Each song can appear in more than one playlist. That's because they're just lists—pointers to your music. Find out more in Chapter 5.

If I sound down on Genres, it's because I've never found it to be a particularly practical way of tapping my music library. Your mileage may vary, and you should feel free to experiment with the Genres sub-menu. You may find it quite helpful, especially if you get all your music from one source (like Zune Marketplace, which is probably your best chance of getting consistent genre categories). To find out more about how to add genre information to your songs, see Chapter 5.

Playlists

Finally, we come to playlists (see Figure 3-1). In Chapter 5 you'll learn all about using and creating them; for now, we'll just focus on the mechanics of the menu (but check out the "What's a Playlist?" section as well). The first item in the list is *not* Shuffle All, but rather Quick List. Unlike playlists you build on your PC using the Zune software, the Quick List is built on the Zune itself. See "The Quick List: The Fastest Way to Find a Song" for more details. Selecting this option displays all your Quick List selections and lets you play one or all of them.

Likewise, selecting a playlist presents you with the usual array of options:

- Play all items in the playlist.

- Add all of the items in a playlist to your Quick List (yes, you can actually add a playlist to your Quick List).

- Send a playlist to another Zune user (again, see Chapter 10).

The twist interface works here the same way it does elsewhere: scroll left or right to cycle through individual playlists.

The Quick List: The Fastest Way to Find a Song

As I'm writing this book, I'm totally hooked on the Lily Allen Brit-pop confection "Smile." It's the first song I look for when I fire up my Zune. The problem is, I currently have about 3,000 songs loaded, and it takes forever to find that particular one by scrolling through my Songs list. Surely there must be a faster way.

One shortcut is to search by artist: That list is quite a bit smaller (though still several hundred entries long). I could also troll the album list—assuming I'm able to remember the name of the album on which "Smile" appears. No, the fastest way to access a favorite song is to first add it to the Zune's Quick List—a customizable playlist that you create on the device itself. Just find the song you want, press OK/Select until you see the song information screen, and then choose Add To Quick List. Now head to the Music > Playlist menu and you'll see Quick List at the very top of the list. Press OK/Select and presto: there's your song. Of course, you can add more than one song to the Quick List. In fact, you can add entire albums, artists, and genres. But that would defeat the purpose of using it to quickly find one or a few favorite tunes.

3

Music Playback Options

Once you've queued up some music to play (your whole library, an album, an individual song, etc.), you may want to delve into some of the Zune's playback options. First, let's examine what you can do with the control pad:

- **Up/down** Raise and lower the volume

- **Left** Press once to return to the beginning of the currently playing song. A quick second press takes you back to the previous song. Hold down the left button to scan backwards through a song, releasing it when you find the spot you want. (This can be particularly helpful if you're playing a podcast or audio book and trying to return to a specific spot.)

- **Right** Press once to skip to the next song in the list. Hold down the right button to scan forward through a song, releasing it when you find the spot you want. (This can be particularly helpful if you're playing a podcast or audio book and trying to jump to a specific spot.)

If you press the OK/Select button while a song is playing, you're presented with an options screen that looks like this.

Let's take a look at these six options and how you can take advantage of them:

- **Rating** For each song that's playing, you can assign a rating of one to five stars—just scroll up one tick until the stars are highlighted, and then press the OK/Select button repeatedly until you've highlighted the desired number. When you're done, you can either do nothing or press the Back button to return to the now-playing screen. Why bother with ratings? For starters, they're synchronized back to your desktop library when you connect your Zune to your PC. That means you can take advantage of them to create special playlists—like, for example, "five-star songs." Find out more about this in Chapter 5.

- **Show song list** When this option is highlighted and you press OK/Select, the Zune shows you all the songs currently queued for playback. This is an interactive list: You can select any song in the list to play it immediately.

■ **Shuffle** This is an on/off toggle. When shuffle mode is on, all selected songs will play in random order. (You'll know it's enabled by the appearance of a little shuffle symbol in the lower-right corner of the screen.) When shuffle mode is off, the songs play back in whatever order they're listed.

■ **Repeat** This is also an on/off toggle. When repeat mode is on, all selected songs will repeat (and you'll see a little repeat symbol in the lower-right corner of the screen). That means that if you play, say, an individual album or playlist, it will repeat when it gets to the end. When repeat mode is off, the selected song(s) will play through once and then stop.

■ **Send** This option sends the currently playing song to a nearby Zune. Find out more in Chapter 10.

■ **Flag** Say there's a song on your Zune that you just despise. You never want to hear it again. You want to remember to delete it the next time you sync. The flag option can help. It assigns a little marker to the song, which is then copied back to the Zune software. In fact, after you assign one or more flags, you'll notice a new Inbox option in the software's navigation pane. Click it to see the songs you've flagged, and then do with them what you will. (Flagging isn't solely for deletion purposes; you can use it as a reminder to recommend a song to a friend, for example, or to add a particular song to a playlist.) Once you've flagged a song on your Zune, you can't unflag it— but it does absolutely no harm to the song, nor does it actually *do* anything to the song except mark it, so don't worry. You can, however, remove a flag using the Zune software. Find out more in Chapter 4.

 *If you do nothing for a few seconds after accessing this options screen, the Zune will automatically return to the now-playing screen. Alternately, you can press the Back button to return to the now-playing screen.*

There's one more playback option worth mentioning: the equalizer. However, because you access it from a different menu, I'm not going to cover it here. Skip ahead to "Use the Settings Menu" if you want to learn about equalizer options right away.

Inside the Now-Playing Screen

Let's take a moment to identify just what you're seeing when you play a song on your Zune. This now-playing screen displays numerous elements: information, gauges, icons, and possibly even some album artwork:

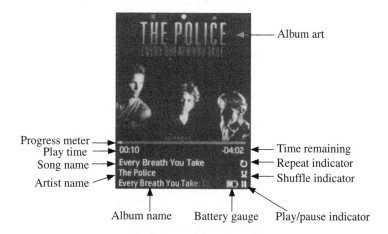

- **Album art** The bulk of the Zune's now-playing screen is taken up by album art. However, some (or all) of your songs may display no artwork at all and show just a colorful placeholder image instead. To find out how to add album art to your songs (a decidedly worthwhile endeavor), see Chapter 5.

- **Progress meter** Shows the current point of playback within the song.

- **Play time** Shows how much time has elapsed for this song.

- **Time remaining** Shows how much time is remaining for this song.

- **Song name**

- **Artist name**

- **Album name**

- ■ **Battery gauge**   Shows how much battery life remains—though not always accurately, in my experience.

- ■ **Play/pause indicator**   A little triangle indicates that music is playing. Two little lines indicate that music is paused.

- ■ **Shuffle indicator**   When this icon appears, your Zune is in shuffle mode.

- ■ **Repeat indicator**   When this icon appears, your Zune is in repeat mode.

Use the Videos Menu

The Videos menu (see Figure 3-2) couldn't be simpler. It's an alphabetical list of all the videos stored on your Zune (complete with their running times, a handy perk). The twist interface doesn't come into play here; the only category is All Videos, so there's nothing to be gained by scrolling left or right.

Thus, you'll be scrolling up or down to find the video you want. When it's highlighted, press OK/Select. The subsequent screen presents you with a bit more information about the video—the date it was added to your Zune, the running time, and a description (if available)—and a single option: Play.

 *Here, the twist interface resurfaces again: you can scroll left and right to cycle through your available videos.*

FIGURE 3-2   The Videos menu presents you with an alphabetical list of your videos. Scroll up or down to select the one you want.

As a reminder, playing a video causes something of a sea change in your Zune: the screen rotates 90 degrees to the right, thus letting you enjoy widescreen videos. Obviously, this will lead you to physically turn your Zune as well (and make you wish for a kickstand or some other method to prop it up at a comfortable viewing angle—see Chapter 11 for information on Zune cases that will do exactly that).

As discussed in Chapter 1, video mode rotates not only the screen, but also the control pad. Specifically, its functions change to match the new screen orientation: left/right becomes up/down and up/down becomes left/right. Everything else stays the same.

Video Playback Options

The Zune has few video playback options (because, really, what more is there to do except adjust the volume and perhaps fast-forward or rewind?). Here's what the control pad does when you're watching a video:

- **Up/down**   Raises and lowers the volume

- **Left**   Press once and the video skips backward seven seconds (a kind of instant-replay). Hold down to rewind the video until you find the desired spot, and then release.

- **Right**   Press once and the video skips ahead 30 seconds (great if you're watching a recorded TV show and want to skip the commercials). Hold down to fast-forward the video until you find the desired spot, and then release.

- **OK/Select**   Press to see a transparent information screen appear over your video. Press again (or wait five seconds), and the screen disappears.

Use the Pictures Menu

The Pictures menu lets you view digital photos, either individually or as part of an automated slideshow. As you'll see upon entering the menu, the twist interface presents you with two sorting options:

- **View by date**   Sorts your photos by the month they were taken.

- **View by folder**   Sorts your photos by folder—specifically, the desktop folder from which they originated when you added them to the Zune software.

The Zune Bookmarks Videos

So let's say you're halfway through watching *The Matrix* on your Zune and decide to take a break, listen to some music, or stop the movie in accordance with FAA regulations (because your flight is about to land). How can you pick up where you left off? Will the Zune force you to fast-forward from the beginning of the movie and hope you can remember the exact spot where you stopped?

Thankfully, no. When you exit a video (meaning the player shuts off or you switch to a different mode), the Zune automatically creates a kind of bookmark. In other words, it remembers your position in the video. The next time you try to play it, you'll see two fairly self-explanatory options:

- Resume
- Play From Beginning

Even better, the Zune will do this for each individual video, not just the last one you were viewing. Unfortunately, it won't do the same for audio files, which creates some definite hassles when you're listening to podcasts and audio books. Hopefully, this will be corrected in a future firmware update. In the meantime, at least you can take a break from watching Neo save the world and later pick up right where you left off.

This is not unlike the Music menu, in that you're simply choosing the way you want to access your photos. Both options have a Play Slideshow selection at the top; select it to launch a slideshow of all the photos in your Zune.

 Your Zune came preloaded with some sample photos, so you should be able to at least explore the operation of the Pictures menu. Of course, you'll no doubt want to add your own photos; head to Chapter 7 to find out how.

3

Once you select a batch of photos (either by date or folder), you're again given the option to play a slideshow. (You can also send photos wirelessly to another Zune user; find out more in Chapter 10.) Alternately, you can drill down a bit further into sub-folders, if they exist. Eventually, you'll see a group of photo *thumbnails*—small versions of each photo in that collection. Thumbnails look like this:

To view a specific photo, hold down the control pad until you see a white box surrounding the first photo. Now the control pad becomes a navigation pad: press it up, down, left, or right until the white box lands on the photo you want. Press OK/Select, and the photo will fill the screen.

 As with video, viewing photos causes your screen to rotate 90 degrees. At the same time, the control pad's functions "rotate" to match. Thus, what was previously up/down becomes left/right, while left/right becomes up/ down. The other controls remain the same. The control pad returns to its previous state of operation after you exit full-screen photo viewing.

Press the Back button to return to the previous screen. Otherwise, the photo will stay on the screen for as long as your Zune has power. Alternately, if you press

OK/Select while viewing a photo (either alone or as part of a slideshow), you'll see an options menu. Let's take a look at those options, which are described in the next section.

Picture Playback Options

While viewing a photo, pressing the OK/Select button launches an options screen containing six items. Here's what they do:

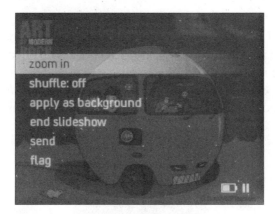

- ■ **Zoom In**   Want to get a closer look at your photo? Select the Zoom In option to enlarge the center portion. From there, you can use the control pad to scroll up, down, left, and right. Notice the small "area box" in the lower-right corner of the screen: It indicates which portion of the photo is currently zoomed. Press OK/Select to zoom out again.

- ■ **Shuffle**   As with music, your Zune can "play" photos in random order. Set shuffle mode to "on" if you want random slideshows; set it to "off" if you want them to play in whatever order they're listed.

- ■ **Apply As Background**   This is one of the Zune's coolest features. By selecting this option, you turn the currently displayed photo into the background image for the entire Zune interface. It's a great way to customize your Zune and give it a unique look. You can easily change the background to something else by loading another photo and selecting this option again.

- ■ **End Slideshow**   Select this option to end the current slideshow and return to the Zune's main menu. Can't you accomplish the same thing with the Back button? Yes, but that merely returns you to the previous screen.

You'd have to press it a couple times (or hold it down for a few seconds) to hit the *main* menu.

■ **Send**   Select this option to beam this photo to another Zune user. Find out more in Chapter 10.

■ **Flag**   Similar to the option discussed in "Music Playback Options," Flag adds an invisible marker to the selected photo. The next time you sync your Zune with your PC, you'll see a list of flagged photos in the Zune software inbox. You can use flags for any kind of reminder or notification; there are no hard and fast rules.

Listen to Music While Viewing Photos

The Zune offers the enviable ability to play music while running a photo slideshow (or just displaying an individual photo). Just start playing a song, and then hold down the Back button to return to the main menu. Navigate to Pictures and start your slideshow or load your photo. It's like your own personal music video. Neat!

Use the Radio Menu

Sometimes, you just want to listen to the radio. Personally, I'm a huge fan of NPR, so I love how the Zune lets me tune into *Fresh Air*, *This American Life*, *A Prairie Home Companion*, and other great shows. There's a whole chapter (Chapter 8, to be exact) devoted to using the Zune's FM radio, so skip ahead if you want to learn how to tune in.

Use the Community Menu

Want to share songs with other Zune users? The Community menu is where it all happens. (See Chapter 1 if you need a refresher on this capability.) Because this isn't something you're likely to do very often, and because there's a whole chapter devoted to it (specifically, Chapter 10), I'm going to keep this short and sweet.

In order to send or receive songs, your Zune's wireless radio needs to be activated—see the next section "Use the Settings Menu" to find out how. Once the wireless radio is turned on, you'll see three options in the Community menu, all of them accessible by scrolling left or right with the control pad:

- **Me** The current status of your Zune
- **Nearby** Scans for and lists any Zunes in the area
- **Inbox** Lists any songs or photos you've received

That's really all you need to know for now about the Community menu. Head to Chapter 10 for complete details on wireless song sharing.

Use the Settings Menu

Finally, we come to Zune settings (see Figure 3-3), where you can tweak various aspects of the device's interface and operation. This is where you can program the Zune to play music in a shuffled order, see how much storage space is available, toggle the wireless transmitter on and off, and more. Most of these settings are extremely self-explanatory, but it says in my job description that I need to give you *everything*. So here goes...

FIGURE 3-3   The Settings menu is the place to modify things like screen brightness and wireless activity.

Wireless

Press the OK/Select button to toggle the Zune's wireless transmitter on and off. When it's on, you'll see a little Wi-Fi icon in the corner of the screen.

To extend your battery life, leave wireless set to off. The only time you'll want to turn it on is when you're in close proximity to another Zune user and want to squirt some tunes. After you're done, turn wireless off again.

Music

Selecting Music leads you to a sub-menu containing three playback-related options:

■ **Shuffle** When set to on, your music will play in random order.

■ **Repeat** When set to on, your selected music (be it an individual song, an album, a playlist, or your entire library) will repeat when it gets to the end.

■ **Equalizer** Your Zune comes with seven equalizer presets designed to enhance audio quality for various kinds of music. Press the OK/Select button to cycle through the presets, which include acoustic, classical, electronic, hip hop, jazz, pop, rock, and none (which is flat). If you modify these settings while music is playing, you'll hear the effects of each equalizer setting as you toggle through them. These are largely a matter of personal preference—there's no right or wrong setting, so experiment!

There's a much quicker way to access the Shuffle and Repeat settings. While you're listening to a song (and the main playback screen is showing), press the OK/Select button. You'll see a screen containing several options, Shuffle and Repeat among them.

Pictures

As with Music, selecting Pictures leads you to a sub-menu, this one containing just two options:

■ **Transitions** When viewing a photo slideshow, the Zune will wait for a predetermined amount of time before switching from one picture to the next. This is where you can set the length of time between photos: anywhere from 3 to 30 seconds. Press OK/Select to toggle through the various choices.

■ **Shuffle** When set to on, your photos will appear in random order.

You can access these settings while viewing a slideshow.

Display

The Display menu contains some of the Zune's most important settings—including one you need when connecting the device to a TV. Let's take a closer look:

3

■ **Themes** This should actually be called Background, as it refers to the background picture that appears behind all menus. The Zune comes with three—amber, haze, and night—but you can also choose any of the photos in your library to use as a background. The instructions for doing so are shown right on the Themes menu, but you can find out more in "Use the Pictures Menu" in this section.

■ **Backlight** To conserve battery life, your Zune's screen will turn off after a predetermined amount of inactivity (meaning you haven't touched any of the controls): 1 second, 5 seconds, 15 seconds, 30 seconds, 1 minute, or never. Press the OK/Select button to toggle through the choices. The shorter the duration, the longer your battery will last between charges. See if you can get by with 5 seconds. If not, bump up the setting until you find one that works for you. If you frequently leave your Zune in a charging cradle, you might want to select "always on" so that you can enjoy your songs' album art.

NOTE *This backlight setting doesn't apply to videos or photo slideshows. For obvious reasons, the screen never goes dark when you're viewing these items. Of course, that's one reason why they contribute to significantly shorter Zune battery life.*

■ **Brightness** Another battery-related setting, Brightness offers you three choices for the brightness of the screen: low, medium, and high. Press OK/Select to toggle between them. I recommend leaving it set to low, again in the interest of longer battery life. It may seem a bit dim at first, but you'll quickly grow accustomed to it.

■ **TV Out** If you connect your Zune to your TV (using either the Zune Home Pack or a third-party accessory), you'll need to toggle the TV out setting to "on." This will disable the Zune's own screen—but you'll see the interface on your TV. As the onscreen instructions inform you, the Zune will stay in this mode until you press Play/Pause to turn the Zune off and then turn it back on again.

■ **TV System** If you live in North America, leave this set to NTSC. If you live in Europe, set it to PAL. If you're not connecting your Zune to a TV, you don't have to bother with this setting at all. 'Nuff said.

Sounds

As you've probably noticed, your Zune makes little beeping sounds as you navigate the menus. If you want to turn these sounds off, press OK/Select.

Radio

This one's too self-explanatory, even for this book. Choose the setting that matches where you are at this moment.

Online Status

When your Zune's wireless transmitter is on, other Zune users can "discover" you (as discussed in "Use the Community Menu" earlier in this chapter). But what will they learn about your Zune's status? It depends on which of these two settings you choose:

- **Basic** Your Zune reveals a simple online status, such as "busy" or "online."

- **Detailed** Your Zune reveals your current activity in detail, such as the name of the song you're listening to or "viewing pictures" if you're looking at photos.

Which one should you choose? It's totally up to you. There's little harm in leaving this set to Detailed, especially if you leave your Zune's wireless transmitter off most of the time.

About

The About menu leads to a sub-menu where you can learn a few choice bits of information about your Zune:

- **Zune** Shows the current firmware version that's installed on your Zune.

- **Storage** This revealing screen shows you how much storage space is used and available, and how many songs, photos, and videos are loaded on your device.

- **Legal** Bo-ring! Unless you enjoy reading legalese.

Well, that's it for the Zune's Settings menu. Now it's time to move away from the device (only for a little while, I promise) and look at the Zune software. Head to Chapter 4; I'll see you there.

How to...

- Use the Zune software interface
- Use the navigation pane
- Use the details pane
- Use the Search bar
- Use the list pane and task selectors
- Play local music
- Play Zune Marketplace music
- Rate songs
- Stream music from your PC to an Xbox 360
- Burn CDs
- Burn an MP3 CD

Now that you know how to use your Zune, it's time to learn something a little more complicated: the Zune software. Let me be brutally honest: This program can be troublesome at times, even annoying. But you're stuck with it, as it's the only way to interface with your Zune player.

In this chapter you'll learn about the three main sections of the Zune software interface. You'll learn how to play songs and videos in the Zune software. And you'll learn how to create CDs from the songs you've purchased in Zune Marketplace.

However, I'm not going to delve into every single aspect of the Zune software. Doing so could easily fill half the book. Instead, I'll focus on basic operation and the areas that are crucial to getting the most from your Zune. In some areas, I'll defer you to later chapters, such as Chapter 5 for learning how to rip songs from CDs—an operation performed in the Zune software, but a subject more suitable for that chapter. The main goal of this chapter is to get you comfortable with navigating the software and peek under the hood at a few of the less obvious features.

Start by installing the Zune software, as described in Chapter 1 and your Zune's quick-start guide.

Use the Zune Software Interface

The first step in using the Zune software is identifying its various elements. Let's take a look at the interface, as shown in Figure 4-1.

Navigation controls
Media selectors   Layout selector   Options menu   Marketplace sign-in   Search bar   Task selectors

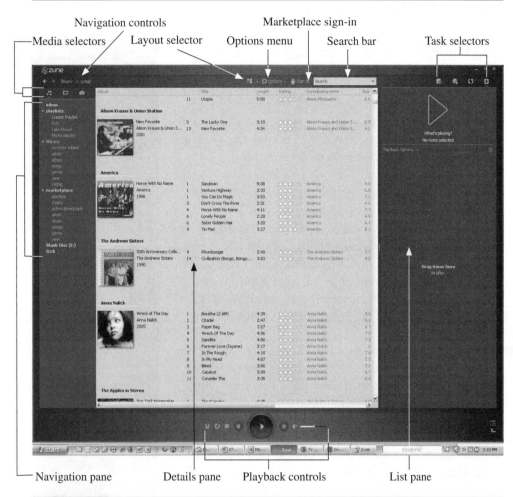

Navigation pane   Details pane   Playback controls   List pane

FIGURE 4-1 Learning the key areas of the Zune software will help you master the program more quickly.

Now let's take a closer look at specific areas of the interface, starting with one of the most important: the navigation pane.

The screenshots in this and upcoming sections show the Zune software with media (music, photos, etc.) already loaded. If you haven't added media of your own, your Zune software may look a bit different. Find out how to add media in Chapter 2.

Use the Navigation Pane

The navigation pane is where you access your media library, Zune Marketplace, and your Zune itself. It's also the place to create and select playlists. This pane occupies the left side of the Zune software interface (see Figure 4-1) and resides beneath three media selectors: one each for music, videos, and photos. Click any of these three icons, and you'll see the navigation pane change accordingly. Let's take a closer look at what you'll find beneath each media selector.

Music

You'll probably spend most of your time viewing the Music area of the navigation pane. As shown in the following screenshot, it usually consists of four key sections—Playlists, Library, Marketplace, and your Zune (represented by whatever name you gave it during the initial installation)—any of which you can collapse or expand by clicking the little triangle next to the section name.

Note that I said the music area *usually* consists of four sections. If you've used your Zune to flag any songs (see Chapter 3), you'll see a fifth section the next time you sync: inbox. Clicking it reveals the flagged items and lets you deal with them however you see fit. (As a reminder, flagging is merely a way of bringing designated songs to your attention on the desktop. You can delete them, reorganize them, do nothing with them, or whatever.) If you've inserted an audio CD in your PC, you'll see it listed in the navigation pane as well.

Here's an overview of the four main sections in the navigation pane's music section.

Playlists As discussed in Chapter 3, a playlist is merely a collection of songs. To create one, click Create Playlist and then type a name into the New Playlist box that appears. From there, you simply drag songs, albums, or artists to that playlist. It really is that easy, although that's not the end of what you can do with playlists—not by a long shot. You'll get the full rundown in Chapter 5.

To listen to an existing playlist, simply double-click it. To do other things with a playlist, right-click and then choose any of the following options:

- **Play**   The same as double-clicking—it plays the entire playlist.

- **Flag**   Flags the entire playlist, though I'm not sure why you'd want to do this. As described previously, you'll immediately see the inbox option appear, with all the flagged songs therein.

- **Add To Now Playing**   If you're already listening to music, this option adds the playlist to the end of the current song list, rather than replacing it.

- **Edit In List Pane**   Choose this option to remove songs or change their order. You'll see the playlist's songs on the right side of the screen in the list pane. To remove a song, click it to highlight it, and then press the DELETE key on your keyboard. (Doing so merely removes the song from that playlist; it doesn't remove it from your library or delete it from your hard drive.) To change song order, click a song and drag it to the desired spot on the list. When you're done making changes, click the Save Playlist button at the bottom of the pane.

- **Rename**   As you might expect, this option lets you rename the playlist.

- **Delete**   Deletes the playlist—and only the playlist. Your songs remain in your library.

- **Open File Location**   Want to find the actual playlist file on your hard drive? Selecting this option opens a window containing Zune playlists, which are little more than text files with a ZPL file extension.

Library   The Library section provides access to the songs stored on your PC, thus allowing you to play them, rate them, add them to playlists, and so on. If some of the categories here look familiar, it's because you encountered them on the Zune itself (see Chapter 3). Indeed, like the Zune, the Zune software offers multiple ways to view your library: by artist, album, song, genre, year, and rating. (The latter two options don't appear on the Zune player, but you can leverage them here to create playlists—again, see Chapter 5.)

If you've recently added media to your library, you'll see another option— the aptly titled Recently Added. Click this to see the songs, videos, or photos that the Zune software recently discovered. This is a great way to direct newly added items to playlists or just to find them in an efficient way.

Click any of the first three options (artist, album, songs), and watch what happens. You'll see your artists, albums, or songs appear in the center section of the Zune software, which is called the details pane. Here's a look at those different views:

There's no right or wrong way to view or interact with your library. You can use any of these options or just head to the search bar (see "Use the Search Bar" later in this chapter).

To quickly play all the music in your library, double-click the Songs category. This saves you having to select all the songs and drag them to the list pane. The result is even better if you turn on the shuffle-play feature by clicking the Shuffle icon in the playback controls.

Marketplace Remember Zune Marketplace? We first talked about it in Chapter 2—it's the built-in online store where you can find, play, buy, and download music. Click Marketplace to access the store, or click any of the following subcategories:

■ **Playlists** Zune Marketplace offers a large selection of "canned" playlists, the idea being to give you quick and easy access to categorical chunks of music. A few examples include Sounds Of India, B.B. King, and Rest & Relaxation. The upper section of the pane shows featured playlists, while the lower section lists Zune Marketplace's dozens and dozens of playlists—in no particular order, unfortunately.

- **Charts**   The Charts section lets you browse Zune Marketplace based on, well, charts: the top-ranked songs, albums, and artists on Zune Marketplace and the well-known Billboard. The latter has its own special section. Click the Year drop-down menu to choose a year's worth of charts (dating back to 1946!), and then click the accompanying drop-down menu to select from dozens of specific charts (such as Top Blues Albums and Hot 100 Airplay) for that year. This is simply another way to browse the Zune Marketplace library to find music you might like.

4

■ **Active Downloads**   After selecting one or more songs or albums to download, click here to track their progress.

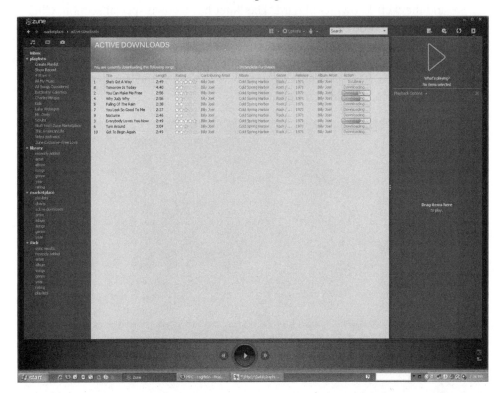

■ **Artist**   As with your own library, you can sort the Zune Marketplace library by artist. By default, this option lists artists by popularity (that is, rating), but you can click any of the three other columns (Album Artist,

Count, and Length) to change the sorting method. Keep in mind that because the Zune Marketplace library is so large (think millions of songs), it might take a minute before the change takes effect.

■ **Album** Lists all the albums in Zune Marketplace. Here you can sort them by even more categories, including Genre, Release Year, and Length. Again, just click one of the columns to choose a sorting method.

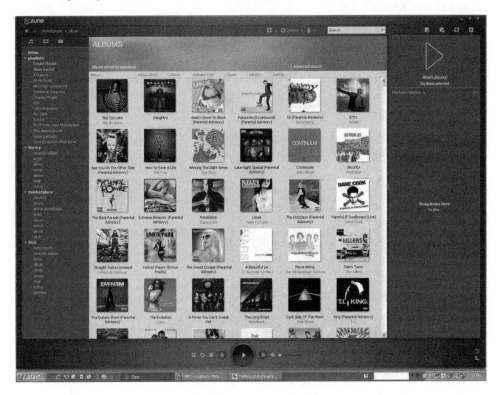

■ **Songs**   Lists all the songs in Zune Marketplace—an extremely lengthy list, to say the least. As with artist and album, you can change the sorting method by clicking one of the available columns.

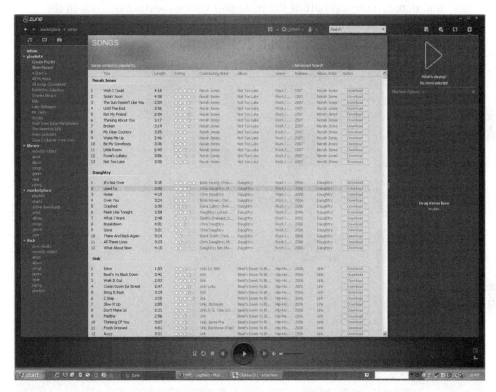

■ **Genre**   Although the Genre area might look a little sparse at first (it shows only nine genres), it's actually a great way to explore Zune Marketplace. Double-click any of the nine choices, and you'll see some highlights from that genre in the top half of the pane and various sorting options in the bar located between the top and the bottom halves. Click Styles to further narrow the genres.

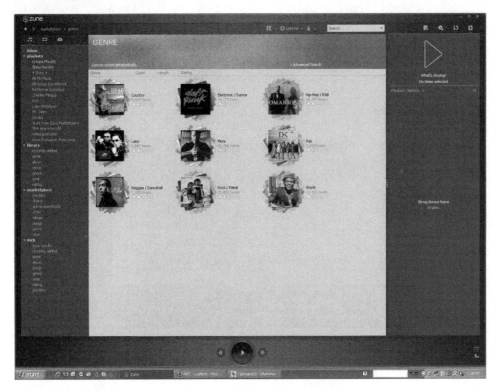

■ **Year**   Lists all the songs in Zune Marketplace by year.

You can move around in Zune Marketplace using any of these options or by clicking Artists, Albums, Playlists, and other items that appear within the list pane. (Think of it as a kind of Web site that operates within the Zune software.) You can also use the Web browser–like navigation controls, which are explained in an upcoming section.

To learn how to download songs from Zune Marketplace, see Chapter 5.

Your Zune   Finally, we come to the section of the navigation pane devoted expressly to your Zune. Of course, if your Zune isn't connected to your PC, you won't see anything listed except for its name (which, in my case, is Rick—clever, no?). Once connected, however, you'll see these selections:

- **Sync Results**   Lets you track the progress of Zune synchronization, both as it happens and after the fact.

- **Recently Added**   Shows the items that were added to your Zune during the most recent sync. (Note that this item appears only if you've recently added items to your Zune.)

- **Artist**

- **Album**

- **Songs**

- **Genre**

- **Year**

- **Rating**

- **Playlists**

The bottom seven items are fairly self-explanatory; see the Marketplace section if you need a refresher. The difference, of course, is that the items you see in the details pane reflect what's on your Zune.

If you don't immediately see these options listed beneath your Zune's name, remember that clicking the little triangle next to it will expand the selections for your navigating pleasure.

Videos

The Videos section of the navigation pane looks and operates just like the Music section, with one main exception: there's no Zune Marketplace category. (Hopefully there will be by the time you read this; Microsoft must be planning to sell Zune videos *someday*.)

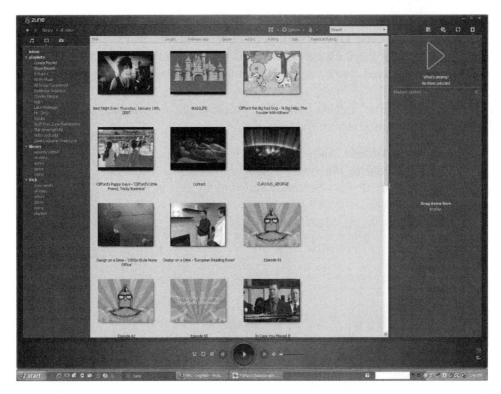

You'll also notice some changes in the Library section, which lists the following choices:

- **Recently Added**   As with the Music section, this category displays all the videos that have been recently added to your library. If you haven't added anything recently, you won't see this option.

- **All Video**   Lists all the videos in your library.

- **Actors**   In theory, this category would list your videos by actor. In practice, it doesn't really work, as there's no "actor" tag that you can apply to video files. Perhaps when Microsoft starts selling videos in Zune Marketplace that will change.

- **Genre**   See Actors.

- **Rating**   As with music, you can assign star ratings to your videos. I'd argue that there's not much value in doing so, unless you use the ratings as a kind of organizational tool (one star is for TV shows, two stars for video podcasts, and so on).

The Videos section also has a Playlist option, but, again, a playlist for videos isn't nearly as useful as one for music. That's because you're not likely to have more than a couple dozen videos on your Zune at any given time. Even so, they can help for things like organizing kids' shows, video podcasts, and the like. Find out more in Chapter 6.

 *Want a sneak peek of how a video will look on your Zune? Double-click it to watch it on your PC.*

4

Pictures

The Pictures section of the navigation pane also looks and operates just like the Music section, but as with the Videos section, there's no Zune Marketplace category. The focus is entirely on photos in your PC's library and on your Zune.

You'll also notice some changes in the Library section, which lists the following choices:

- **Recently Added**   As with the Music section, this category displays all the photos that have been recently added to your library. If you haven't added anything recently, you won't see this option.

- **All Pictures**   Lists all the photos in your library.

- **Keywords**   Neither the Zune nor the Zune software allows you to assign keywords to your photos. In theory, then, the Zune software would retrieve keyword information from the photo files themselves—assuming you'd assigned any. (Keywords, also known as tags, are an organizational tool used by some desktop photo organizers.) But even with photos that have keywords, I haven't seen any evidence that the Zune software properly recognizes them. Check my blog (zunebook.wordpress.com) for updates on this issue.

- **Date Taken**   Sorts your photos by the year they were taken. Double-click any year to see a further breakdown of photos by dates.

- **Rating**   Although you can't rate photos on your Zune itself, you can rate them in the Zune software—according to the Help file, anyway. In my tests, I was unable to assign ratings to my photos. Chalk it up to a bug in the software or your intrepid author doing something wrong. (Nah...couldn't be that.) As noted previously, check my blog to see if I've uncovered anything helpful about this.

- **Folder**   Sorts your photos by the folder from which they were imported.

Like its Music and Videos counterparts, the Photos section has a Playlist option. Building a photo playlist is akin to creating a slideshow of exactly the pictures you want, which might be a worthwhile endeavor. See Chapter 7 for more details.

You can view photo slideshows right on your PC. While viewing any group of photos in the details pane, double-click any single photo to start the slideshow. When you're done, click the little left-pointing arrow in the upper-left corner of the screen.

Use the Details Pane

The details pane (see Figure 4-2) is where all the action happens—it's the place that shows the selected contents of your library, playlists, and Zune, and the various virtual aisles of Zune Marketplace. It changes depending on what you click, of course, and offers you different ways to view your music for certain category selections.

Of course, the details pane does more than show things—it also lets you select media to play, copy to playlists, add to your Zune, and so on. Within Zune

4

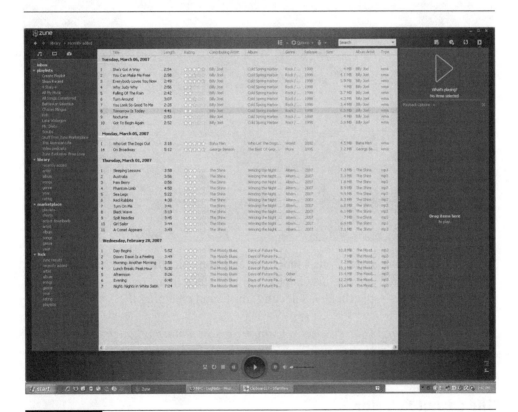

FIGURE 4-2   When you click a selection in the navigation pane, the results appear in the details pane.

Marketplace, you use the details pane to browse the catalog; buy, play, and download songs and albums; and tell friends about music you've discovered.

To find out more about Zune Marketplace options like this one, see "Play Zune Marketplace Music" later in this chapter. For now, let's focus on the library aspects of the details pane—specifically, selecting music and changing the layout.

The bulk of this discussion is going to focus on music, though the concepts and procedures are fairly similar for videos and photos. See Chapters 6 and 7, respectively, to learn more about working with those kinds of media.

The Layout Selector

Up near the top of the Zune software interface, smack dab in the center, lies the layout selector—a button that lets you choose between three different views for your library (see Figure 4-1).

The views are as follows:

◼ Icon

◼ Tile

◼ Details

I could explain the differences between them, but it's easier just to show them:

Icon view

Tile view

Details view

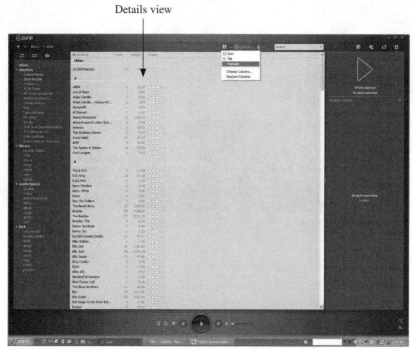

As you can see, the three views simply show your library with different levels of detail. You can click the layout selector button to cycle between them, or click the little arrow next to it and choose the one you want. There's no right or wrong view; experiment with them and see which you like best for perusing your media.

 *Not all three views are available for all areas of your music library. In some cases, there might be only two views, and a few categories limit you to just one view.*

Use the Search Bar

If you're like most users, your music library includes hundreds, if not thousands, of songs. So when you're absolutely dying to hear, say, Fountains of Wayne's "Mexican Wine," you don't want to waste valuable time scrolling and clicking your way through the song or artist lists. Wouldn't it be better if you could just type "mex" and, poof, there's the song? That's the idea behind the Search bar, which enables you to perform quick and easy searches of your media library.

The Search bar is located at the top of the screen. Plan on spending a lot of time here; there's simply no better way to find items in your library.

There's nothing complicated about using Search: just start typing the name of a song, artist, or album. You'll quickly notice that searches are dynamic. As you type, the Zune software narrows the search with each additional letter. That's in contrast to the "old-fashioned" way of searching for data, which was to type a phrase, press ENTER, and hope for the best. This way, you're likely to find what you're after with just a few keystrokes. Watch this "in action" in the following screenshots as I go looking for the aforementioned Fountains of Wayne song. With each letter I type, I get closer to the song, and after just three letters I've found it.

Album		Title		Length	Rating	Contributing Artist	Size	Type	Bit Rate
10,000 Maniacs									
Blind Man's Zoo	1	Eat for Two		3:31	⭐⭐⭐	10,000 Maniacs	4.8 MB	mp3	192 ...
10,000 Maniacs	2	Please Forgive Us		3:24	⭐⭐⭐	10,000 Maniacs	4.6 MB	mp3	192 ...
Soft Rock	3	The Big Parade		4:01	⭐⭐⭐	10,000 Maniacs	5.5 MB	mp3	192 ...
1989	4	Trouble Me		3:14	⭐⭐⭐	10,000 Maniacs	4.4 MB	mp3	192 ...
	5	You Happy Puppet		3:38	⭐⭐⭐	10,000 Maniacs	5 MB	mp3	192 ...
	6	Headstrong		4:16	⭐⭐⭐	10,000 Maniacs	5.8 MB	mp3	192 ...
	7	Poison in the Well		3:08	⭐⭐⭐	10,000 Maniacs	4.3 MB	mp3	192 ...
	8	Dust Bowl		4:12	⭐⭐⭐	10,000 Maniacs	5.7 MB	mp3	192 ...
	9	The Lion's Share		3:03	⭐⭐⭐	10,000 Maniacs	4.2 MB	mp3	192 ...
	10	Hateful Hate		4:31	⭐⭐⭐	10,000 Maniacs	6.2 MB	mp3	192 ...
	11	Jubilee		6:07	⭐⭐⭐	10,000 Maniacs	8.4 MB	mp3	192 ...
ABBA									
ABBA - Gold: Greatest ...	3	Take A Chance On Me		4:01	⭐⭐⭐⭐	ABBA	3.7 MB	mp3	128 ...
ABBA	4	Mamma Mia		3:44	⭐⭐⭐⭐	ABBA	3.4 MB	mp3	128 ...
Rock/Pop	9	Money, Money, Money		3:08	⭐⭐⭐⭐⭐	ABBA	2.9 MB	mp3	128 ...
1993									
Adam Sandler									
What The Hell Happene...	6	The Chanukah Song		3:44	⭐⭐⭐⭐	Adam Sandler	3.4 MB	mp3	128 ...
Adam Sandler									
Comedy									
1996									
Alanis Morissette									
Jagged Little Pill	1	All I Really Want		4:44	⭐⭐⭐	Alanis Morissette	6.5 MB	mp3	192 ...
Alanis Morissette	2	You Oughta Know		4:09	⭐⭐⭐⭐⭐	Alanis Morissette	5.7 MB	mp3	192 ...
Rock	3	Perfect		3:07	⭐⭐⭐	Alanis Morissette	4.3 MB	mp3	192 ...
1995	4	Hand In My Pocket		3:41	⭐⭐⭐	Alanis Morissette	5 MB	mp3	192 ...
	5	Right Through You		2:55	⭐⭐⭐	Alanis Morissette	4 MB	mp3	192 ...
	6	Forgiven		5:00	⭐⭐⭐	Alanis Morissette	6.8 MB	mp3	192 ...
	7	You Learn		3:59	⭐⭐⭐	Alanis Morissette	5.4 MB	mp3	192 ...
	8	Head Over Feet		4:27	⭐⭐⭐	Alanis Morissette	6.1 MB	mp3	192 ...
	9	Mary Jane		4:40	⭐⭐⭐	Alanis Morissette	6.4 MB	mp3	192 ...
	10	Ironic		3:49	⭐⭐⭐	Alanis Morissette	5.2 MB	mp3	192 ...
	11	Not The Doctor		3:47	⭐⭐⭐	Alanis Morissette	5.2 MB	mp3	192 ...
	12	Wake Up		4:53	⭐⭐⭐	Alanis Morissette	6.7 MB	mp3	192 ...
	13	You Oughta Know (Altern...		8:12	⭐⭐⭐	Alanis Morissette	11.2 MB	mp3	192 ...

A few other things to note about Search:

- The Search tool works within whatever media category is selected: Music, Videos, or Photos.

- If you use Search while viewing the Zune Marketplace, it will look only in Zune Marketplace, not your library.

- If you perform a search of your library and the Zune software finds no matches, it will automatically search Zune Marketplace.

- The search results will display differently, depending on the selected view (see the previous section, "The Layout Selector").

- You can click the down arrow next to the Search bar to narrow the results or to see the results of the Zune Marketplace search (if they're not already displayed in the details pane).

■ Don't forget to clear the Search bar (by clicking the little x) when you're done; otherwise, you'll see only search results when you try clicking different areas of the navigation pane.

Use the List Pane and Task Selectors

Finally, we come to the list pane, which occupies the right side of the Zune software. What you see here depends on what option is highlighted in the Task Selectors toolbar at the top of the pane; but for the most part, it displays whatever media you've selected recently. If you're listening to music, for instance, you'll see the queued list of songs. If you've selected media to sync to your Zune, you'll see it listed here.

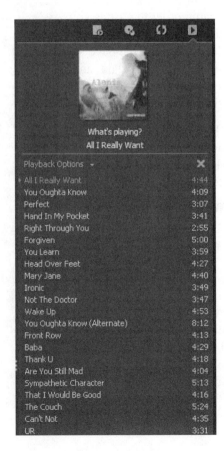

Let's talk about the four task selectors and how they affect the list pane:

■ **Create And Edit Playlists**   Although you can create a playlist by clicking the eponymous option in the navigation pane, here you get more control and a better look at what's actually in the playlist. Just drag whatever media you want (songs, photos, etc.) from the details pane to the list pane. Each time you drop in additional media, it will fall into the lineup wherever you drop it. You can reorder the list as you see fit by dragging items to the desired spot. When you're done, click the Save Playlist button, as shown on the right, and give the new playlist a name. Find out more about playlists in Chapter 5.

■ **Burn Files To Disc**   Click this task to create an audio CD from the songs currently in the list pane. Find out more in the upcoming section, "Burn CDs."

■ **Sync Content To and From Your Zune Device**   This is the place to queue items you want added to your Zune. For example, if you've elected not to auto-sync your video library (see Chapter 2), you'll need to manually select videos to copy. Click this task, open your video library using the navigation pane, and drag the desired videos from the details pane to the list pane. Click Start Sync to begin the synchronization process as shown next.

■ **Now Playing** When you select one or more songs, videos, or photos to play in the Zune software, the list appears here. You can double-click any item to jump directly to it or drag items to adjust the play order. Clicking the X in the upper-right corner of the pane clears all entries (just from the pane, not from your library). At any time you can click the Playback Options arrow to save the Now Playing list as a playlist. You can also clear the list, view visualizations, or select an equalizer setting.

 *While listening to music in the Zune software, move your mouse pointer over the little graphic equalizer in the lower-left corner of the screen. After a moment, a small box will appear displaying the* bit rate *of the current song. (See Chapter 5 to learn more about bit rates.)*

Modify the Interface

Although you can't change much about the Zune software interface (sorry, you're stuck with the rather drab color scheme), there are a few helpful tweaks you can make. For example, you can resize the list pane to make it wider. Why bother? The before and after are shown on the next page.

As you can see, the wider pane contains more information than just song name; ratings and lengths are now visible as well. Even better, you now have the option to rate each song as it plays (accomplished by clicking the desired number of stars next to each song name). In the narrower, starless view, you had to right-click the song and choose Rate from the accompanying menu.

To resize the list pane, click the three small dots midway down the left side of the pane, and then drag that border to the left (or right, if you want to make it narrower again). You can perform similar resizing on the navigation pane, though there's less value in doing so. Finally, within various Zune Marketplace views in the details pane, you can adjust the sizes of the upper and lower halves of the pane by dragging the center line up or down. Here's an example:

Playing Music on Your PC

Although the Zune software exists primarily to feed media to your Zune player and provide a Zune Marketplace storefront, it's also a capable music player. In fact, it's not unlike Windows Media Player 11, the music manager/player built into the Windows Vista operating system (and available for download for Windows XP users). If you're sitting at your desk and want to enjoy some music, just fire up the Zune software.

The software can play songs stored on your PC (that is, your local library) or streamed from Zune Marketplace (assuming you have a Zune Pass—see Chapter 2). Before I show you how to do both, let's take a quick look at the playback controls.

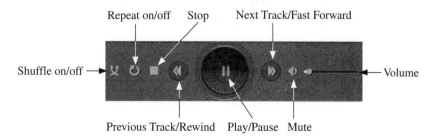

 *There are times when all but the Previous Track, Play/Pause, and Next Track buttons become invisible. I'm not sure of the rhyme or reason behind this, but rest assured that the remaining controls will become visible again when you point your mouse at that area.*

Playing Local Music

Ready to listen to your music? The Zune software can play anything or everything in your library. Let's look at the steps for several common scenarios:

- **Shuffle-play all your music**   Regrettably, the Zune software lacks the Shuffle All option that's so prevalent on the Zune itself (see Chapter 3). But it's not hard to accomplish the same thing. In the navigation pane, in the Library section, right-click Songs and then select Play. By default, all your songs will begin playing in the default order, which is alphabetically by album. To randomize them, click the Shuffle icon in the playback controls at the bottom of the screen.

- **Play one album**   If the list pane isn't empty, click the little x to clear the now-playing list. In the navigation pane, click Album and then find the one you want in the details pane. From here you have several options: You can double-click the album, right-click the album and choose Play, or drag the album to the list plane. The end result is the same: the album begins playing immediately.

- **Play a playlist**   This is probably starting to seem obvious by now, but to listen to a playlist, right-click it and choose Play.

- **Play your choice of songs**   Remember that you can drag any song(s) you want from the details pane to the list pane. (Incidentally, this is also how you build a playlist.) Once you've compiled a list of the songs you want, just click the Play/Pause button in the playback controls.

Remember, too, that you can adjust playback order just by dragging songs within the list pane. You can also turn any queued selection of songs into a playlist by clicking the Playback Options arrow and choosing Save Playlist As.

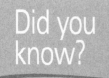

The Origins of the Zune Software

If the Zune software looks a bit familiar, that's because it's built on the same core as Windows Media Player 11. Indeed, except for a few cosmetic differences, the two programs function quite similarly. If you're already experienced with Windows Media Player 11, you should have an easy time transitioning to the Zune software.

The two programs can easily coexist on your PC—you don't have to use one exclusively over the other. In fact, you can use Windows Media Player to play songs you've downloaded or purchased from Zune Marketplace; that's how connected the two programs are.

Playing Zune Marketplace Music

This option requires you to have a Zune Pass subscription, which, as we discussed in Chapter 2, gives you full access to the Zune Marketplace library. You can not only download songs to copy to your Zune, but also stream songs directly from Zune Marketplace—much like tuning in a radio station. The difference here is that you choose the songs, albums, artists, and/or playlists you want to hear.

   Without a Zune Pass subscription, you can still stream music—but only 30-second snippets of each song, which is not my idea of the ideal jukebox.

As you know from reading about the navigation pane and Search bar, it's easy to stroll through Zune Marketplace's virtual aisles. As for actually playing the music you find, that's even easier. Let's walk through a few common scenarios to help illustrate how it all works:

■ **Play one song**   While looking at the song list (in the bottom half of the details pane) for any artist, album, playlist, etc., you can queue any single song for playback by right-clicking it and choosing Play. You can also double-click the song, but that will add all other listed songs to the queue.

■ **Play an album**   While viewing an album listing, you should see a Play Album link in the top half of the details pane. One click is all it takes to add the album to the queue. You can also follow the instructions for playing a single song. Double-clicking any song in the album list will add them all to the Now Playing queue.

■ **Play all songs from one artist**   Want to hear every Billy Joel song available in Zune Marketplace? Do a search and then click the 504 Songs link that appears in the details pane. You'll see a list of all Billy's tunes. Then follow any of the usual procedures to get them all in the queue.

■ **Play a playlist** While browsing Zune Marketplace playlists, double-click the one you want and then click the Play button in the upper half of the details pane.

4

Simply put, playing songs in Zune Marketplace isn't much different from playing them from your local music library. The best way to learn your way around is to explore and experiment.

 *To learn how to buy and download songs from Zune Marketplace, see Chapter 5. In the meantime, Microsoft has a good Web page devoted to Zune Marketplace activity: http://tinyurl.com/36w7ox.*

Rating Songs

As you learned in Chapter 3, you can use your Zune to rate songs in your library on a scale of one to five stars. The advantage of doing so is that you can use these ratings to create specialized playlists or even to organize your songs in a certain way. (Find out more in Chapter 5.)

There are several ways to rate songs in the Zune software. You can:

- Right-click a song title (either in the details pane or list pane), click Rate, and then choose a rating of one to five stars.

- While viewing a song list in the details pane, point your mouse at the stars alongside any given song, and then click the rating you want.

- You can rate songs in the list pane just as you would in the details pane, provided the former is wide enough that you can actually see the stars and point your mouse at them. See "Use the Zune Software Interface" earlier in this chapter for more details.

Any ratings you apply to songs in your library will be applied to songs on your Zune—and vice versa.

Want to give an entire album (or any batch of songs) the same rating? Select all the songs (done by holding down the CTRL key while clicking each one), right-click any song in the selection, and choose Rate. Click the rating you want, and presto—fast-batch ratings.

Stream Music from Your PC to Your Xbox 360

Got an Xbox 360? You lucky reader, you. If you're *really* lucky, it's connected to your home theater system, meaning you're enjoying widescreen gaming and roof-rattling stereo sound. Whatever your setup, you may want to leverage one of the Zune software's more interesting capabilities: streaming your music library to your Xbox.

This is not the same thing as streaming music from your Zune player to your Xbox, which is covered in Chapter 12.

Why bother? Simple: It lets you enjoy your music library in a different room of the house (assuming, of course, that your computer and Xbox aren't occupying the same entertainment center). This can be especially great in the aforementioned scenario, where your Xbox is connected to some killer speakers. Here's what you need to make this possible:

- ■ A home network (meaning you have one or more computers connected via a router)

- ■ A wired or wireless connection between your Xbox 360 and your router (which you probably already have if you're an Xbox Live subscriber)

With that equipment in place, it's a simple matter to configure the Zune software and your Xbox to communicate and, well, share! Start with the Zune software:

1. Click Options | Library | Media Sharing.

2. Select the Share My Media check box.

3. Select the Music check box (and Video and/or Pictures if you want to share those, too).

4. If desired, give your media library a name other than the one listed. (You might want something more specific, like "Rick's PC Zune Library.")

5. Select the Share With All Xbox 360s option.

6. Click OK.

That takes care of the PC side of things. Now head to your Xbox, open the Dashboard, and follow these steps:

1. Select Media.

2. Select Music (or, if you enabled other kinds of media for sharing, Pictures and/or Video).

3. Select Computer—namely, the one on your network that has the Zune software installed.

4. Choose the songs, albums, artists, etc. you want to play.

That's all there is to it! You'll be glad to know that streaming your library has little impact on your computer; you can still use it like normally would. In fact, the Zune software doesn't even indicate that there's any streaming in progress—it happens entirely behind the scenes.

Also, keep in mind that for streaming to work, your PC must remain on. This may sound obvious, but you'd be surprised at how many people overlook this fact.

Burn CDs

When you buy music from Zune Marketplace (as opposed to "renting" it with a Zune Pass), it's only natural to want something tangible for your money. After all, many of us grew up buying LPs or CDs, so trading hard-earned cash for invisible bits and bytes may seem a trifle unsatisfying. Of course, there are practical considerations as well. A CD doubles as a backup of your purchase, just in case your hard drive suffers a catastrophic failure. What's more, a CD can play just about anywhere: car stereos, boom boxes, even other PCs.

For the purposes of this discussion, we're talking about audio CDs—the kind you'd get at a music store and that play in pretty much any player. To learn about burning MP3 CDs, which are a bit different, see the next section.

The Zune software makes it easy to burn audio CDs using purchased content from Zune Marketplace or existing content from your music library (or both, if you care to mix and match). Before we get started, however, you'll need to make sure that your PC has a key piece of hardware: a CD or DVD drive capable of burning discs. These are commonly known as CD-RW or DVD±RW drives. If you're not sure if your computer has the right kind of drive, consult the manual. If it doesn't, you can add one pretty inexpensively. An internal DVD burner (which can also burn CDs) should run you no more than $30 to 40, while external models (which plug into a USB port) sell for around $50 to 60. See Figure 4-3 for an example of the latter.

Of course, you'll also need some blank CDs. My advice is to buy the cheapest 80-minute CD-R media you can find (which usually means buying a spindle of 50 or 100 discs), but, really, any blank CD will do. You could opt for rewriteable (or CD-RW) media, but with write-once CD-Rs being so inexpensive, I honestly don't see the point.

FIGURE 4-3   If your PC doesn't already have a CD burner, you can add one like this external BusLink model.

But I digress. Here's how to burn a CD with the Zune software:

1. Start the program and then insert a blank CD into your CD/DVD burner. The list pane should automatically switch to the Burn Options view, showing you how many minutes' worth of space are available on the disc.

2. Using the navigation pane, find whatever music you want to burn: an album, individual songs, a playlist, etc. (Remember that you can't burn songs downloaded with a Zune Pass, only those purchased outright from Zune Marketplace. Of course, you can also burn any unprotected tracks stored in your library.)

3. Drag the desired songs to the list pane. As you do, you'll notice the CD Gauge start to fill up, indicating how much space is still available.

4. If you've selected more songs than will fit on the CD, the Zune software will automatically "span" the extra songs to a second disc (and, if

necessary, a third, a fourth, and so on). In other words, you can select as many songs as you want, and the software will spread them out over as many discs as it takes.

5. Click Start Burn and grab a cup of coffee while the Zune software burns your new CD(s).

When the process is finished, your PC should spit out the new disc. Take it for a spin in your favorite CD player (or just pop it back into the PC) to make sure it works.

Burn an MP3 CD

When you create an audio CD, the Zune software converts your MP3, WMA, and other compressed music files into much larger audio files, which is why each disc can hold only a couple dozen songs, at most. However, the software can also produce MP3 CDs, which are essentially ordinary data CDs filled with unconverted MP3s. The advantage to doing so is that a single CD can hold upwards of 150 songs—roughly 10 times what you get from an audio CD. The disadvantage is that not all CD players can recognize MP3 CDs. What's more, if you copy Zune Marketplace purchases to an MP3 CD, they'll play only on a PC that's authorized to download the licenses for those songs. Thus, its overall value is questionable. And let's not forget that your Zune more or less obviates the need for CDs anyway, so you may not want to bother.

If you do, simply click the Burn Options arrow above the list pane, and select Data CD. You'll see that a lot more songs will now fit on your blank disc. From there, just proceed as before.

To learn more about data CDs, see the Zune's Help file.

The Zune Software Plays CDs, Too

When you insert an audio CD into your PC, the Zune software can play it for you. In fact, you'll see the album name in the navigation pane, the song list in the details and list panes, and possibly even the album's cover art. Better still, the software can "rip" songs from the disc and add them to your library—a great way to build up your Zune music collection. Find out more in Chapter 5.

Part II

Pack Your Player

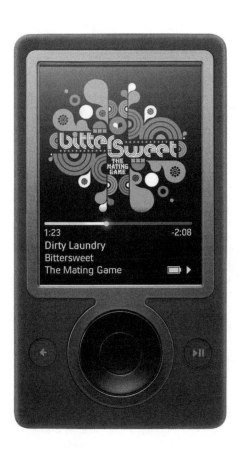

Chapter 5

Music

How to...

- Download subscription music
- Buy songs from Zune Marketplace
- Convert songs from other online services
- Buy unprotected music online
- Convert audio files to a Zune-compatible format
- Rip songs from CDs
- Rip songs from cassette tapes
- Create a new playlist
- Use song tags and album art

Now that you know how to use your Zune and the Zune software, it's time to get down to business—the business of filling that puppy with music. You've got 30 gigabytes' worth of space at your disposal, enough to hold thousands of songs. But where will these songs come from? Most likely, they'll come from a mixture of sources, including your existing library, audio CDs, online stores, and, of course, Zune Marketplace. Let's take a look at these and other sources for Zune music.

Get Music from Zune Marketplace

You first learned about Zune Marketplace in Chapter 2. As a reminder, there are two ways to retrieve music from this massive online store:

- Buy songs and albums, which are then downloaded to your PC and copied to your Zune.
- Subscribe to Zune Pass, which entitles you download unlimited tracks.

As discussed in Chapter 4, you can also stream music from Zune Marketplace, but that's more like listening to the radio. It doesn't actually download songs to copy to your Zune.

The end result of these two methods is the same: Song files get downloaded to your PC and then copied to your Zune. Let's take a closer look.

Download Subscription Music

In case you missed it in Chapter 2, a $15-per-month Zune Pass entitles you to download all the music you want from Zune Marketplace's library of over three million songs. Not convinced? Look in your Zune box: You should find a promotional card offering a free 2 week trial, which will give you enough time to explore the service and download a few thousand songs of your choosing.

No, you can't just let the trial expire and then keep the songs forever. As mentioned previously, Zune Marketplace songs have a kind of built-in monitoring system that knows if your subscription is still paid up. If not, the songs will simply stop playing after 30 days. Hey, don't look so annoyed—they're just keeping you honest, after all. If you do decide to stop your subscription, consider flagging your favorite tracks (see Chapter 3) to remind yourself to buy them later.

With an active Zune Pass subscription in place, it's a simple matter to download individual songs or entire albums.

Download Individual Songs

Ready to start downloading? Let's start with one song.

1. Sign into Zune Marketplace.

5

2. Browse Zune Marketplace or search for a particular song, artist, or album. Ultimately, you want to see one or more songs listed in the bottom half of the details pane.

3. Click the Download button for the song you want to download. Note that you may have to slide the scroll bar to the right to make this button visible.

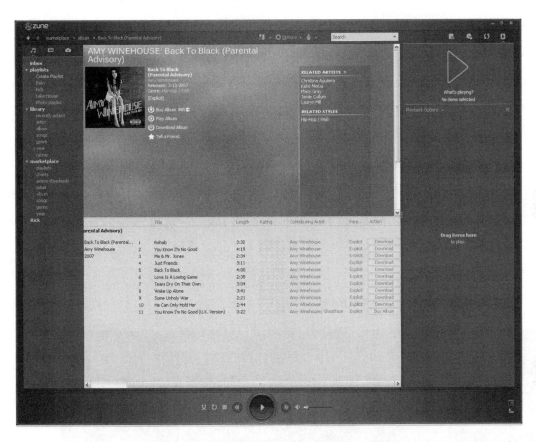

4. Wait a minute or two while the song downloads. You can see its progress in the Download button, which turns into a status gauge.

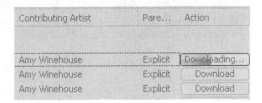

5. When the download completes, the song automatically gets added to your library and copied to your Zune on the next sync (assuming you've configured the Zune software to auto-sync your music library).

If you want to make the Download button more readily accessible, resize or remove a few of the columns in the lower half of the details pane. For instance, you may find the Contributing Artist and Parental Rating columns superfluous. To remove them, right-click any column and select Choose Columns. Clear the check boxes for those two columns, and then click OK. Alternately, select the Hide Columns Automatically option, which will ensure that the Download button is visible and that no scrolling is required.

Download an Album

Sure, you could click Download for each and every song in an album, but why click a dozen or more times when you could click just once? Here's the process to download an entire album, using Amy Winehouse's *Back to Black* as an example:

1. Sign into Zune Marketplace.

2. Type **back to black** in the Search bar. In a moment, you should see the following in the details pane:

3. Click the 4 Albums link, and then double-click the entry for Amy Winehouse's *Back to Black*. You'll then see the following album page:

4. Now just click Download Album in the top half of the details pane. Look in the lower half, and you'll see that all the Download buttons have been "activated." You can monitor their progress there or click the Active Downloads link in the navigation pane.

5. When the downloads are done, the songs automatically get added to your library and copied to your Zune on the next sync (assuming you've configured the Zune software to auto-sync your music library).

Wash, rinse, repeat! Remember, you've got unlimited access to Zune Marketplace, so don't be afraid to go nuts. Download anything and everything you want to hear. If you try something and don't like it, just delete it—no harm done.

Songs downloaded as part of a Zune Pass won't be automatically deleted from your computer if you let the subscription expire—you just won't be able to play them. If you want to clear up that space on your hard drive, open the folder that contains the tracks and delete them manually.

Buy Songs from Zune Marketplace

Even if you're not a Zune Pass subscriber, you can still purchase music from Zune Marketplace. Why bother? The chief reason would be to burn a CD (see Chapter 4), something you can't do with Zune Pass downloads. Alternately, if you're planning to end your Zune Pass subscription but there's music you want to keep permanently, you can buy it outright. (Learn more about these considerations in Chapter 2.)

My Top Five "New" Artists

One reason I'm so fond of Zune Pass is that it enables me to discover new music like never before. In the old days, you had to listen to the radio or watch MTV if you wanted to be exposed to new artists. Now, all it takes is a few clicks, and I can listen to the complete catalogs of tens of thousands of artists—new and old alike. Consequently, I thought I'd share five of my most recent discoveries.

- **Brendan Benson** I can't get enough of this guy's "power pop"—his most recent album, *Alternative to Love*, ranks among my all-time favorites. I dare you to resist jamming along to "Spit It Out" or belting out the words to "Feel Like Myself."

- **Lily Allen** Normally, I'm not one for cheeky Brit-pop, but I can't help loving Allen's amusing blend of sweet melodies and acerbic lyrics. I've even got the music video for the track "Smile" on my Zune; I downloaded it from YouTube (see Chapter 6). Fun stuff.

- **The Shins** I credit actor Zach Braff with introducing me to this band, which has a decidedly unique sound and some catchy alt-pop tunes.

- **Bruce Springsteen** Obviously "The Boss" is no newcomer, but he's never released anything like 2006's *We Shall Overcome: The Seeger Sessions*. This rowdy collection of folk tunes covers evokes a bit of Bob Dylan with a good helping of the *O Brother, Where Art Thou?* soundtrack.

- **Amy Winehouse** Clearly I'm a sucker for pretty British vocalists. Like Lily Allen, Amy Winehouse dishes out biting, clever lyrics. But her deep, soulful voice begs comparison to Billie Holiday, and a good many of the tunes on her *Back to Black* album evoke that smoky jazz sound of the '40s and '50s.

Allow me to give you a quick refresher on how Zune Marketplace purchases work. As I bemoaned before, you can't just pay 99 cents per song or $9.99 per album and be done with it, as you can with virtually every other online music store on the planet. Instead, Microsoft forces you to buy *points*, which you then exchange for music. It may seem pointless, but at least it's not complicated.

Here's how it works: You buy a predetermined number of points that stay in your account like, well, money. Then you "spend" those points when you buy music. As of press time, Microsoft is offering the following points packages:

- $5—400 points

- $15—1,200 points

- $25—2,000 points

- $50—4,000 points

As discussed in Chapter 2, there's no real advantage to buying larger blocks of points up front, so you might as well hang on to your money and just buy small blocks of points as you need them.

Want to give a Zune user the gift of points? You can buy prepaid points cards. Look for them wherever you can buy other kinds of digital music gift cards, such as Best Buy and Circuit City.

Add Points to Your Account

Before you can buy music from Zune Marketplace, you'll need to stock your account with some points. Here's how:

1. Sign into Zune Marketplace.

2. Click the Zune Marketplace sign-in button again, and this time select Account Management.

3. Click the Purchase Points button. (If you have a prepaid card you bought or received as a gift, click Redeem Prepaid Card, and follow the instructions.)

4. Choose your desired denomination, and then click Next.

5. Enter your credit card information. (If you're uncomfortable with this, then you're definitely a candidate for buying prepaid cards. However, I'm of the opinion that online purchases—especially through Microsoft—are 99.99 percent secure.)

6. Click Purchase, and you're done! You should now see your available points in the main Account Management screen.

NOTE *You can also access your account via Microsoft's Zune site (www.zune .net). Click the Sign In button, and provide your user ID and password, just as you would in the Zune software.*

Buy Songs and Albums

Once you've got some points in your account, you're all set to start buying music.
The process is almost exactly the same as downloading songs via Zune Pass,
with a couple of tiny exceptions. Here's the scoop, again using Amy Winehouse's
dazzling *Back to Black* as an example:

1. Sign into Marketplace.

2. Type **back to black** in the Search bar.

3. In the details pane, click the 4 Albums link, and then double-click the entry
   for *Back to Black*. You'll see the following album page:

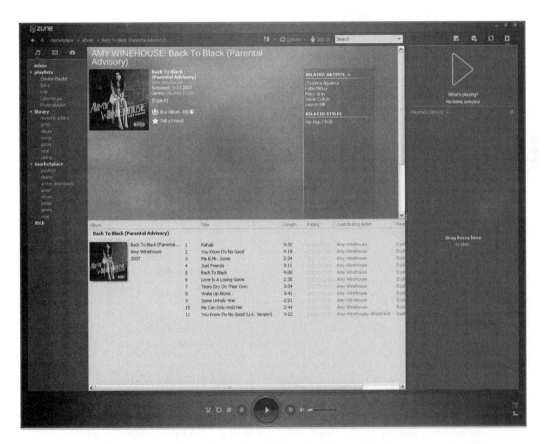

4. If you want to buy the entire album (well worth it, I assure you), click
   the Buy Album link in the top half of the details pane. Note the "price"

that's listed there: the Winehouse album will cost you 880 points, which works out to about $10. After clicking that link, you'll see a box asking you to confirm the purchase. Click Confirm, and the Zune software will immediately begin downloading the songs to your library.

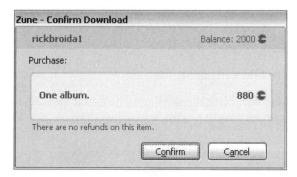

5. If you'd rather buy an individual track, just right-click it in the details pane, and choose Buy from the pop-up menu. Again you'll see a box asking you to confirm the purchase. Click Confirm to buy and download the song.

To monitor the progress of your downloads, you can click the Active Downloads link in the navigation pane. When the downloads are done, the songs automatically get added to your library and copied to your Zune on the next sync (assuming you've configured the Zune software to auto-sync your music library).

Where to Score Cheap CDs

If you've decided that you prefer CDs to Zune Marketplace, don't pay those ridiculous retail prices. Instead, take advantage of these Web resources to score dirt-cheap and even free CDs to add to your collection:

- **Amazon Marketplace** Amazon usually has great deals on CDs, but you can often do even better by clicking the See Offers link, which will lead you to private sellers. Just keep in mind that you'll pay around $3.50 for shipping from these vendors, which may offset any savings.

- **DeepDiscount.com** This site tends to have some of the Web's best deals on CDs, and as an added perk, shipping is free. However, it's Media Mail shipping, so it'll probably take a week or two for your CD to arrive.

- **Lala** Want to trade old, unwanted CDs for new ones? That's the idea behind Lala (www.lala.com), a CD-swapping service that charges just $1 per trade. I've used this before, and while it's not always easy to trade crummy old discs for cool new stuff, it's definitely worth checking out.

There's often a price advantage to buying an entire album, most of which cost 880 points. Individual tracks cost 79 points apiece, so if an album has more than 12 tracks (and you intend to buy them all), you're definitely better off buying the whole thing.

Convert Songs from Other Online Services

Zune Marketplace isn't the only game in town. There are lots of other online music stores, including BuyMusic, iTunes, Napster, Rhapsody, and Yahoo Music Unlimited. However, as you learned in Chapter 2, songs purchased from those stores aren't compatible with the Zune due to their digital rights management (DRM) protections.

Just as I was finishing work on this book, Apple announced plans to remove DRM protections from songs from the EMI record label. That's a huge deal, as it means those tracks will be playable on your Zune (which supports Apple's AAC file format). Time will tell if other labels follow suit, but it's definitely good news for users who want more than one online-store option when shopping for music.

So what if you've already spent big bucks on music from one or more of these stores? What if your iPod died and you decided to replace it with a Zune? Are you completely out of luck? Do you have to buy all those songs a second time?

The answer, I'm happy to report, is no. Ideally, you'd subscribe to Zune Pass, which would allow you to download from Zune Marketplace all the songs you purchased from other services. However, that's rental, not ownership. If you want to convert songs purchased elsewhere, there's a relatively simple solution. It goes like this:

1. Using whatever software is recommended or required by the service that sold you the songs, burn the songs to CDs.

2. Using the Zune software, rip those CDs like you would any other (as described in the upcoming section, "Rip Songs from CDs").

That's all there is to it! This two-step process may be a bit of a hassle, but it does rid you of that annoying DRM protection, leaving you with MP3 or WMA files you can copy and play as you please.

NOTE *There is one downside to this burn-and-rip solution: Sound quality takes a minor hit. That's because you're starting with files that are already compressed, meaning some of the original audio data has already been removed. When you rip the songs from the CDs, they're being converted and compressed a second time, further degrading the original audio. Personally, I can't hear much difference between the DRM-protected songs and the CD-ripped versions, but if you have a keen ear, you might not be happy with the results. Hey, I didn't say it was a perfect solution.*

Wait a Second, I Thought the Zune Could Play AAC Files!

As you learned in Chapter 2, the Zune can play not only MP3 and WMA files, but also AAC files—the kind traditionally used by iPods. That being the case, shouldn't the Zune be able to play songs purchased from iTunes, which are delivered in AAC format? You're forgetting one thing: DRM. Just as music purchased from Zune Marketplace is copy-protected, so are the tunes sold by iTunes (the exception being those songs from the EMI catalog, which were recently made available without DRM). You can still burn them to CDs and rip them to MP3 or WMA format using the method described in the previous section, but you can't just copy them straight to your Zune.

There is, however, an exception: If you've used iTunes to rip CDs, the resulting AAC-formatted songs *can* be copied straight to your Zune.

Are There Any DRM-Free Alternatives?

Not all online music stores employ DRM. If you're looking for Zune-compatible music that's totally free of restrictions, there's one place I highly recommend: eMusic (www.emusic.com). Unlike iTunes, Zune Marketplace, and other well-known digital music stores, eMusic (seen in Figure 5-1) delivers unrestricted, unprotected MP3s. How many CDs can you burn with them? As many as you want. What portable players do they support? All of them. In short, they're like the MP3s you'd rip from your own CDs, making other stores' heavily armored downloads seem particularly draconian.

You can sign up for a two-week trial and download 25 free songs, no strings attached. After that, eMusic charges between $9.99 and $19.99 per month. The three available subscription plans include a fixed number of downloads each month: 30 for $9.99, 50 for $14.99, and 75 for $19.99. That works out to 33 cents per track or less—quite a savings over what you pay at most other online stores. Plus, you get to keep the songs even if you cancel the subscription, which is not true of subscription services like Zune Pass.

There's a hitch, of course. You can't buy tunes a la carte; non-subscribers can't buy music at all; and if you want more songs than your subscription plan includes, you have to wait till next month or buy "booster packs"—10 extra downloads for $4.99, 25 for $9.99, and so on. Thankfully, these don't expire like your monthly allotment; they stay in your account for as long as you're a paying subscriber.

Another Great Way to Discover New Music

As I've espoused already, a Zune Pass makes it possible to discover all kinds of great music, new and old alike. But don't ignore old-fashioned discovery tools, like radio. Specifically, NPR's weekly *All Songs Considered* show brings you the best of what's new, with full-length track samples from each featured album or artist. The show introduced me to Brendan Benson and Fountains of Wayne, two of my favorites.

Visit NPR's Web site (www.npr.org) to see where and when you can hear the show in your area or to stream it directly to your PC. Even better, subscribe to the *All Songs Considered* podcast, which lets you listen to the show on your Zune. See Chapter 9 to learn more about podcasts.

FIGURE 5-1 If you want music downloads that don't saddle you with DRM restrictions, try eMusic.

There's another hitch—selection. Although eMusic boasts more than 1.5 million tracks, the majority of them come from lesser-known indie artists. However, there's enough mainstream material to satisfy casual music fans. I used up my first month's download credits on Cat Power, Miles Davis, and The Raconteurs, to name a few.

To use eMusic with your Zune, just configure its Download Manager utility to save songs into one of the Zune software's monitored folders. After you download your eMusic tunes, fire up the Zune software and sync your Zune—it's as simple as that.

Obviously, you get quite a bit more bang for the buck from Zune Pass, but you also get saddled with restrictions. Not so with eMusic. So do yourself a favor and give it a try. It's quite possibly the *fairest* music store around.

Rip Songs from CDs

Chances are good that you own some CDs—perhaps more than some. I know people who've amassed hundreds of them over the years. And I know plenty more who refuse to buy music online, instead preferring the tangibility and versatility of store-bought CDs. Indeed, there's something to be said for buying music on traditional media (see "CDs vs. Digital Downloads" later in this chapter).

As you may know, it's possible to copy songs from your CDs to your PC and, ultimately, your Zune. This involves a process called *ripping*, which not only copies the songs, but also converts them to PC-friendly digital files. There are countless programs that can rip CDs, but you need look no further than the Zune software, which makes simple work of it.

Before we get started, however, you're going to need to make a few decisions about the digital files you're going to create:

- Where to store them on your hard drive

- What audio format to use

- What bit rate to use

All three of these options can be set in the Zune Options menu, which is shown in Figure 5-2.

To get there, click Options > Rip > More Options. Let's start with the location for ripped songs.

Choose Where to Store Ripped Songs

By default, the Zune software will save ripped songs to My Documents > My Music > Zune. To save them somewhere else, click the Change button (see Figure 5-2), and choose the desired folder (or create a new one). Does it matter where you save

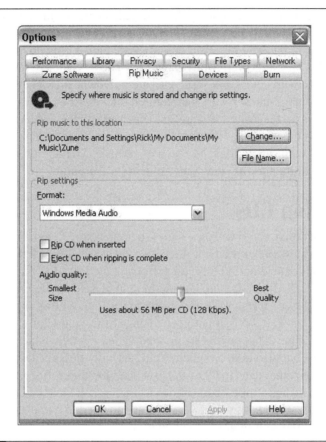

The Zune Options menu is where you modify settings for the CD-ripping process.

ripped songs? Not really, but the default folder has an advantage because it's already being monitored by the Zune software. Consequently, ripped songs will automatically find their way into your music library and, ultimately, onto your Zune.

If you decide to save ripped songs somewhere else (I've long kept my music in a folder called "MP3s" on the root directory of my hard drive), you may want to add that folder to the Zune software's monitor list. Here's how:

1. With the Options window still open, click the Library tab, and then click the Monitor Folders button.

2. In the subsequent window, click Add Folder and then navigate to the folder you want to monitor. Be prepared to wait a while, as the Zune software will rescan *all* monitored folders after you click OK.

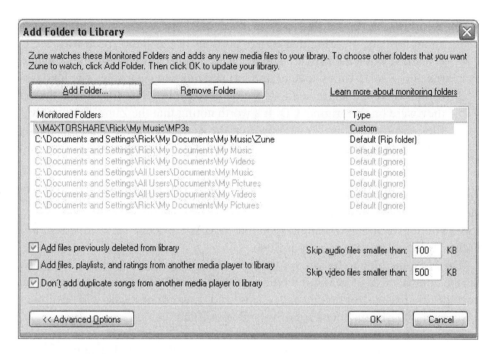

Now, all songs ripped to that folder will get added to your library in the Zune software. You're one step closer to being ready to rip.

Choose an Audio Format

The Zune software gives you a choice of three different audio formats for ripping your CDs. Here's a quick overview:

- ■ **MP3** The universal standard for digital audio. MP3 files are compatible with just about every computer and portable music player on the planet (including iPods).

- ■ **Windows Media Audio** WMA for short, Microsoft's answer to MP3 offers an interesting advantage: the same audio quality in roughly half the space. That means you can get the same fidelity from, say, a 2.5-megabyte (MB) WMA file as you can from a 5-MB MP3. Of course, given that your PC has almost limitless storage and your Zune has a whopping 30 gigabytes (GB), this is less of a consideration than it was back in the days when portable players had only 128 MB of available space. Still, if you have a really large library of CDs to rip, you may want to consider WMA.

■ **Windows Media Audio Lossless** Both MP3 and WMA are compressed audio formats, meaning that certain portions of the audio spectrum are discarded when the files are created. This is done to make the files smaller (usually 8 to 10 times smaller, in fact) and more manageable. The lossless format is an uncompressed format that keeps your audio files as pristine as they were on the original CD. It's worth noting that the Zune cannot play files encoded in this format; however, the Zune software will automatically convert them should you attempt to copy them to the player.

So, which format should you choose? That's a tough one. Keep in mind that you can mix and match MP3s and WMAs on your Zune; you're not limited to one or the other. It's quite all right if, say, you already have some MP3s you ripped previously and now want to switch to WMA. The Zune software doesn't discriminate, and neither does your Zune.

There's something to be said for the universal compatibility of MP3, but I also like the compactness of WMA. I wouldn't bother with WMA Lossless, unless you have specific reasons for doing so, as a single CD's worth of music will occupy upwards of 700 MB on your hard drive and your Zune.

 *If you're attempting to create a permanent digital archive of your CDs, consider ripping your entire library using the WMA Lossless format and then converting those files to MP3s or standard WMAs for copying to your Zune. That way, you'll have CD-quality digital files you can burn back CD, convert to any future formats that might come along, and so on.*

My advice is this: If you own an iPod (or think you might in the future), go with MP3. iPods don't play WMA files, and likely never will. Ripping to MP3 assures a universal compatibility of your song files, meaning you'll be able to play them on pretty much *any* device—including, it should be noted, a growing number of global positioning system (GPS) receivers, cell phones, etc. However, if you plan on being a Zune user now and forever, you're not concerned with other devices, or you have a particularly large CD library, choose WMA. You'll be able to fit nearly twice the amount of music on your Zune as you could if you went with MP3.

NOTE *The songs you get from Zune Marketplace are DRM-protected WMA files. That's just for your information; it really has no impact on how you rip your CDs.*

Of course, the size of each song file depends on what *bit rate* you choose, and that's your final consideration before you start ripping.

Choose a Bit Rate

The last option you need to choose is audio quality, which is determined by a slider at the bottom of the Options window (see Figure 5-1). What you're actually doing here is selecting a bit rate for ripped songs—that is, the amount of audio data that will be retained in each compressed audio file. The formula is simple: The higher the bit rate, the better the sound quality, and the larger the file.

Feel free to experiment with different settings, but I'm going to make this simple:

5

■ **MP3**   If you've chosen MP3 as your format, set the slider to 256 Kbps. That'll give you sound quality that's just about on par with CDs. Of course, if you want the best possible fidelity from the MP3 format, bump it up to the highest setting (320 Kbps).

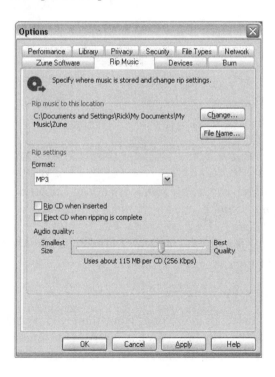

■ **WMA** If you've chosen WMA, set the slider to at least 128 Kbps, which is roughly the equivalent of a 256-Kbps MP3. But I recommend bumping it to the maximum (192 Kbps), which will still give you smaller files than MP3s while providing better sound quality.

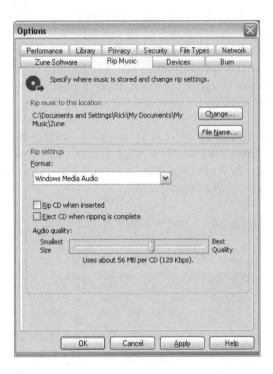

"Sound quality" is a highly subjective thing. The bit rates I've suggested are those that sound good to me; your mileage may vary. I recommend ripping a sample CD, copying the songs to your Zune, and evaluating the sound quality. If it doesn't meet your expectations, raise the bit rate and rip the CD again.

Rip Your First CD

Now that you've wrangled all the settings (something you probably won't need to do again), it's time to start ripping. This is a surprisingly simple procedure; you can probably figure it out without me. Just in case you can't, though, here's the rundown on ripping:

1. Start the Zune software.

2. Insert the CD into your drive.

3. Wait a moment while the software scans the CD. Assuming your computer is connected to the Internet, the software should be able to look up the album name, cover art, and song list.

4. By default, the Zune software will switch views to display the contents of the CD. Notice that the navigation pane now lists the album title. It will also select all the tracks (as indicated by the check boxes next to each track title) and start playing the CD.

5. Click the Start Rip button at the bottom of the details pane. The Zune software will start copying the contents of the CD to the folder you specified earlier and converting the songs to the selected format and bit rate.

Some commercial audio CDs have copy protection that may prevent you from ripping them. Yes, I agree that this is totally unfair, as the process is protected under fair-use laws. If a CD causes you trouble, try a Google search to see if someone has devised a workaround that will allow you to rip it.

It shouldn't take more than 5 to 10 minutes to rip a CD, but ultimately, the time depends on the speed of your PC and CD/DVD drive. They might get the job done in as little as 2 to 3 minutes. Of course, if you have several hundred CDs to rip, this could easily turn into a weekend project. I know a few people who have paid the local teenager 50 bucks or so to sit at their PCs and swap discs.

TIP   *You can save a smidgen of time by enabling two automation options: Rip CD Automatically When Inserted and Eject CD After Ripping. Both are accessible by clicking Options > Rip and then clicking each option in turn. A check mark will appear to indicate the option is enabled.*

CDs vs. Digital Downloads

The novelty of the 99-cent song has worn off. The ugly reality of DRM has settled in. The music-download revolution is over. It's time to go back to buying CDs.

Is it? Zune Marketplace, along with iTunes, Rhapsody, and a host of other online stores, sells tracks for 99 cents apiece (often less if you buy an album's worth), while a CD *still* costs upwards of $16 at the mall or other store. Plus, you have to pay sales tax and, you know, *go* to the mall (where you'll probably buy more than just a CD). Ah, but is it worth it? Should you spend that little extra to buy your music in tangible form? Or should you stick with bits and bytes?

Let's take a closer look at these two methods of music distribution and weigh the pros and cons of each.

CDs: Priced anywhere between $9.99 and $16.99 (if you buy them new), CDs are universally compatible and easy to use, and you can rip them to whatever format and bit rate you want. Plus, they're usually packed with liner notes, lyrics, artist photos, etc.

On the downside, they typically cost more than downloads, and you have no choice but to buy the whole album. Some discs come with anti-rip copy protection, and all discs are susceptible to scratches (which can impede playback). Finally, you have to go a store (or pay shipping) to get CDs, and once you have them, you have to store them.

Not long ago, having grown drunk with download power on my Zune Pass, I was all ready to cart my CD collection to the dump. Who needs easily scratched analog media and perpetually cracked cases when I can store all my tunes on my PC and carry them with me on my Zune? Well, a funny thing happened on the way to Mt. Trashmore: I remembered why I fell in love with CDs in the first place. They sound great, they play anywhere, and they come with extra goodies you don't get with digital downloads, like liner notes and song lyrics.

But best of all, I like being able to rip my CDs to whatever format I want at whatever bit rate I want. That makes them compatible with *all* portable players, unlike digital downloads (which tend to be iPod-only, Zune-only, etc.) Am I willing to pay extra for all these benefits? Well, no, but I now scour hard in search of used or otherwise discounted discs. With a little bargain-hunting (eBay, Half.com, and Amazon Marketplace for purchases; Lala.com and Swapacd.com for trades), I can usually score a CD for a lot less than the $9.99 digital-download price.

Downloads: With prices of 99 cents per song or $9.99 per album, downloads tend to be cheaper than CDs, and they're delivered instantaneously. Plus, online stores like Zune Marketplace carry much larger selections than brick-and-mortar stores.

Unfortunately, DRM is a nightmare, and you're locked into whatever bit rate and file format the store (in this case, Zune Marketplace) chooses. What's more, if your purchased tunes get lost or damaged, replacing them can be a hassle.

I could easily fill a second book on the evils of DRM, which treats users like thieving children. That said, I realize it's a necessary evil, especially for subscription-download services like Zune Pass. But when I buy a song or album outright, I'd like to be able to do what I want with it: burn it to an unlimited number of CDs, play it on an unlimited number of computers, copy it to an unlimited number of portable players, and so on.

Thankfully, there's a way to circumvent these annoying protections—see "Convert Songs from Other Online Services" earlier in this chapter. In the meantime, whether you subscribe to Zune Pass or not, consider *buying* your music on CDs and then ripping the songs to your PC for playback on the Zune. Digital downloads are fast, convenient, and reasonably priced, but there can be too many hassles.

Rip Songs from Cassette Tapes

If you're over 30, chances are good that you've got some old tape cassettes sitting around collecting dust. Wouldn't it be great if you could resurrect those antiques, if you could make that music live again on your Zune? You can, and here's where you find out how.

 *You can resurrect your old vinyl albums as well, though the process is a bit more involved. For a really good tutorial, visit this Web site: http://tinyurl. com/28kdfq.*

Before you invest what is sure to be a considerable amount of time, ask yourself if it wouldn't be more cost-effective to simply sign up for a Zune Pass. I don't mean to sound like a total Microsoft shill, but by paying that $14.99 per month, you'll probably be able to download the digital versions of all your old tapes.

That said, you've already invested money in this media, so why not get your money's worth by bringing it into the digital age?

Why Bother?

Okay, I'll 'fess up: Tapes sound fairly crummy compared with CDs and digital downloads. Sure, they were fine when we didn't know any better, but they're expressly an analog media. If you're a fidelity snob (it's okay—some of my best friends turn their noses up at cassettes), you probably won't be happy with the quality of your converted Def Leppard tapes.

On the other hand, we're not talking AM radio, here—if the tapes are in reasonably good condition, you can expect reasonably good audio. And if you're resurrecting audiobooks, kids' tapes, out-of-print material, or even bootleg recordings, fidelity really isn't an issue. The ultimate goal is simply to let this music be heard again.

In fact, once you learn how to "rip" tapes, you may want to start looking for cheap deals on them. By trolling garage sales, eBay, and other resale sources, you can score some serious bargains on audiobook cassettes that cost a fortune on CD. So this is not only a practical exercise, it's potentially a money-saving one as well.

What You Need

To copy your tapes to your PC for digital archiving, you'll need exactly three things:

- A cassette player. I dug out my old Walkman, which I found perfectly suited to the task, but you could also use a tape deck (provided it's part of or connected to an amplifier of some sort).

- A stereo patch cord. Specifically, you need a cable that connects your Walkman's headphone jack to your sound card's line-in jack. You can get one at Radio Shack for around $5.

5

■ Audacity (http://audacity.sourceforge.net), an open-source, cross-platform
   program that makes simple work of recording and editing audio. It's
   available for Windows, Macintosh, and Linux. If you plan to turn your
   tapes into MP3 files, make sure to get the LAME MP3 encoder as well;
   there's a link to it on the Audacity download page.

Getting Started

After installing Audacity, you'll need to tweak a few settings. First, open the
Preferences window (accessible from the Edit menu), and bump the Channels
setting from one to two. In the same window, click the File Formats tab, and
configure Audacity for use with the LAME MP3 encoder you downloaded.
Click the Find Library button, and then navigate to the folder on your hard drive
containing the file Lame_enc.dll. Finally, choose a bit rate for your recordings.
128 kilobytes per second (Kbps) is more than ample for audiobooks, but for music,
consider doubling it to 256 Kbps.

   Now it's time to check your line-in connection and audio levels. Put a tape in
your Walkman and start playing it; you should hear sound coming from your PC's
speakers. Click the input level meter, and select Start Monitoring to see a live
meter. Then you can adjust the input volume using the slider to the right.

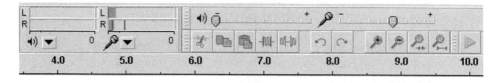

Keeping in mind that your first recording may require some trial and error, rewind your tape to the beginning, click Record in Audacity, and then start the tape. If it's music, you needn't record each song individually, starting and stopping your tape player along the way. Instead, let Audacity record the whole side. Then use the Selection tool to highlight a song (you'll be able to tell where it ends by the few seconds of flatline, which indicate silence), and export the selection as an MP3 (or whatever file format you choose).

If it's a book on tape, you might want to divide the recording into, say, 10-minute segments so it's easier to navigate. This makes organization a bit more complicated, as you'll need to name and tag your MP3s so they'll play sequentially; I recommend something along the lines of *01-Stephen King-The Stand.mp3*, *02-Stephen King-The Stand.mp3*, and so on.

After you've saved your MP3s, you'll want to use the Zune software to update the tag information so that the tracks appear correctly on your Zune. Find out more in the upcoming section "Use Song Tags and Album Art" and in Chapter 13. In the meantime, however, save or move your newly created MP3s to a folder that's monitored by the Zune software.

Understanding Playlists

Your Zune can hold thousands of songs. As you learned in Chapter 4, you can sort those songs using a handful of criteria: artist name, album, song title, and so on. However, there's a much better way to organize and access your music: *playlists*.

A playlist is simply a list of songs that you create. It's a concept that can be a little tricky to grasp at first, so let me give you a few examples:

■ **Songs from the '80s** Feeling nostalgic? You could create a playlist like this to hold all your Huey Lewis and the News, Cyndi Lauper, Duran Duran, and other music from that glorious decade.

- **Piano jazz** Suppose you're in the mood for some Thelonious Monk, Diana Krall, and the like. You can use a playlist to group similar artists or musical styles.

- **Top-rated songs** Want to listen to the cream of your music library crop? How about a playlist that contains only those songs you've rated five stars? (See the upcoming section on auto playlists for this one.)

- **New music** Here's a playlist that'll give you easy access to the stuff you've recently downloaded from Zune Marketplace (or ripped from CDs).

- **Green Day** I have a pretty large Green Day collection. Sometimes, I want to play the whole thing without having to navigate the music library. This playlist (which could be for any artist, of course) lets me hear all my Green Day songs in a hurry.

- **Kids' music** I keep a few CDs' worth of kids' music on my Zune for when I'm in the car with my family. To make these songs easy to find, I have a special playlist for them.

- **Podcasts** If you decide to take podcasts along on your Zune (see Chapter 9), you'll definitely want to create some playlists for them. Otherwise, they may be just about impossible to locate in your song library.

Get the idea? A playlist can be anything you want it to be. They're easy to build, and they're not limited in any way. Each song can appear in more than one playlist. That's because they're just lists—pointers to your music.

In Chapter 4, you learned how to create a Quick List—an on-the-fly playlist that's assembled and stored on your Zune. Mostly, however, you'll want to use the Zune software to create and manage playlists. Let's get started.

Create a New Playlist

There are several ways to create a playlist using the Zune software. Perhaps the easiest is to click Create Playlist in the navigation pane, and then type a name in the New Playlist box that appears. From there, you simply drag songs, albums, or artists to that playlist.

Another option is to click the Create And Edit Playlist button in the list pane. Once again, it's a drag-and-drop affair:

you drag songs, albums, or artists to the pane. The difference here is that you can then reorder the songs to your liking (by dragging them to specific spots within the list). When you're done, click the Save Playlist button at the bottom, and give your new playlist a name.

Similarly, you can take any list of songs in the Now Playing list and turn it into a playlist. Just click the Playback Options button near the top of the list pane, and choose Save Playlist As.

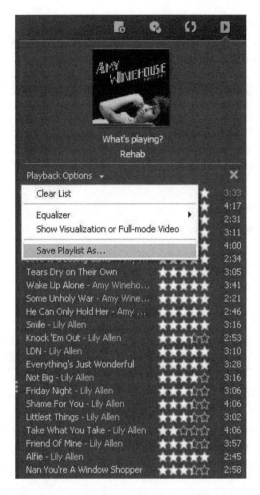

One of the coolest options is the auto playlist, which creates a playlist based on certain criteria. Find out more in the next section.

Auto Playlists

A traditional playlist is one that you cobble together manually, picking and choosing the albums or songs that you want. An auto playlist is created automatically based on one or more criteria. The best way to understand this is to walk through the process of creating one. Let's build an auto playlist called "Five Star Songs."

1. In the navigation pane, right-click Playlists and choose Create Auto Playlist.

2. Click the first big green plus sign to select criteria. As you'll see in the list that appears, this can be anything from artist to date added to rating to play count. Select My Rating.

3. Notice that a new line has appeared: "My rating <u>is at least</u> <u>4 stars</u>." You can click either of the underlined portions to make adjustments. In this case, click 4 Stars and select 5 Stars. (You could also change Is At Least to Is, but it's not necessary.)

4. In the Auto Playlist Name field, type a name for this playlist, and then click OK.

5. You'll see the new playlist in the navigation pane. Click it, and you should see all songs that you've rated five stars. (That's assuming you've rated any songs at all. If not, see Chapter 3 to learn how.)

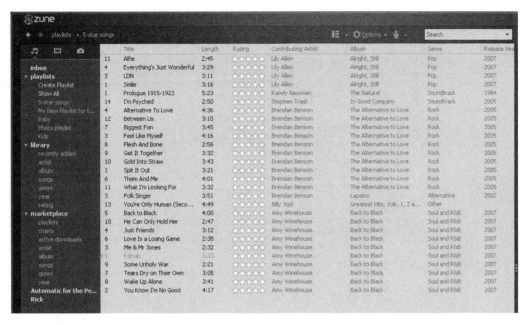

		Title	Length	Rating	Contributing Artist	Album	Genre	Release Year
	11	Alfie	2:45	☆☆☆☆☆	Lily Allen	Alright, Still	Pop	2007
	4	Everything's Just Wonderful	3:29	☆☆☆☆☆	Lily Allen	Alright, Still	Pop	2007
	3	LDN	3:11	☆☆☆☆☆	Lily Allen	Alright, Still	Pop	2007
	1	Smile	3:16	☆☆☆☆☆	Lily Allen	Alright, Still	Pop	2007
	1	Prologue 1915-1923	5:23	☆☆☆☆☆	Randy Newman	The Natural	Soundtrack	1984
	14	I'm Psyched	2:50	☆☆☆☆☆	Stephen Trask	In Good Company	Soundtrack	2005
	4	Alternative To Love	4:36	☆☆☆☆☆	Brendan Benson	The Alternative to Love	Rock	2005
	12	Between Us	3:10	☆☆☆☆☆	Brendan Benson	The Alternative to Love	Rock	2005
	7	Biggest Fan	3:45	☆☆☆☆☆	Brendan Benson	The Alternative to Love	Rock	2005
	3	Feel Like Myself	4:16	☆☆☆☆☆	Brendan Benson	The Alternative to Love	Rock	2005
	8	Flesh And Bone	2:56	☆☆☆☆☆	Brendan Benson	The Alternative to Love	Rock	2005
	9	Get It Together	3:32	☆☆☆☆☆	Brendan Benson	The Alternative to Love	Rock	2005
	10	Gold Into Straw	3:43	☆☆☆☆☆	Brendan Benson	The Alternative to Love	Rock	2005
	1	Spit It Out	3:21	☆☆☆☆☆	Brendan Benson	The Alternative to Love	Rock	2005
	6	Them And Me	4:01	☆☆☆☆☆	Brendan Benson	The Alternative to Love	Rock	2005
	11	What I'm Looking For	3:32	☆☆☆☆☆	Brendan Benson	The Alternative to Love	Rock	2005
	3	Folk Singer	3:51	☆☆☆☆☆	Brendan Benson	Lapalco	Alternative	2002
	13	You're Only Human (Seco...	4:49	☆☆☆☆☆	Billy Joel	Greatest Hits, Vols. 1, 2 a...	Other	
	5	Back to Black	4:00	☆☆☆☆☆	Amy Winehouse	Back to Black	Soul and R&B	2007
	10	He Can Only Hold Her	2:47	☆☆☆☆☆	Amy Winehouse	Back to Black	Soul and R&B	2007
	4	Just Friends	3:12	☆☆☆☆☆	Amy Winehouse	Back to Black	Soul and R&B	2007
	6	Love Is a Losing Game	2:35	☆☆☆☆☆	Amy Winehouse	Back to Black	Soul and R&B	2007
	3	Me & Mr Jones	2:32	☆☆☆☆☆	Amy Winehouse	Back to Black	Soul and R&B	2007
	1	Rehab	3:33	☆☆☆☆☆	Amy Winehouse	Back to Black	Soul and R&B	2007
	9	Some Unholy War	2:21	☆☆☆☆☆	Amy Winehouse	Back to Black	Soul and R&B	2007
	7	Tears Dry on Their Own	3:05	☆☆☆☆☆	Amy Winehouse	Back to Black	Soul and R&B	2007
	8	Wake Up Alone	3:41	☆☆☆☆☆	Amy Winehouse	Back to Black	Soul and R&B	2007
	2	You Know I'm No Good	4:17	☆☆☆☆☆	Amy Winehouse	Back to Black	Soul and R&B	2007

That's it! You've just created a playlist based on a specific criterion: song rating. Now let's do one that's a bit more complex, containing songs you haven't played in at least 30 days, but only those with the word "baby" in the title. (I know, it's a silly example, but it demonstrates just how specific you can get with auto playlists.)

1. Repeat steps 1 and 2 from the previous example. This time, however, select Date Last Played. Notice that its default setting is Before Last 30 Days.

2. Click the green plus sign again, and choose Title. Click Click To Set and type **baby**.

3. Give the playlist a name, and click Finish to see the results. It might contain a handful of songs, or it might contain none. However, the Zune software will continue to monitor your library for songs that meet the criteria. Thus, after some time elapses, one or more songs with the word "baby" in the title might appear there, provided you haven't played them in at least 30 days. Neat, huh?

The sky's pretty much the limit with auto playlists. You can add as many criteria as you want, tweaking each one to match exactly what you want. I encourage you to experiment with them, because even if you build an auto playlist that doesn't give you the desired results, no harm done—just delete and start over, or try fiddling with the settings.

For auto playlists to work effectively, it's crucial that your songs have accurate tags. Find out more in the upcoming section "Use Song Tags and Album Art."

Syncing Playlists

By default, the Zune software will automatically sync new playlists to your
Zune. If you'd rather pick and choose the playlists to sync, you'll need to turn off
automatic syncing. Here's how:

1. Connect your Zune to your PC.

2. In the navigation pane, right-click your Zune's name, and choose Set Up Sync.

3. Select the Sync This Device Automatically check box if it's not already
selected.

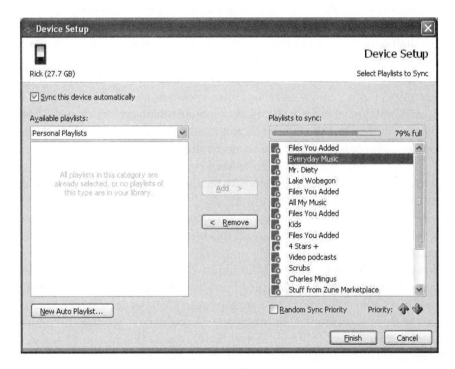

4. In the pane on the right, click a playlist you no longer want to sync, and
then click the Remove button in between the two panes.

5. Repeat as necessary. Click Finish when you're done.

Deleting and Renaming Playlists

Don't want a playlist anymore? Just right-click it in the navigation pane, and choose Delete. Keep in mind that deleting a playlist will *not* delete the songs it contains, nor will it remove those songs from your Zune. They'll still be in your library; you're deleting only the list that points to them.

To rename a playlist, right-click it in the navigation pane, click Rename, and then type the new name. Again, no changes are made to the songs themselves.

Use Song Tags and Album Art

Ever wonder how the Zune software knows so much about each song in your library? It shows information like album, artist, genre, release year, length, track number, and so on. You might think all this data comes from each song's file name, but you'd be wrong.

An audio file (such as an MP3 or WMA) contains not only the actual song, but also categorical information—*ID3 tags*, also known as metadata—about that song: name, artist, album, and so on. (It can also contain album art, which we'll discuss shortly.) It's critical that the tags be accurate; otherwise, neither the Zune software nor the Zune player will be able to sort or identify songs correctly.

If you get all your music from Zune Marketplace, you're all set—the songs are delivered with album art and complete tag information. Same goes for songs ripped from CDs using the Zune software. As discussed earlier in the chapter, the software fetches album art and song information from the Internet the moment you insert the CD. When you rip the disc, all this information is applied to the newly created audio files.

However, if you have music in your library that came from other sources—for example, friends, peer-to-peer download services like KaZaa (which are illegal, but, hey, I'm not here to judge), and perhaps even pre-Internet CD rips—there's a chance the tags are incomplete or inaccurate. If you're having a hard time locating music you know is in your library, it may be for exactly that reason. (For example, I've seen songs that had the wrong artist name, a misspelled title, etc.)

Fortunately, it's not hard to fix MP3 and WMA tags. It can, however, be a little time-consuming. See Chapter 13 for all the details.

Chapter 6

Video

How to...

- Copy DVDs to your Zune
- Watch TV shows on your Zune
- Watch other videos on your Zune
- Add video podcasts to your Zune
- Download YouTube videos

Think the Zune's great at playing music? Like the saying goes, you ain't seen nothing yet. If you're in the mood for a movie, TV show, music video, or even just some home movies of your daughter's dance recital, the Zune is only too happy to oblige. It's time to put that nice, big screen to good use.

In this chapter you'll learn how to copy videos from a variety of sources to your Zune. Unfortunately, none of those sources include Zune Marketplace. At the time of this writing, Microsoft still hasn't added any video content; the store remains music-only for now. I have to assume that will change, but I can't understand all the foot-dragging. Apple offers a robust selection of TV shows, movies, and music videos for sale via its iTunes store. Alas, you can't buy videos from iTunes and play them on your Zune; they're copy-protected, just like iTunes music.

Fortunately, while we're waiting for Microsoft to come to its senses, you can indeed put movies, TV shows, and more on your Zune.

Understanding Video Formats

You may wonder why you can't just copy any video to the Zune, why there's a need for conversion and compatibility and all that. As with audio files like MP3 and WMA, video files are created using several different formats. The content itself might be identical, but the containers are a bit different. For example, YouTube videos are streamed using the FLV format, which is exclusive to that service. Movies sold by iTunes are distributed in MP4 format. Windows Media Center PCs record TV shows using a format called DVR-MS. And, sad to say, the Zune player supports only one video format: Windows Media Video (WMV).

However, the Zune software can automatically convert videos in the MPEG4 and H.264 formats (meaning files that have MP4, M4v, and MOV extensions). That's key, because it opens the door to video podcasts and other video sources.

NOTE *According to Microsoft, future Zune updates will add "native" MPEG4 and H.264 support to the player, meaning the Zune software won't have to convert those kinds of files before copying them over. That's good news, because conversion can take a considerable amount of time. Hopefully, said update will already have been applied to your Zune by the time you read this, courtesy of an automatic firmware update.*

You don't need to have a full understanding of all these different formats. The key thing to realize is that the Zune can play most kinds of video, but some—DVDs, for example—require you to jump through a hoop or two first.

Copy DVDs to Your Zune

With a screen that's nearly twice the size of the video iPod's, the Zune is much better-suited to watching movies on the go. I'm not going to say it's a fantastic experience (this isn't a 50-inch plasma, after all), but if you're sitting on a long flight or running on the treadmill, it's leaps and bounds better than nothing.

As I've said in previous chapters, at some point in the future, you'll undoubtedly be able to buy (or rent) movies from Zune Marketplace, much as you can from iTunes. That'll be an easy, point-and-click solution, just like downloading music. Even so, movies will probably be on the pricey side (as they are at iTunes), and what happens if there's a movie you already own on DVD? It hardly seems fair that you should have to buy it twice.

If you'd rather not wait for Zune Marketplace, or if you just want to make your movie collection mobile, there are plenty of options at your disposal. Numerous software developers have released programs designed expressly for copying DVDs to the Zune. Of course, these require an investment of $25 to 30. It's also possible to copy DVDs using freely available tools—although they're not nearly as easy to use. Let's take a look at both options so you can decide which is right for you.

Comparing Commercial Software

A Google search of "DVD to Zune" produces upwards of a dozen different programs, all promising the same thing: one-click conversions of your DVDs. A few vendors were kind enough to let me try out their software; I used one of my favorite movies, *Contact*, as the test DVD for all of them.

M2Convert for Zune

M2Convert for Zune ($29.99) has perhaps the easiest interface of any program of its kind. Just click the Open DVD button, and then select your DVD. Of course, you can tweak a few settings along the way, including the output folder for converted DVDs and the size (which is set to Auto by default).

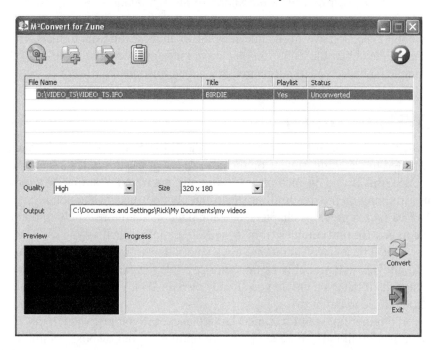

I encountered a few problems with the software. First, it's slow: a 2-hour movie took about 5 hours to convert. A faster computer and/or DVD-ROM drive would probably get the job done quicker, but to me that still seems excessive. Second, the aspect ratio of the converted movie wasn't quite right—it came out vertically stretched, though just slightly. So much for "auto." I was also disappointed that when I posted this issue on M2Solutions' support forum, it never received a reply from a tech.

DVD Ripping: Is It Legal?

Most commercial DVDs are copy-protected using a technology known as Content Scrambling System (CSS). Fortunately, it's pretty easy to work around CSS, as evidenced by the myriad programs that can copy DVDs. Okay, but is that legal? Well, it's a pretty gray area. In fact, as of this writing, there's a pending court case that may answer this question once and for all. (Hopefully, the judge will have half a brain and realize the meaning of "fair use.")

My feeling is that if you legally purchased a DVD, you should have the right to do with it as you please—including copying it to your Zune. That said, it's not against the law to buy any of the programs mentioned here, and there's really no way for you to get in trouble by using them. It's kind of like creeping through a red light at 3 a.m. when there's not another car in sight: It may violate the letter of the law, but if no one gets hurt and no one even finds out, where's the harm?

Because I was converting a letterboxed movie (one with a 16:9 aspect ratio), I tried adjusting M2Convert's size setting to 320×180, and that solved the aspect-ratio problem. However, about halfway into the converted movie, the audio became noticeably out of sync with the video. The same thing happened with other movies I tried. As a result, it's difficult for me to recommend this program, though your mileage may vary.

NOTE *One product I strongly recommend avoiding is Okoker DVD to Zune Converter. In my test of the trial version, it produced nothing but a green screen. What's more, it doesn't even convert to WMV—only MP4, meaning the Zune software would have to convert it a second time while copying it to your Zune. Don't bother with this one.*

Pocket DVD Wizard

This program has been around for years, and I've been a fan since the days when I used it to copy DVDs to my Palm and Pocket PC handhelds. The good news is that Pocket DVD Wizard can convert DVDs for a number of different devices, not just the Zune. You can use it to create videos for your iPod, personal digital assistant (PDA), smart phone, Sony PSP, and so on. The bad news is that it doesn't work on commercial DVDs—that is, most/almost all movies. You can use it for unprotected DVDs, such as those you've burned yourself, but not for, say, *The Matrix*.

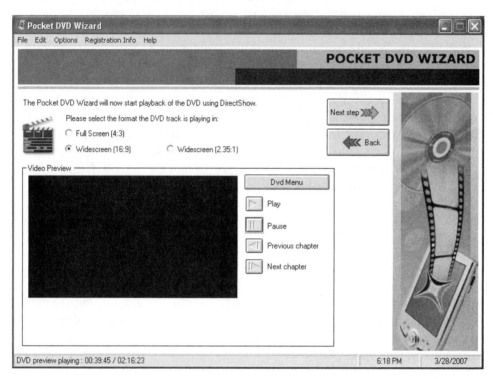

PQ DVD to Zune Converter

One of the best ways I've found to copy a movie to your Zune is with PQ DVD to Zune Converter. All it takes is a few clicks and a couple of hours. That may sound like a lot, but most of the other programs I tried took 4 to 5 hours to convert a DVD. Plus, it's quite easy to use, though I do recommend lowering the video bit rate to around 500 kilobits per second (Kbps). When I converted a movie using the default setting (around 1,200 Kbps), the Zune software had to perform a secondary conversion on it before copying it to the Zune. I tried again with the lower bit rate, and it copied right over.

DVD to Zune Converter sells for $29.95. For an extra 10 bucks, you can add the company's Zune Movie Video Converter, which can convert virtually any kind of video file to a Zune-compatible format (namely, WMV). You'll find out more about file conversions in the sections to come, but, suffice it to say, it's well worth the extra $10 if you're planning to buy DVD to Zune Converter anyway.

Xilisoft DVD to Zune Converter

Yes, a lot of these programs are called "DVD to Zune Converter." Xilisoft's product is a bit more flexible than PQ DVD to Zune Converter, as it can convert not just to WMV, but also to MP4 and other formats (meaning you can also use it with your iPod). However, it's definitely the slower of the two programs, so you'll have to weigh that in your decision. But I can easily recommend Xilisoft DVD to Zune Converter; it did a great job converting my movies for Zune viewing. It's $29.

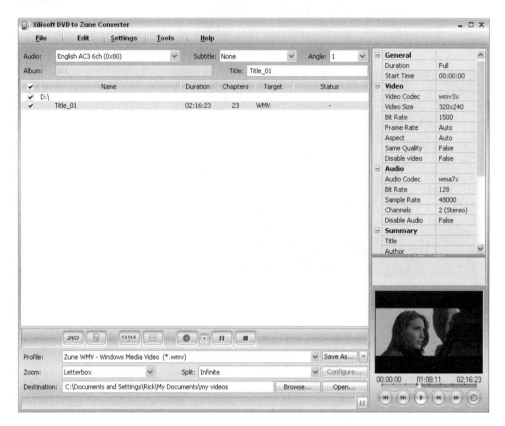

Using a Free Solution

If you'd rather not pay for software to copy DVDs to your Zune, you can get the job done with a handful of free programs. The one I prefer is called DVD-WMV, which turns DVDs into Windows Media Video files. To use it, you'll need to download and install two items:

- Windows Media Encoder 9 (http://tinyurl.com/jv9yx), which will work entirely behind the scenes for this operation.

- DVD-WMV (www.dvd-wmv.com), which does all the heavy lifting.

Actually, you'll want to check out the complete system requirements at the DVD-WMV Web site, as you may need to install additional components as well. For example, you'll need the Windows .NET Framework 2.0 (which you might already have) and a program called DVD Decrypter, but the latter is included with your DVD-WMV download. You will, however, have to install it manually after installing DVD-WMV—look for the Setup DVD Decrypter icon on your desktop.

Once you've installed all your software (and rebooted Windows, just to be on the safe side), plop a DVD into the drive and fire up DVD-WMV. Then follow these steps:

1. Click the Settings tab. Change the output folder to one that's monitored by the Zune software, such as My Documents | My Videos. In the DVD Drive field near the lower-right corner, make sure that the correct drive letter is selected.

2. Click the First Encode tab, and select the Custom First Encode Options check box.

3. Change both the audio and video modes to Constant Bit Rate (CBR).

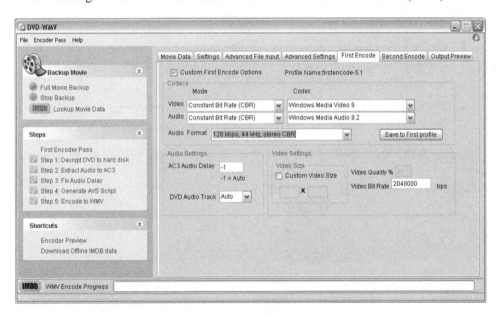

4. Set the video codec to Windows Media Video 9 and the audio codec to Windows Media Audio 9.2.

5. Set the audio format to 128Kbps, 44kHz, Stereo CBR.

6. In the Video Size box, select Custom Video Size, and change the numbers to 320 × 240. (If your video ends up vertically stretched, try 320 × 188.)

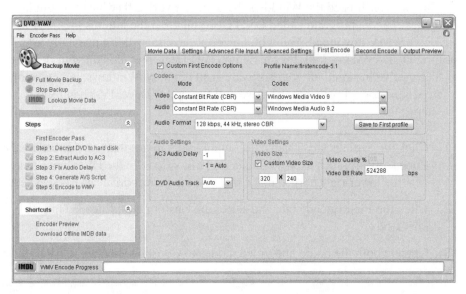

7. In the Video Bit Rate box, type **524288**, which translates to 512 Kbps. You can experiment with different numbers, but I find this an acceptable video quality, one that works well with the Zune.

8. Click the Movie Data tab, and enter the name of the movie. You can click Query IMDB if you want to fetch more details from the Internet.

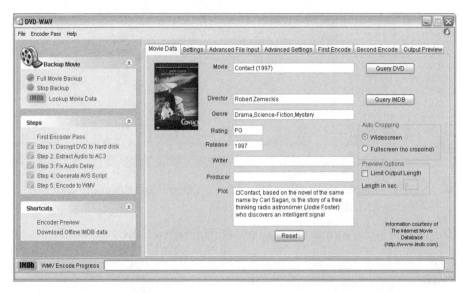

9. On the left side of the DVD-WMV window, click Full Movie Backup—and be prepared to wait. The process will probably take a good 2 hours for each movie, if not a little longer.

When it's done, fire up the Zune software. Your newly converted DVD should appear in the video library. Copy it to your Zune, sit back, and enjoy.

TIP *If you encounter any problems, visit the DVD-WMV forums (www.dvd-wmv .com/Forum/) to pick the brains of other users.*

My Top Five TV Shows for Zune Viewing

I'll watch a movie on my Zune, but I'd rather watch TV shows. One reason is that I think most movies are better suited to large screens, whereas TV shows feel more "comfortable" on a Zune-size screen. But I also think there's *so* much good TV these days, and so few good movies. Hence, my picks for the best shows to record on your Media Center PC (or rent on DVD) and transfer to your Zune for on-the-go entertainment:

- *The Office*   I never, ever thought the American version could hold a candle to the BBC original, which ranks among my all-time favorite shows. But it's surprisingly inventive, well written, and well acted. The American *Office* is rapidly turning into a classic in its own right.

- *The Shield*   I didn't start watching this show until it was already 5 years old—but that's the beauty of TV on DVD. This is, without a doubt, one of the most compelling cop shows ever. A word of warning: It's also violent, graphic, and seriously grim. But, um, in a good way.

- *Coupling*   You'll probably need to hit Netflix to find this British import, which was derived from *Friends* (which, incidentally, was itself derived from a British show). *Coupling* is laugh-out-loud funny, and its twist-at-the-end plotting will make you marvel at British cleverness.

- *Firefly*   It only ran for one season (half a season, in fact), but this is one of the best sci-fi shows ever to hit the airwaves. It's funny, endearing, and criminally short-lived. I own the entire series on DVD. It's that good.

- *Heroes*   At a time when dramatic trailblazers like *Battlestar Galactica* and *Lost* (two other favorites—don't get me wrong) are starting to show their age, *Heroes* comes along as a breath of fresh air. And it has a full season yet to go before it hits that inevitable third-season slump.

Watch TV Shows on Your Zune

Heroes? Scrubs? 24? Battlestar Galactica? The Sarah Silverman Project?
The Daily Show? All on your Zune? It's true. It's possible. The dream can be yours.
(I sorta like TV, in case you hadn't guessed.) Although Zune Marketplace is just as
bereft of TV shows as it is movies, there are, thankfully, other sources.

Indeed, there are three primary ways to get TV shows onto your Zune:

- **Rent the DVDs** and copy them using one of the methods described in the
  previous section. This is definitely the path of least resistance, though it
  doesn't help you with shows that are currently airing.

- **Copy them from a Media Center PC.** This is my favorite method, as it
  enables me to watch on my Zune anything I've recorded on my PC. Find
  out more about this option in the next section.

- **Download them from the Internet**, and then convert them to a Zune-
  compatible format. Using a program called Bittorrent, you can find just
  about any TV show. I'll leave it to you and a bit of Googling to figure
  out how, as this activity definitely crosses a legal line. Keep in mind, too,
  that most shows distributed in this way are encoded using formats known
  as Divx and Xvid, both of which will require conversion before they're
  viewable on a Zune.

The Ultimate Source for TV Shows: Media Center PCs

I'm a huge fan of Media Center PCs. I have one at the heart of my home
entertainment center. Basically, it's an ordinary PC that has a TV tuner card
installed, meaning it can function like a Tivo (or cable-TV DVR) and record TV
shows. Because those shows are stored on its hard drive in digital format, it's a
fairly simple matter to copy them to the Zune for on-the-go viewing.

Interested? Let me start by giving you some details on how (and why) you might
want to buy a Media Center PC or overhaul your current model with TV capabilities.
Then we'll get into the nitty-gritty of copying recorded shows to your Zune.

What's a Media Center PC?

The simplest definition of a Media Center PC is one that includes software for
managing your music, movies, videos, and, possibly, TV shows. This software
might be the operating system itself, as in the case of Windows XP Media Center

Edition 2005, Windows Vista Premium, and Windows Vista Ultimate. Specifically, these versions of Windows operate like any other, except that they come with Microsoft's Media Center software—a couch-friendly, remote-operable interface for accessing all your media.

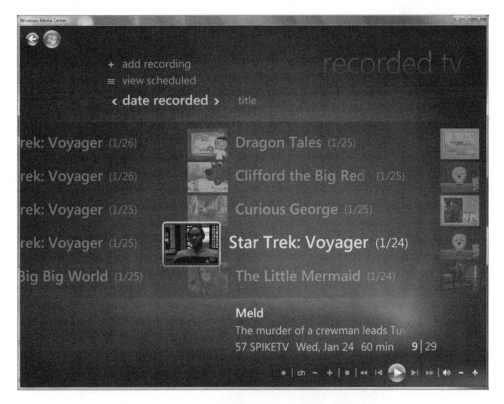

Third-party programs are also available that can add Media Center capabilities to your PC. Some of these include Beyond TV, MediaPortal, and Sage TV. For our purposes, however, we're going to focus on the Windows options, in part, because they're much more ubiquitous (remember, they're included with the three aforementioned versions of Windows, so you may already have one), and, in part, because they're the ones I like best.

The key hardware ingredient is a TV tuner—an add-on card that plugs into your PC. Windows Media Center can't play or record shows without one. If your system didn't come with a tuner, you can add one. Look for one with both analog *and* high-definition (HDTV) inputs, which will give you the best of both worlds: standard-def shows from your cable or satellite feed and high-def (HD) shows from over-the-air (OTA) broadcasts. As for the tuner itself, consider the $129.99

ATI TV Wonder 650, which installs in a Peripheral Component Interconnect (PCI) slot. No room in your PC? The $99 Hauppauge WinTV-HVR-950 (see Figure 6-1) plugs into a Universal Serial Bus (USB) port and records analog or OTA high-definition TV. Get two if you want both. (Windows Media Center supports up to four tuners, internal or external.)

For the ultimate Media Center experience, consider installing an HD antenna. Yes, it's true, rabbit ears are back. If you want free, over-the-air HDTV in your living room, you'll need to connect an antenna to your PC. What kind of antenna, and where should you put it? AntennaWeb.org offers recommendations based on your location (and lets you know how many stations you should expect to pull in). You might need nothing more than powered rabbit ears, or you might have to install an outdoor antenna and run wire to your PC. It can be a hassle, sure, but it beats paying the cable company steep monthly fees for HD.

Copying TV Shows from a Media Center PC to Zune

I could fill a whole book on Media Center PCs, so I'll have to leave it to you to handle the hardware end of things and learn how to record shows on your PC (it's incredibly easy, I promise). The next step is to copy recorded TV shows to your Zune, which requires a few steps (and possibly some extra software).

FIGURE 6-1   To play and record TV on your PC, plug in a TV tuner like the Hauppauge WinTV-HVR-950.

Watch TV Shows on Your Zune

The Zune and TV go together like peanut butter and jelly. Like the Captain and Tennille. Like teens and angst. Okay, maybe that's taking it a little too far, but there's no question the Zune makes an awesome portable television.

Of course, it's not a television in the traditional sense—it can't tune in live broadcasts, and it doesn't come with a remote (though you *can* get a remote for your Zune—see Chapter 11 for details). Instead, the Zune enables you to view TV shows that you've recorded on your PC.

Yes, your PC. I touched on this a bit in Chapter 6. By adding a special TV tuner to your PC, you can record TV shows on the hard drive, much like a TiVo does. The trick lies in getting those shows (which are really just computer files like any other) onto your Zune. You can't just import them into the Zune software like you can music, photos, and some other kinds of video files.

That's really too bad, because the Zune and TV go together like...well, you get my point. Unlike movies, TV shows are created with relatively small screens in mind. Plus, they're shorter than movies, so they won't drain your battery as quickly. And let's not forget the awesome selection of shows on the airwaves these days: *30 Rock, Battlestar Galactica, Heroes, Lost, The Office, The Shield*...shall I go on? Movies? Who needs 'em!

Now that I've whetted your TV appetite, let's take a look at what you need to watch your favorite shows on the go.

NOTE

At some point in the future, you'll probably be able to buy TV shows from Zune Marketplace, much like iPod users can from the iTunes Store. My solution is better, as it provides access to unlimited TV and costs nothing (except what you're already paying for cable). Well, okay, you may have to spring for a TV tuner, but you don't pay anything to record shows with it.

What You Need

To watch TV on your Zune, you'll need three basic ingredients:

- A PC running one of these three operating systems: Windows XP Media Center Edition 2005, Windows Vista Premium, or Windows Vista Ultimate (see Figure 1)

- A TV tuner that plugs into that PC, either internally or externally

- A "hack" that tweaks the Zune software to make it recognize recorded TV shows

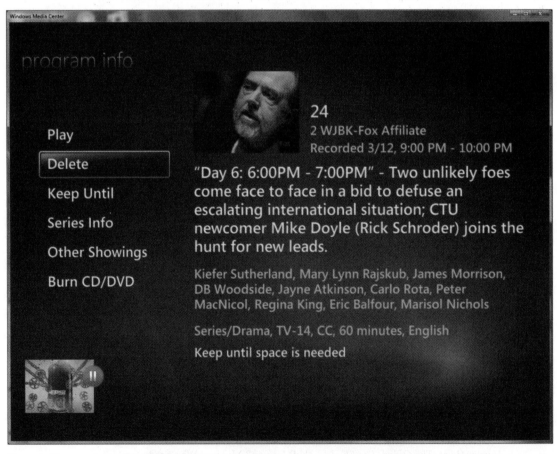

Figure 1. Many versions of Windows include Microsoft's Media Center software, which, when paired with a TV tuner, can record TV shows.

Chapter 6 covers the first two items in detail, so head there if you want to learn more about Windows Media Center and/or TV tuners. As for the hack, it's the work of an enterprising Zune user, who posted the information (and the tiny download you need) on the Zune Boards Web site (http://tinyurl.com/2qprp3).

> **NOTE**
>
> You'll need to register with the site to gain access to the download. It's free and easy—and it'll also enable you to post messages on the various Zune Boards forums, a definite plus (see Chapter 13).

Install the Multi-Extension Support Mod

Get ready to have some fun: You're about to become a hacker! Not in the breaks-into-bank-servers-and-steals-account-numbers sense, but in the tweaks-software-to-do-something-it-couldn't-previously-do sense. Don't worry: This isn't illegal. It won't void your Zune's warranty. It won't make you a bad person. And based on my experience, it won't mess up your system or Zune software in any way. As the saying goes: It's all good.

> **CAUTION**
>
> Gotta put a disclaimer here: This hack is a little snippet of computer code that modifies the Zune software, so it could potentially cause problems. It's not supported by Microsoft, so if you do run into trouble, they won't be able to help you. That said, you can always reinstall the Zune software if necessary. And I have zero qualms about recommending this; I've installed it on two computers, and it's worked flawlessly.

> **NOTE**
>
> If you've configured the Zune software to automatically copy all videos to your Zune (as described in Chapter 2), you'll probably want to disable that option before importing your TV shows. Each show can take upwards of an hour to convert, and if you've got a few dozen shows, well, you do the math—it could take days to synchronize your Zune. Plus, the player probably won't even have enough storage space to accommodate all the shows.

The Multi-Extension Support Mod was actually created to enable the Zune software to support a lot more file types than it currently does. For our purposes, we're interested only in the DVR-MS format, which is what Windows Media Center uses for recorded TV shows. After installing the Multi-Extension Support Mod, the Zune software will be able to recognize (though not play) DVR-MS files and convert them for viewing on your Zune.

Here's how to make it happen:

1. Head to the Zune Boards page containing the Multi-Extension Support Mod (http://tinyurl .com/yqarcx). Remember, you need to register with the site in order to gain access to the download.

2. Scroll down a bit until you see the Download This .Zip File link (see Figure 2). Click it to download the Multi-Extension Support Mod.zip file. Make sure to take note of where you're saving this file on your hard drive.

3. Exit the Zune software, if it's running. Open the downloaded ZIP file, and extract the contents (it doesn't matter where). You should

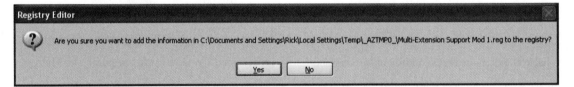

Figure 2. The Multi-Extension Support Mod can be found within the text of a post on the Zune Boards message site.

have two files, each a tiny program. Double-click each one in turn to run it.

🔲 Multi-Extension Support Mod 1.reg
🔲 Multi-Extension Support Mod 2.reg

4. For each program, you'll see an alert box asking if you want to add it to the registry. Have no fear: Click Yes.

7. Click the Add Folder button, and then navigate to the Recorded TV folder on your hard drive (see Figure 3). Click to highlight the folder, and then click OK. Click OK a second time to return to the Zune software—and be prepared to wait. It'll take the software a while to re-index your library (which, alas, it does every time you add or remove a folder).

Registry Editor

? Are you sure you want to add the information in C:\Documents and Settings\Rick\Local Settings\Temp_AZTMP0_\Multi-Extension Support Mod 1.reg to the registry?

Yes   No

5. Run the Zune software.

6. Now we're going to add your PC's Recorded TV folder (which is where shows are stored) to the Zune software's list of monitored folders. You already learned how to do this in Chapter 2, but since you're already here, let's go through the steps again. Start by pressing F3 to display the Add Folder to Library dialog box.

8. When the Zune software has finished indexing your library, head to the video section. You should see all your recorded TV shows (see Figure 4).

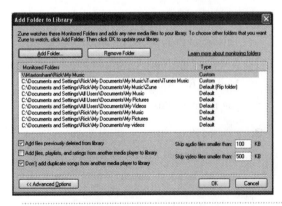

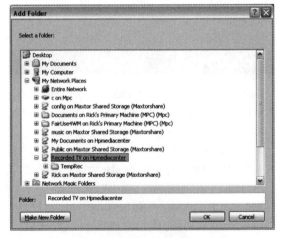

Figure 3. Use the Zune's Add Folder option to add your Recorded TV folder to the list of monitored folders.

4

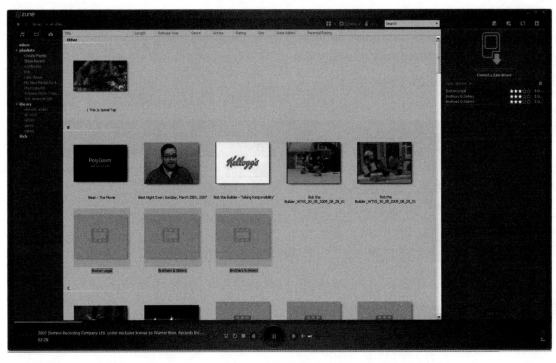

Figure 4. Presto! Now the Zune software can recognize recorded TV shows.

9. All that's left is to copy one or more shows to your Zune! If you haven't already done so, connect the Zune to your PC. Then just drag one or more shows to the Sync list (as you would with any video files), and then click Start Sync.

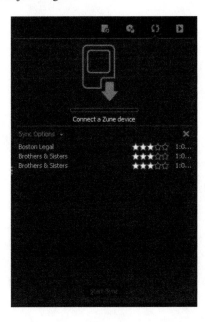

10. Be prepared to wait. Videos take a long time to convert. In my experience, a single half-hour TV show takes about 30 minutes, though your mileage may vary, depending on the speed of your PC.

11. Once the synchronization process is complete, disconnect your Zune and head to the Video menu. You should see your newly converted show(s)! Watch and enjoy.

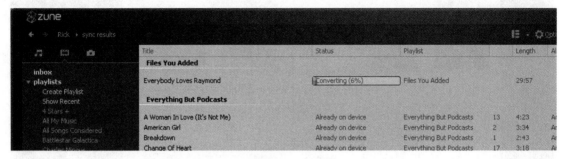

TIP

The Multi-Extension Support Mod also adds Zune software support for DivX and Xvid video files, which, like DVR-MS files, would normally require a pass through third-party conversion software before being copied to your Zune.

Windows Media Center records shows in a video format called DVR-MS. This is just a slight variation of the popular MPEG-2 format, but it's different enough to cause trouble. In an ideal world, the Zune software would be able to automatically convert DVR-MS files to the Zune-friendly WMV format. For whatever stupid reason, it can't. (Yeah, I'm bitter about this. Windows Media Player, the Zune software's kissing cousin, has no problem converting DVR-MS files for other *non-Microsoft* devices, so there's no legitimate reason the Zune software can't do this for the Zune.)

According to my contacts at Microsoft, the Zune software will gain this capability down the road. When it does, it should be as simple as adding your Recorded TV folder to the list of monitored folders and then choosing whatever shows you want to synchronize to the Zune.

There are several ways to perform this conversion:

- **Commercial software** I'm particularly fond of Roxio's MyTV ToGo ($29.99), which integrates with the Windows Media Center interface (see Figure 6-2) and allows you to manually select shows for conversion. It can also automatically convert selected shows right after they're recorded. Then there's PQ DVD to Zune Video Suite ($39.95), which, in addition to ripping DVDs, can convert DVR-MS files (among other file types) to WMV.

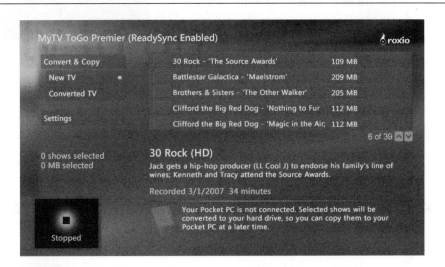

FIGURE 6-2 Roxio's MyTV ToGo operates inside the Media Center interface. It can convert recorded shows to WMV for Zune viewing.

■ **Homebrew software**   At press time, I'd just started tinkering with a new freeware program called ZuneTVWatcher, which automatically converts all recorded shows to WMV and queues them for Zune synchronization. It's a great little utility, though, for the moment, it's all or nothing. You can't choose which shows or episodes you want to convert. The program simply converts every recorded show on your hard drive.

■ **Windows Vista**   If you have Windows Vista, you can use an included program—Windows Movie Maker—to convert Media Center recordings. Even better, because it's a video editor, you can chop out all the commercials before sending them to your Zune.

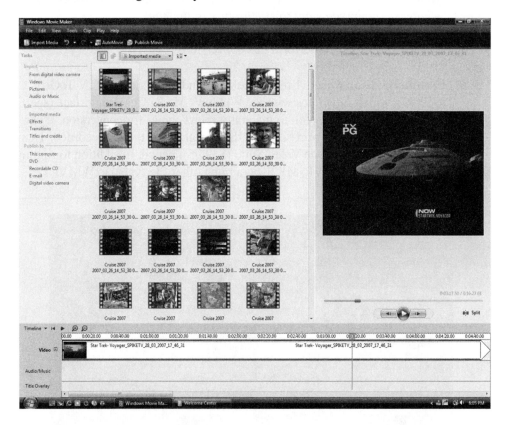

Watch Other Videos on Your Zune

Movies? Check. TV shows? Check. Now it's time to tackle other kinds of videos:
Internet downloads, home movies, video podcasts, and even YouTube clips. You
can watch just about any kind of video on your Zune, though some sources do
require third-party software for downloading and/or conversion.

Internet Downloads, Home Movies, and More

Videos can land on your PC from a wide variety of sources. You might have home
movies you've created, movie trailers you've download from the Web, or perhaps
some of those hilarious foreign TV commercials your friends e-mail you. As with
TV and movies, you can copy those videos to your Zune—though some of them
might require a little attention first.

6

As you learned in the first section of this chapter, the Zune can play any WMV
video files, and the Zune software can convert any M4V, MP4, and MOV files
to that format. That should cover the bases for the majority of videos. However,
any videos in the AVI, MPEG-1, MPEG-2, RM, or other formats will need to be
converted with third-party software.

Video-Conversion Software

One option is the aforementioned PQ DVD to Zune Video Suite, which can convert
just about anything to WMV (including DVR-MS TV shows, a nice perk). If you'd
rather not pay $40 for the software, there are, of course, free alternatives. One of
them is the aptly named SUPER, which can also convert any format to any other
format. (It's not great with DVR-MS, however, so use ZuneTVWatcher instead.)
The program even comes with a Zune-specific output filter that will convert your
videos to Zune-friendly specs.

TIP

*The SUPER Web page (http://www.erightsoft.com/SUPER.html) can be a
little confusing. To find the program, you'll need to scroll all the way to the
bottom and click the Start Download SUPER link. On the following page,
click the Download And Use link. On the page after that, scroll all the
way down, and choose one of the Download Now links. Yes, I agree this is
highly ridiculous. But, remember, the software is free, so who cares about
a few download hassles?*

Here's how to use SUPER to convert a video:

1. Install and run the program.

2. Click the Select Output Container drop-down menu, and choose Microsoft Zune. That's it! You're done. Okay, well, not really, but you're almost done. This single selection sets all the necessary parameters for converting videos to Zune-compatible WMV.

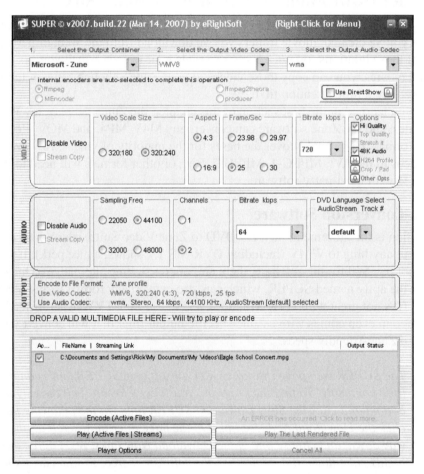

3. Open Windows Explorer or your file manager of choice. Navigate to the video you want to convert, and then drag it to the large empty pane in the bottom of the SUPER window. You'll see the file name appear there along with a check mark.

4. Right-click anywhere in the SUPER window, and choose Output File Saving Management. Choose a folder for the converted video (I recommend something like My Documents > My Videos).

5. Click the Encode button, and be prepared to wait—file conversion can take time.

6. When SUPER finishes the job, fire up the Zune software, and sync the newly converted file to your Zune.

Add Video Podcasts to Your Zune

Some of the very best video content you'll find for your Zune comes in the form of video podcasts. Also known as vidcasts and vodcasts, video podcasts are videos delivered online and on demand. Many of them are distributed on a daily or weekly basis; you "subscribe" to them much like you would a newspaper. Video podcasts can be anything: collections of old cartoons, clips from TV shows, news programs, and so on. Some examples include the following:

- **NBC Nightly News**   The entire 22-minute broadcast of last night's news with host Brian Williams. Perfect for catching up on the news while, say, riding the train to work.

- **HBO Documentary Films**   Watch entire documentaries and selected segments from HBO's impressive series.

- **Rocketboom**   A popular video blog covering everything from news to technology to Internet culture.

- **MTV News: Daily Headlines**   Daily news updates on what's happening in music, video, movies, and more.

- **Channel Frederator**   Like cartoons? This video podcast serves up new animated goodness every week. It's one of my favorites.

- **National Geographic Video Shorts**   Just like it sounds: 2- to 5-minute clips from National Geographic's awesome shows.

These are just the tip of the iceberg. There are thousands of video podcasts out there—some good, some not so good—and you can easily add them to your Zune.

 *This section is devoted specifically to video podcasts. To learn about audio podcasts, see Chapter 9.*

Well, okay, adding podcasts isn't as easy as it *should* be. At press time, the Zune software lacked any kind of support for podcasts, video or otherwise. That means you'll have to turn to "outside" solutions. I'm told by Microsoft that the Zune software will include podcast capabilities in the future, meaning it should be quite simple to subscribe to, download, and copy video podcasts. For now, however, let's look at other ways to get the job done.

 Most video podcasts are distributed in MOV or M4V format, which means the Zune software will need to convert them before copying them to your Zune. There's nothing you can do about this; it's just the nature of the video podcast beast. However, a planned firmware update will add native support for these formats to the Zune itself, so conversion will no longer be necessary. That'll make for much faster syncing of video podcasts.

FeedYourZune

To my knowledge, FeedYourZune is the world's only podcast program designed expressly for the Zune. Unfortunately, in my opinion, it's not the world's best podcast program. FeedYourZune is slow, limited, and not particularly user-friendly. It doesn't come with any instructions, and there's no online help to be found. But it does work, and the price is right: It's free.

Here's a quick tutorial on using FeedYourZune to, well, feed your Zune (with video podcasts):

1. Install the program (http://feedyourzune.com).

2. Look under the Sample Channels folder for Rocketboom. (FeedYourZune refers to each video podcast as a channel.) Drag Rocketboom down to My Channels. You'll see it added to the list.

3. Under My Channels, right-click Rocketboom and choose Download. This will download all available episodes of the podcast. Alternately, click Rocketboom to see each available show in the bottom-center pane. Click Get Next to any episode(s) you want to download.

4. When the downloads are complete, fire up the Zune software, and look in the Videos > Recently Added section. You should see your newly downloaded video podcasts. FeedYourZune deposits them in the default video folder monitored by the Zune software.

5. Connect your Zune, wait a few moments, drag one or more podcasts to it, and then sync.

Of course, you're not limited to FeedYourZune's handful of sample channels. You can also add other video podcasts, either by searching for them with the program's search tool or pasting the address of a podcast's "feed." Unfortunately, the search tool is such a slow, buggy disaster that it's almost unusable. But if you can find the feed address for a desired podcast (this is usually available from the podcast's Web site), just copy it, press CTRL+SHIFT+A in FeedYourZune, and then press CTRL+V to paste it.

Much as it seems desirable to use FeedYourZune because, well, it has Zune in the name, there's a much better alternative. It's called iTunes.

iTunes

Believe it or not, you can use Apple's iTunes software to deliver video podcasts to your Zune. Why would you want to? Because iTunes has a world-class podcast library, and because it's excellent at managing podcast downloads and subscriptions. What's more, it offers both video and audio podcasts (more on the latter in Chapter 9). Here's how to take advantage of an Apple product for your Microsoft product:

1. Install and run iTunes.

2. Click iTunes Store and then click Podcasts.

3. Scroll down a bit until you reach the Video Podcasts section in the center portion of the screen. Browse the various categories and shows until you find something that sounds appealing. Click it.

4. Click the Subscribe button if you want a subscription to the podcast (meaning new shows will automatically be downloaded as they're made available), or just click Get Episode for each individual episode you want to download.

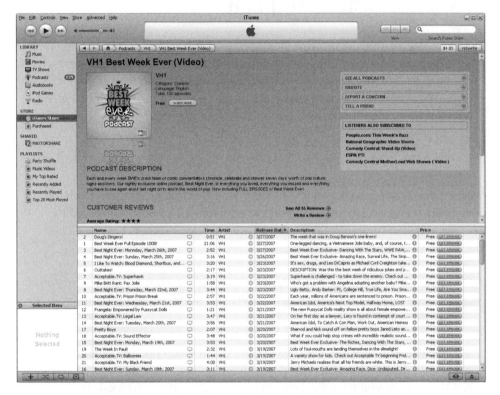

5. By default, iTunes downloads video podcasts to a folder that should already be monitored by the Zune software: My Documents > My Music > iTunes > iTunes Music > Podcasts. (Remember, the Zune software monitors *all* subfolders within My Music.) Thus, when you fire up the Zune software and head to Videos > Recently Added, the podcast(s) should appear there. Drag them to your Zune, and sync.

If you subscribe to any video podcasts, remember that you'll have to run iTunes regularly so it can download the latest episodes.

Other Options

If you're already using a "podcatching" program to manage and download podcasts (Juice and MyPodder are popular ones), there's probably no need to

Videos Always Resume From Where You Left Off

Suppose you're midway through Doug Liman's criminally underrated movie *Go* and you accidentally click the Back button. Are you now forced to restart the movie and fast-forward until you manage to get close to the same spot? Nope. The Zune automatically remembers your position in any video you're watching, so if you turn off the Zune or switch to music, for example, you'll have no problem picking up where you left off.

switch to FeedYourZune or iTunes. Just use your existing program to fetch the video podcasts you want, and save them in a folder that's being monitored by the Zune software (or tweak the Zune software to start monitoring your default podcast-download folder).

 *Even the whole folder-monitoring thing isn't essential. You can drag any video podcast from any folder to the Zune software, and it'll queue up for synchronization.*

Likewise, if you visit the Web site for any given video podcast, you can probably download individual episodes without having to use any special software at all. Of course, if you want the convenience of automatic downloads (by way of subscriptions), you'll need FeedYourZune, iTunes, or some other program.

Download YouTube Videos

Anything that plays on YouTube can play on your Zune. That's thanks to a nifty little Internet Explorer plug-in called Zunemytube. (Alas, it's not available for Firefox, my browser of choice, but I'm willing to jump ship for this particular task.) Here's how to use it:

1. Download and install Zunemytube.

2. Fire up Internet Explorer, head to YouTube, and choose a video you want to save. (I recommend anything from the *Mr. Deity* series.)

3. Click the ZuneIt button in Internet Explorer's toolbar. Don't be alarmed if nothing seems to happen. Zunemytube operates entirely in the background.

4. Wait a few minutes while Zunemytube downloads the video, converts it to WMV format, and deposits it in the My Videos > YouTube folder—ready for syncing the next time you fire up the Zune software. Note that there's no way to monitor the progress of these steps, but in my experience, it usually takes just a few minutes for the process to finish.

TIP *Zunemytube also works with Google Video! Of course, Google's recent purchase of YouTube means that Google Video will probably get folded into it before too long and cease to exist. But for now, it's still there, and you can "Zune it."*

Where to Find It

Web Site	Address	What's There
Apple	www.apple.com/itunes	iTunes
eRightSoft	http://www.erightsoft.com/SUPER.html	SUPER video converter
FeedYourZune	www.feedyourzune.com	FeedYourZune
DVD-WMV	www.dvd-wmv.com	DVD-WMV
M2Solutions, Inc.	www.m2solutionsinc.com	M2Convert for Zune
PQDVD.com	www.pqdvd.com	PQ DVD to Zune Converter
Roxio	www.roxio.com	MyTV ToGo
SourceForge	http://tinyurl.com/y2oomb	Zunemytube
The Coding Workshop	www.pocketdvdwizard.com	Pocket DVD Wizard
Xilisoft	www.xilisoft.com	DVD to Zune Converter
ZuneTVWatcher	http://zunetvwatcher.jconserv.net/index.php	ZuneTVWatcher

Chapter 7

Pictures

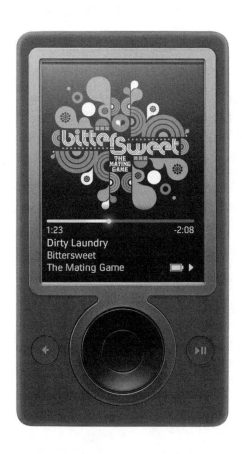

How to...

- Add pictures to your Zune
- View pictures on your Zune
- Play music during a slideshow

If a picture is worth a thousand words, then your Zune is worth...well, let's just say it's a lot of words. That's because the device doubles as a portable photo album, able to store a potentially huge library of images. In this chapter you'll learn how to put pictures on your Zune, view them, and even enjoy music while watching a slideshow.

Add Pictures to Your Zune

Just like music and movies, pictures can find their way on to your Zune only via the Zune software. If you've configured the latter to auto-sync your pictures (as discussed in Chapter 2), then all pictures added to your monitored folder(s) will automatically be copied to your Zune during the next synchronization. You can also manually add photos to the Zune software by dragging them from any folder on your hard drive (see the next section).

> NOTE
> *The Zune software (and the Zune itself) is compatible with only one digital photo file format: JPEG. That's not a bad thing, as virtually every digital camera on the planet stores photos in the JPEG format, and it's also an almost universal standard for images posted on the Internet. If you have photos in a different format, you can convert them to JPEG using any number of free programs. I highly recommend IrfanView (www.irfanview.com).*

I think that given the volume of digital photos most users are taking these days (I don't know about you, but I've got thousands of them), the smarter move is to manually sync. That way, you can pick and choose just the pictures you want. Not sure how your Zune software is configured? Here's how to determine the sync status for pictures:

1. Run the Zune software, and connect your Zune. Wait a few moments while it performs its initial sync.

2. In the navigation pane, right-click your Zune's name, and choose Set Up
Sync. The Sync This Device Automatically check box should be selected.

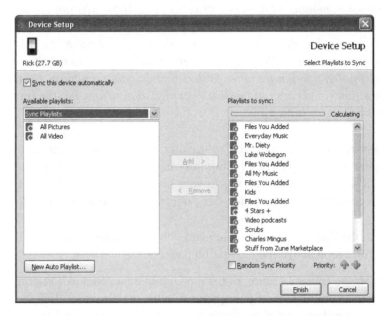

3. In the window on the right (titled Playlists To Sync), you should see one
or more playlists. Look for one called All Pictures. If it's *not* there, the
Zune software will not automatically sync your pictures—you'll have to
add them manually. If you want to enable automatic synchronization of
pictures, proceed to step 4.

4. In the Available Playlists field, click the arrow to access the drop-down
menu, and then choose Sync Playlists. In the window below, click All
Pictures and then click the Add button that's in between the two windows.
Finally, click Finish.

Once again, if you've enabled auto-synchronization of all pictures, the only
remaining step is to instruct the Zune software to monitor hard drive folders
that contain pictures. To add new folders, press F3. (See Chapter 2 if you don't
remember the finer points of folder monitoring.)

Just because you enable auto-synchronization doesn't mean you have to copy every photo on your hard drive to your Zune. Ultimately, only the photos in monitored folders will get copied. Thus, why not create a special folder just for photos you want copied to your Zune? For example, I frequently download new wallpaper images. I save them in a folder called Wallpapers, which I've configured the Zune software to monitor. I've also configured it to ignore other folders that do contain photos. Now, all my new downloads are automatically copied to my Zune, but the rest of my photo library stays put.

Let's assume, however, that you're sticking with manual synchronization. You can configure the Zune software to monitor one or more photo-bearing folders, but that will simply add those photos to your library (just like adding music and videos). To actually copy photos to your Zune, you'll need to do the following:

1. With the Zune software running and your Zune connected, click the View Pictures icon above the navigation pane.

2. Under the Library section of the navigation pane, click All Pictures. If you don't see thumbnails of your pictures in the details pane, click the View Layouts button, and choose either Icon or Tile.

3. In the upper-right corner of the Zune software window, above the list pane, click the Sync icon.

4. Drag one or more photos from the details pane to the list pane.

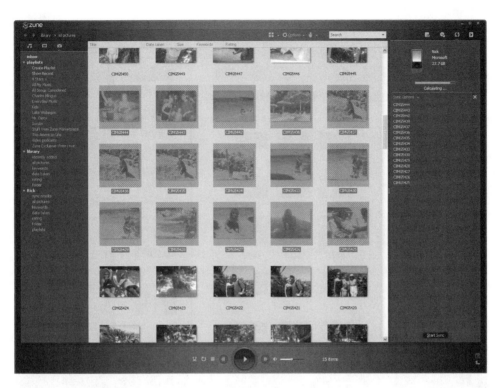

5. Sync your Zune.

To select more than one photo at a time, hold down the CTRL key while you click each photo. Once you've made your selections, release the CTRL key. Then drag the selection of photos to the list pane. If you want to quickly select several photos in a row, hold down SHIFT and click the first and last selections on the list. This will highlight all the ones in between as well.

Add Pictures from Outside the Zune Software

Want to add pictures that aren't part of your Zune software library? No problem. Using your preferred Windows file manager, just open the folder containing the pictures, and drag them from that folder to the list pane in the Zune software (see Figure 7-1). They'll get queued for synchronization just as though you'd dragged them from the library.

FIGURE 7-1   You can drag photos from an outside folder to the Zune software.

   *You can't drag photos from an optical disc or memory card to the Zune software; they must be copied to a folder on your hard drive first.*

Adjust Zune Photo Sizes and Resolutions

At this point, you probably have a few technical questions about copying photos to your Zune. For instance, if your digital camera snaps 10-megapixel images that result in files of about 4 megabytes (MB) apiece, won't those photos consume an inordinate amount of space on your Zune? What's more, if the Zune's screen resolution is a mere 320 × 240 pixels and you copy over a three-megapixel image (which has a whopping resolution of approximately 2,048 × 1,536 pixels), what will happen? Some kind of freakish implosion, perhaps?

Relax. The Zune and Zune software are quite adept at handling photos of all sizes and resolutions. Whenever you sync a photo to the Zune, the Zune software automatically creates a copy of it and resizes that copy to fit the confines of the screen. In other words, it shrinks it to 320 × 240 pixels, which results in a significantly smaller file size (roughly 10-30K). That means you can store thousands of pictures on your Zune and they'll barely make a dent in the 30-gigabyte (GB) hard drive.

Interestingly, if you've configured the Zune software to auto-synchronize your pictures, it will automatically perform this resizing during periods of inactivity. That way, the pictures will copy much faster the next time you sync, instead of having to be converted "on the fly" during the synchronization process.

Use the Zune Photo Library

When you select View Pictures in the Zune software and look under the Library section, you'll notice six options:

- Recently Added

- All Pictures

- Keywords

- Date Taken

- Rating

- Folder

Although several of these are self-explanatory, a few may not be. See Chapter 4 for a complete description of each item. Remember—you can sort by each of those fields simply by clicking the term at the top of the column.

View Pictures on Your Zune

As discussed in Chapter 3, the Zune stores its pictures in the Pictures menu (big surprise, huh?). As you'll see upon entering the menu, the twist interface presents you with two sorting options:

- **View By Date**   Sorts your photos by the month they were taken

- **View By Folder**   Sorts your photos by folder—specifically, the desktop folder from which they originated when you added them to the Zune software

This is not unlike the Music menu, in that you're simply choosing the way you want to access your photos. Both options have a Play Slideshow selection at the top; select it to launch a slideshow of *all* the photos in your Zune. (Remember, you haven't drilled down into a particular folder or collection yet, which is how you'd select a specific group of photos for a slideshow.)

Once you select a batch of photos (either by date or folder), you're again given the option to play a slideshow. (You can also wirelessly send photos to another Zune user; find out more in Chapter 10.) Alternately, you can drill down a bit further into sub-folders, if they exist. Eventually, you'll see a group of photo *thumbnails*—small versions of each photo in that collection. Thumbnails look like this:

To view a specific photo, press the control pad down until you see a white box surrounding the first photo. Now the control pad becomes a navigation pad: Press it up, down, left, or right until the white box lands on the photo you want. Press OK/Select, and the photo will fill the screen.

> **NOTE** *As with video, viewing photos causes your screen to rotate 90 degrees. At the same time, the control pad's functions "rotate" to match. Thus, what was previously up/down becomes left/right, while left/right becomes up/down. The other controls remain the same. The control pad returns to its previous state of operation after you exit full-screen photo viewing.*

Press the Back button to return to the previous screen. Otherwise, the photo will stay on the screen for as long as your Zune has power. Alternately, if you press OK/Select while viewing a photo (either alone or as part of a slideshow), you'll see an Options menu. Let's take a look at those options, which are described further in the next section.

Use Picture Playback Options

While viewing a photo, pressing the OK/Select button launches an Options menu containing six items. Here's what they do:

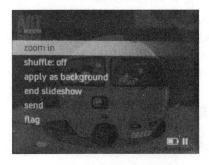

- ■ **Zoom In**   Want to get a closer look at your photo? Select the Zoom In option to enlarge the center portion. From there, you can use the control pad to scroll up, down, left, and right. Notice the small "area box" in the lower-right corner of the screen. It indicates which portion of the photo is currently zoomed in on. Press OK/Select to zoom out again.

- ■ **Shuffle**   As with music, your Zune can "play" photos in random order. Set shuffle mode to "on" if you want random slideshows; turn it "off" if you want them to play in whatever order they're listed.

- **Apply As Background** This is one of the Zune's coolest features. By selecting this option, you turn the currently displayed photo into the background image for the entire Zune interface. It's a great way to customize your Zune and give it a unique look. You can easily change the background to something else by loading another photo and selecting this option again.

- **End Slideshow** Select this option to end the current slideshow and return to the Zune's main menu. Can't you accomplish the same thing with the Back button? Yes, but that merely returns you to the previous screen. You'd have to press it a couple of times (or hold it down for a few seconds) to hit the *main* menu.

- **Send** Select this option to beam this photo to another Zune user. Find out more in Chapter 10.

- **Flag** Similar to music playback options, Flag adds an invisible marker to the selected photo. The next time you sync your Zune with your PC, you'll see a list of flagged photos in the Zune software inbox. You can use flags for any kind of reminder or notification; there are no hard and fast rules.

Play Music During a Slideshow

The Zune offers the enviable ability to play music while running a photo slideshow (or just displaying an individual photo). Just start playing a song, and then hold down the Back button to return to the main menu. Navigate to Pictures, and start your slideshow or load your photo. It's like your own personal music video. Neat!

Where to Find It

Web Site	Address	What's There
IrfanView	www.irfanview.com	A free image-editing program that can convert pictures to the JPEG format

Part III

Get More From Your Zune

Chapter 8

FM Radio

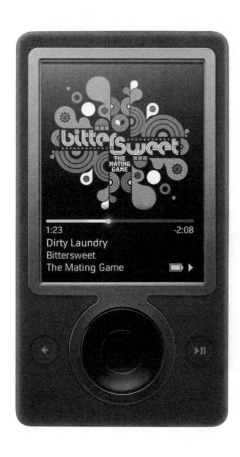

How to...

■ Tune in FM stations

■ Add or remove station presets

■ Tune to station presets

■ Use radio playback controls

■ Understand RBDS

■ Use your Zune with your car stereo

One big advantage your Zune has over Apple's current crop of iPods is its built-in FM radio. With it you can tune in music, news, sports, talk radio, NPR programs, and more (pretty much like every other radio on the planet). Personally, there are times when I'm happy to take a break from my music library and listen to something live and unexpected.

The Zune functions a bit differently in radio mode than it does when you're playing content stored on the hard drive. Fortunately, it's not the least bit difficult to use. Let's take a look at the Zune's crackerjack FM capabilities (see Figure 8-1).

FIGURE 8-1   The Zune features a built-in FM tuner so you can listen to the radio.

 *As noted in Chapter 1, the Zune's headphones double as an antenna for the radio. Thus, if you're listening to your Zune through, say, a stereo dock or your TV, you'll need to leave the headphones plugged in. The only exception would be a speaker dock with its own antenna, though I don't know of any currently on the market.*

Tune in FM Stations

I'm sure you can figure out how to access the Zune's radio, but just in case: From the home screen, scroll to Radio and press OK/Select. Presto: radio! As with music and video playback, pressing the control pad up and down raises and lowers the volume.

Ah, but what happens when you press it left and right? By default, the Zune operates in seek mode, meaning that a right or left press jumps the tuner to the next or previous in-range station on the FM dial. (Okay, "dial" is kind of an outdated term, here, but cut me some slack—in my youth, radios had dials!)

If you'd rather tune your Zune manually, you need to disable seek mode. Here's how:

1. From the tuner screen, press OK/Select.

2. In the Options menu that appears, scroll to Seek and press OK/Select to turn it off.

3. Press Back to return to the tuner (or just wait a few seconds).

Complicated, huh? Now, when you press the control pad right or left, the Zune moves one channel up or down the dial. In other words, if you're currently tuned in to 99.1, a right-press of the control pad bumps you to 99.3. A second press moves to 99.5, and so on. This kind of precision can be useful when you're trying to tune in to a particularly frequency but the seek mode is having trouble locking onto it (perhaps because it's just slightly out of range).

 *If you hold down the control pad while pressing right or left, the Zune will quickly scan up or down the dial.*

8

Add or Remove Station Presets

Like your car stereo, the Zune lets you save your favorite stations so that you can quickly jump to them. These *presets* are easy to add:

1. Tune to the desired station.

2. Press OK/Select.

3. On the subsequent Options menu, you'll see Add [Station] To Presets. Press OK/Select.

In other words, all you have to do is tune to a station and press OK/Select twice. If you want to remove a preset, the steps are identical. (The Options menu will say Remove [Station] From Presets.)

You can spot presets on the Zune's FM dial by the little white lines that appear. The Zune allows you to set an unlimited number of presets, though obviously you wouldn't want to create more than, say, 20. Otherwise it's no different from just stepping up the dial one frequency at a time.

There's an even faster way to save a preset: Just hold down the OK/Select button for 2 seconds. You'll immediately see a little white line appear on the FM dial. The same method works for removing a preset.

Tune to Station Presets

Once you've added one or more presets to your Zune, it's a simple matter to hop between them. From the tuner screen, press the OK/Select button. You'll see the radio options screen and your list of presets (which appear in ascending order). Scroll to the one you want, and press OK/Select.

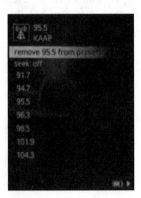

Use Radio Playback Controls

You already know how the control pad functions when you're listening to the radio. What about the Zune's other controls? The following list explains them in detail:

- ■ **Play/Pause** When the Zune is in radio mode, the Play/Pause button turns into a Mute button. Press once to mute the audio; press it again to un-mute it.

- ■ **Hold Switch** It works with radio, too, locking out the player's controls so that you don't accidentally switch stations or send the volume soaring.

Understand RBDS

While you're listening to the radio, you may start to see snippets of information appear above and below the FM dial. This information might include the station's call letters, the type of program (talk, rock, etc.), and possibly even the name of current song and/or artist.

8

This is the Radio Broadcast Data System, or RBDS. Some stations in the United States leverage this system to broadcast small amounts of information over the airwaves, and the Zune can display this information as well. It's not exactly satellite radio (which, as you may know, provides a wealth of data along with the audio), but it's still pretty cool.

NOTE *The type and amount of information you'll receive varies from one station to the next. Some stations don't broadcast RBDS at all.*

Use Your Zune with Your Car Stereo

As you'll discover in Chapter 11, it's possible to wirelessly feed audio from your Zune to your car stereo—great for listening to music while driving. However, to do so, you'll need an FM transmitter, which broadcasts Zune audio to an unused radio frequency. Why can't you use the Zune's built-in FM tuner to accomplish the same thing? Because it's a receiver, not a transmitter. In other words, the Zune can receive FM radio signals, but it can't broadcast them.

Find out more about making a Zune-car connection in Chapter 11.

Chapter 9

Podcasts and Audiobooks

How to…

- Find podcasts

- Load podcasts on your Zune

- Play podcasts on your Zune

- Find audiobooks for your Zune

- Play audiobooks on your Zune

- Rip audiobooks from CDs and tapes

As touched upon in previous chapters, your Zune is capable of playing podcasts—audio and video programs that originate from various amateur and professional sources. Podcasts open the door to a world of rich content, far beyond plain old music and movies. In this chapter you'll learn everything you need to know about finding, loading, and playing podcasts. I'll also help you get started with audiobooks—the digital equivalent of books on tape. The Zune is a little weak in this department, but the option is there for users who are willing to work around the hassles.

What's a Podcast?

In its simplest definition, a podcast is an audio or video program that's distributed online. These programs are designed for playback on portable devices like the Zune; however, because they're created using common digital formats (such as MP3 for audio and MOV for video), they can also be played on PCs just as easily.

Think of a podcast as a radio or TV program that you can download. Here are some examples of some popular audio podcasts:

- **NPR: *Car Talk's Call of the Week***   Although you can't get the entire *Car Talk* show in podcast form (yet), you can at least get the "call of the week"—usually a 5- to 9-minute segment.

- **NPR: *Wait Wait…Don't Tell Me***   The popular NPR quiz show.

- ■ *Learn Spanish with Coffee Break Spanish*   That's right, a podcast that teaches you a foreign language.

- ■ *ESPN Baseball Today*   Daily highlights and postgame reports from ESPN.

- ■ *Grammar Girl's Quick and Dirty Tips for Better Writing*   An entire podcast devoted to improving your writing skills.

- ■ *Audiobooks with Annie*   Each podcast is a chapter from a public-domain book, such as *The Adventures of Huckleberry Finn* and *Pride and Prejudice*.

These are just the tip of the iceberg. You can find podcasts devoted to a huge range of subjects, and the best news of all is that the vast majority of them are free. The same is true of video podcasts. However, I'll be looking at audio podcasts for most of this chapter. To learn about the video stuff, see Chapter 6.

Remember, a podcast is just an audio file, different from music only in terms of its content. However, you may want to explore some different methods of organization so that your podcasts don't get lumped in with your music during shuffle play. Find out more in the upcoming section, "Organize Podcasts into Playlists."

9

Now, without further adieu (this chapter has had quite enough adieu, thank you), let's learn how to find podcasts and put them on your Zune.

Find Podcasts

At this writing, the Zune software offers no provision for finding or downloading podcasts. Microsoft has promised to remedy this disappointing shortcoming in a future release, but for now you'll have to look to other solutions.

There are dozens of programs that enable you to "subscribe" to podcasts, meaning the software automatically downloads new episodes of a given show as they become available. (Alternately, you can pick and choose individual shows to download.) How can you decide which program to use? Allow me to make a rather surprising recommendation: Apple's iTunes.

I know it sounds crazy, but hear me out. iTunes includes an excellent podcast library, and you can easily subscribe to any shows that aren't already listed. What's more, Apple recently started selling unprotected music, meaning you can now use iTunes as a secondary source for music for your Zune. So now you have two reasons to install iTunes on your PC.

 *Installing iTunes will have no effect on the Zune software—they're just two different programs that both happen to be music managers/stores. However, the first time you run iTunes, you'll likely see a message asking if you want to make it the default audio player. Make sure to say no; otherwise, you could end up with some hassles when trying to play music in the Zune software.*

Let's take a look at how you'll use iTunes to locate, subscribe to, and manage podcasts.

Install iTunes

To install iTunes on your PC, just head to Apple's Web site (www.apple.com/itunes), click the Download iTunes button, and follow the instructions. The software is free to download and use (though, obviously, you'll have to pay up if you decide to buy any music).

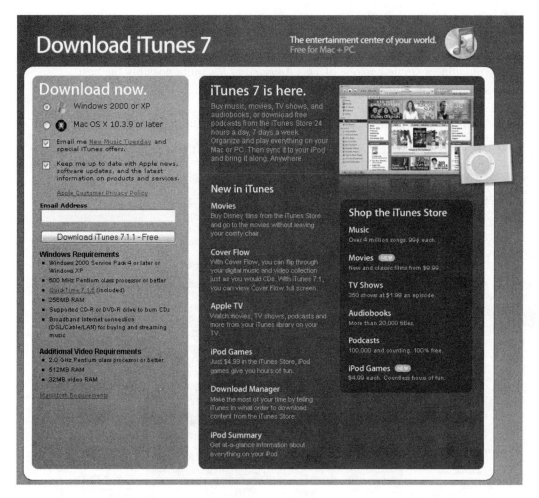

It's worth noting that the system requirements for iTunes are similar to those of the Zune software:

■ 256 megabytes (MB) of random access memory (RAM)

■ 500-megahertz (MHz) Pentium processor or faster (trust me, you'll want something a *lot* faster)

■ Windows 2000 Service Pack 4 or later or Windows XP (the software can also run on Windows Vista, though as of this writing, that operating system is not yet officially supported by iTunes)

You'll also need to install the latest version of Apple QuickTime (this is included with iTunes and will install automatically).

Run iTunes

Once you've installed iTunes, run the program. Let's walk through the steps of downloading a single episode of *This American Life*, quite possibly the best podcast money can't buy.

1. In iTunes navigation pane on the left side, click iTunes Store.

2. In the iTunes Store area near the upper-left corner of the screen, click Podcasts.

3. Look for the Top Podcasts section on the right; you should see This American Life at (or near) the top of the list. Click the link for the podcast.

4. You'll see the podcast page for the show. There should be a single episode listed in the bottom pane. Click Get Episode, and the podcast will begin downloading immediately.

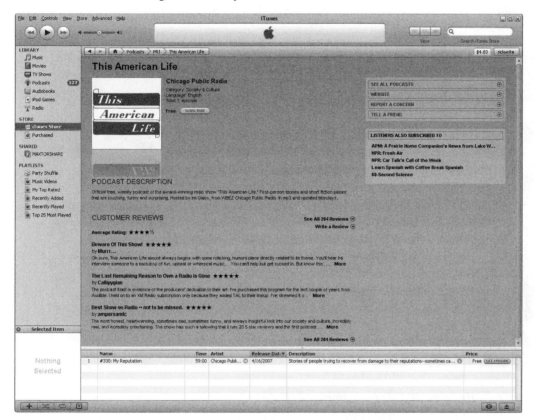

5. You can monitor the download progress by clicking Downloads in the navigation pane. You can also click the Podcasts entry under Library in the same pane to see your podcast downloads and subscriptions.

That's all there is to it! At this point, you're probably wondering how this downloaded podcast is going to end up on your Zune. Well, I'll tell you: By default, iTunes saves podcasts in a subfolder of your My Music folder—which is monitored by the Zune software. Head to the next section to find out more.

Load Podcasts on Your Zune

Now it's time to add your podcasts to the Zune software so that they can be copied to your Zune. As noted in the previous section, iTunes stores downloaded podcasts in a My Music subfolder, meaning they should be recognized by the Zune software (which monitors My Music and all subfolders therein) as new additions.

To test this theory, start the Zune software, and click the Recently Added item under Library in the navigation pane. You should see your newly downloaded podcast(s).

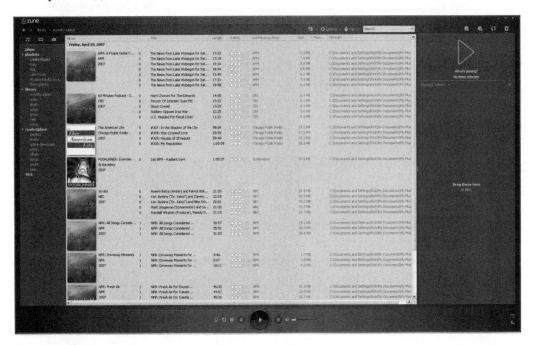

 *If you've disabled monitoring of the My Music folder for some reason, you'll need to add iTunes' podcast folder to the monitor list. To do so, press F3, click the Add Folder button, and then navigate to the proper folder (which is most likely My Documents | My Music | iTunes | iTunes Music | Podcasts).*

Organize Podcasts into Playlists

By default, all newly added audio files (podcasts included) will get copied to your Zune the next time you synchronize. However, a little organization is in order. Podcasts often have funky ID3 tags (see Chapter 5), which can make them difficult to locate on your Zune. Thus, consider creating one or more playlists for your podcasts (again, see Chapter 5). Here's an example:

I've created playlists for *60 Minutes*, *A Prairie Home Companion*, and *This American Life*. All I have to do is drag each podcast to the appropriate playlist and synchronize my Zune. Now I can easily find the podcasts I want.

 This doesn't solve the problem of podcasts entering the mix when you use the Zune's "shuffle all" option for listening to music. This is one more reason why Microsoft needs to release a firmware update so that the Zune player differentiates podcasts from music. Fortunately, this is in the works; hopefully, it will already have happened by the time you read this. In the meantime, see the upcoming section, "Keep Podcasts Out of Your Music Library."

Unfortunately, there's no easy way to manage podcasts, to track which ones you've already played. Until Microsoft updates the Zune software to support podcasts directly, all you can do is keep a mental record and then delete the "used" podcasts from the software (which will, in turn, delete them from your Zune the next time you synchronize).

Keep Podcasts Out of Your Music Library   Although the Zune can't differentiate podcasts from music, there is a way to keep the two separate. The solution lies in auto playlists, which we first discussed in Chapter 5. What you can do is create a playlist that automatically excludes all podcasts, leaving everything else (namely, your music). It's a bit of a hassle to set up, but to me, it's worth the effort. Nothing bugs me more than listening to my music library on shuffle-play and suddenly

9

getting interrupted by the voice of *A Prairie Home Companion*'s Garrison Keillor (who I otherwise dig). Here's how to create this playlist:

1. In the Zune software's navigation pane, right-click Playlists and choose Create Auto Playlist.

2. Give this new playlist a name, ideally something descriptive, like "Everything But Podcasts" or "All My Music."

3. Click the first green plus sign, and choose Genre from the menu.

4. Right beside Genre, click Is and choose Is Not.

5. Click Click To Set, and choose Podcast from the menu. Click OK to create the playlist.

6. The Zune software will immediately switch to the new playlist so that you can review its contents. You shouldn't see any podcasts, only music.

7. Sync your Zune to copy over the new playlist.

8. To shuffle-play all your music, just play the new playlist (making sure that shuffle mode is turned on, of course—see Chapter 3 if you can't remember how to do that).

Whether or not this works properly depends on your podcasts being tagged correctly (see Chapter 5). In other words, the Genre tag for each podcast must be set to "podcast"; otherwise, the Zune software won't know it's a podcast and won't exclude it from your new playlist. Most of the podcasts I've downloaded via iTunes were tagged correctly, but there were a few exceptions. Fortunately, it's quite easy to modify the Genre tag for any problematic podcast(s). Here's how:

1. In the Zune software, browse your library until you find your podcast(s), or just click the appropriate playlist, assuming you created one as described previously.

2. Right-click a podcast and choose Edit Track Info. To select more than one podcast, hold down the CTRL key while clicking each one. Then right-click any of the selected podcasts, and choose Edit Track Info.

3. In the dialog box that appears, click the Genre check box, and then type the word **podcast** into the blank field.

4. Click OK and you're done. Presto! The Zune software has modified the Genre tag for the podcast(s), which will now be excluded from your new auto playlist.

My Five Favorite Podcasts

If you're new to podcasts, perhaps you're not sure which ones to try first. I've whipped together a list of my five favorites; you're guaranteed to enjoy at least some of them. (Note that this is not a money-back guarantee. If you don't like the choices, well, you've got problems. Or maybe I do. It's anybody's guess.)

- *All Songs Considered*   Host Bob Boilen plays entire tracks off new albums from established and unknown artists alike. The first time I listened to this show, I heard the music of Brendan Benson, who quickly became one of my all-time favorite artists.

- **Anything from NPR**   You can now get a wealth of NPR shows and segments in podcast form, including *Story of the Day, Driveway Moments, Talk of the Nation*, and *StoryCorps*. This stuff alone can stock your Zune with hours of riveting listening.

- *Battlestar Galactica*   For fans of the show, there's no better listening than creator Ronald D. Moore's podcast dissecting each episode. You'll get behind-the-scenes secrets, explanations for various plot points, and sometimes even visits from various cast members.

- *Fresh Air*   One of NPR's longest-running and most popular shows, *Fresh Air* features interviews with musicians, actors, politicians, newsmakers, and other luminaries.

- *This American Life*   My all-time favorite radio show is now available in podcast form. You'll definitely want to subscribe to this one, as you can't go back and download the previous weeks' episodes.

Play Podcasts on Your Zune

Once you've copied some podcasts to your Zune, it's a simple matter to play them: Just find the desired podcast (hopefully, you've organized them into playlists, as discussed in the previous section), and then play it like you would a song or video. However, there's one caveat to keep in mind: The Zune won't remember your place in the podcast the way it will in a video. In other words, it doesn't bookmark audio files—not yet, anyway. The Zune can resume from where it left off after going into standby mode, but if you switch to a different track or activity while in the middle of a podcast, you'll lose your place. Hopefully, Microsoft's future firmware update will remedy this issue.

Because the Zune lets you fast-forward through a track with relative ease (see Chapter 3), you should be able to return to where you left off in a podcast. The trick is to remember your spot. Before you switch activities or turn the Zune off, look at the playback time and make a mental note of the number. If you're 29 minutes into the podcast, for example, just remember 29 and you'll know how far to fast-forward when you return to it later.

Find Audiobooks for Your Zune

If podcasts are a good source of listening material, *audiobooks* are even better. Audiobooks are the digital equivalent of books on tape. They're books read aloud by an actor or author. For my money, there's no better way to pass a long car trip than to listen to an audiobook.

Sadly, Zune Marketplace doesn't sell audiobooks (one area where it falls short of iTunes, which does sell them). Likewise, the Zune doesn't support media purchased from Audible.com (see Figure 9-1), one of the Web's best source for audiobooks. (Score one more for the iPod, which does support Audible.) With any luck, Microsoft will offer audiobook sales and support in the future.

In the meantime, you're left with a handful of other solutions—and a caveat. The caveat is the same as for podcasts: The Zune doesn't automatically bookmark your spot, so if you're listening to a 9-hour audiobook, for example, navigation can really cause problems. Finding your spot again after switching to another activity is a major hassle. However, there's a way to work around this, so let's take a look at some of the sources for audiobooks you can play on your Zune:

■ **Audible.com**   I can't speak highly enough of this service. Audible carries a huge library of fiction, nonfiction, and other spoken-word books, which you can buy piecemeal or download as part of various subscription plans. You'll have to do a bit of fiddling to get the books (which are protected files) to play on your Zune (see the upcoming section, "Convert Audible Files into MP3s), but I think it's worth the effort.

FIGURE 9-1 Audible.com carries an excellent selection of audiobooks, but you'll have to jump through a few hoops if you want to play them on your Zune.

- **Books on tape and books on CDs** You may have a library of old books on tape you'd like to hear again, or perhaps you've checked out audiobook CDs from the library. Either way, you can copy them to your Zune. See the upcoming section, "Rip Audiobooks from CDs and Tapes."

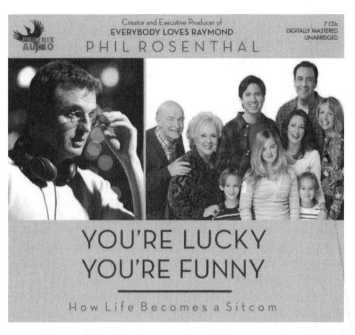

- **AudioBooksForFree.com**   Its name notwithstanding, this site doesn't actually provide audiobooks for free. Instead, it offers public-domain works (such as *The Count of Monte Cristo* and *20,000 Leagues Under the Sea*), read by professional actors/narrators, for a low price—usually $3 to 7 per book. What's nice is that the site delivers the books already split up into multiple MP3s, which helps with navigation.

- **Your public library**   In addition to audiobook CDs that you can check out, many public libraries now offer MP3-format audiobooks you can download. This is arguably your best option, as the books are free, of course, and they're already in MP3 format—no conversion required. (There are exceptions: Some libraries distribute their audiobooks as digital rights management (DRM)-protected WMA files, which may or may not work on your Zune.)

- **Podcasts**   As you learned in an earlier section ("What's a Podcast?"), there's at least one podcast that consists of audiobooks.

- **LibriVox.com**   This site offers over a thousand audiobooks that are free to download. The catch, if you want to call it that, is that the books are all public-domain works, like *Tom Sawyer* and the novels of Jane Austen. What's more, they're read by volunteers, not professional voice talent, so the quality isn't always stellar. Still, the downloads are divided into chapters, they're Zune-friendly MP3s, and they're free. Sounds like a pretty good deal, no?

Find out more about these options—and how to use them with your Zune—in the sections to come. Let's start with Audible.

Want to download a batch of public-domain audiobooks that are already split into pieces and recorded in Zune-compatible WMA format? Head to the "free" section at Simply Audiobooks (http://tinyurl.com/2dqem7). You'll find about a dozen titles, including Mark Twain's The Stolen White Elephant, *Jack London's* Call of the Wild, *and T.S. Eliot's* The Waste Land. *Good stuff!*

Download Audiobooks from Audible.com

Whether I'm driving 20 minutes across town or 20 hours across the country, I always keep a generous supply of audiobooks in the car. Back in the day, that meant spending big bucks on cassettes—without even knowing if I'd like the book—or digging through the local library's paltry collection.

Now, thanks to our old friend the Internet, I get audiobooks delivered to my PC and pay significantly less for the privilege. The service that makes this possible is Audible.com, one of the Web's oldest stores and best-kept secrets.

Launched in 1997, Audible (see Figure 9-1) boasts over tens of thousands of hours' worth of downloadable content—everything from fiction and nonfiction books to radio programs and even newspapers. Among the titles currently available: *The Da Vinci Code*, Barack Obama's *The Audacity of Hope*, loads of Stephen King novels, and even some exclusive content not available elsewhere (like comedian Julia Sweeney's funny, insightful *Letting Go of God*).

Most of Audible's books are unabridged, unlike many cassettes and CDs. And, needless to say, the site carries a much larger selection than any bookstore. It's basically the Amazon of audiobooks.

The service supports a wide range of portable devices, but, alas, the Zune isn't currently one of them. (I spoke with Audible, and they couldn't confirm any plans to add Zune support. The ball's in Microsoft's court.) However, it is possible to burn your own CDs, and that's where there's a ray of hope in the otherwise bleak Audible-Zune landscape. It's a time-consuming and occasionally error-prone process—especially if you're copying, say, a 12-hour book (which would require roughly 12 blank CDs)—but it does make it possible to copy Audible content to your Zune. More on that in a minute.

You can purchase Audible content piecemeal—fiction and nonfiction titles cost upwards of 60 percent less than their CD/cassette counterparts—or sign up for an AudibleListener plan. The Gold plan ($14.95/month) includes one credit per month (which can be redeemed for a single audiobook). That's a pretty good deal, considering that many titles sell for a lot more than $14.95 if purchased piecemeal. The Platinum plan costs $22.95 per month and includes two credits per month. Both plans entitle you to free weekly audio selections, a 30-percent discount on additional purchases, and a free digital audio newspaper (*The Wall Street Journal* or *The New York Times*).

Using Audible with Your Zune

So let's say you decide to sign up for an AudibleListener plan or just buy a few audiobooks outright. If Audible doesn't support the Zune and the Zune doesn't support Audible downloads, did you just waste your money?

No, of course not—I wouldn't do that to you. In fact, there are two ways to convert Audible content to a Zune-compatible format:

■ Burn the books to CDs using Audible's software, and then rip those CDs using the Zune software. This is exactly the same as ripping an audio CD, as described in Chapter 5. You'll end up with MP3 files, which, as you know, are compatible with any player, the Zune included.

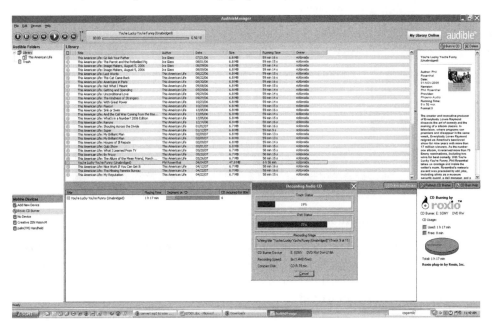

■ Use special software to convert the Audible audiobook files directly to MP3s. Find out how in the next section.

Convert Audible Files into MP3s   If you'd rather not go to the trouble of burning a bunch of audiobook CDs and then ripping them to create MP3s for your Zune, there's a somewhat more streamlined method you can employ. It requires a program called Replay A/V (www.applian.com), which captures all audio played through your computer's sound card and creates MP3 files from it. Here's the nutshell version of how this works:

1. Run the Audible Manager software.

2. Install and run Replay A/V.

3. Click the Open Recording Wizard button. Follow the prompts to record what you're hearing (the bottom option).

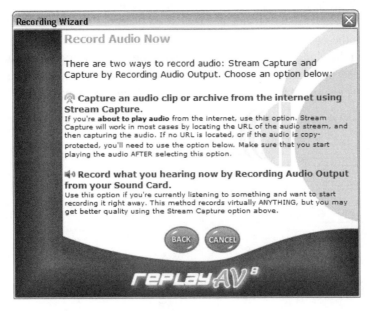

4. Switch back to Audible Manager, and then play the audiobook.

5. Mute your PC's speakers, and go about your business until the audiobook has played through. Obviously, this can take several hours (the book plays in real time), so it's the kind of operation you might want to start, say, before heading off to bed.

Before you get started, make sure to close down other programs that might inadvertently "sneak" audio into your recordings (like e-mail and instant-messaging software that pings when new messages arrive).

That's all there is to it. When you're done, you'll have an MP3 audiobook file you can copy to your Zune. And because Replay A/V can automatically split tracks at designated intervals, you can create MP3s that span, for example, 20 minutes apiece, which makes for much easier navigation of your audiobook.

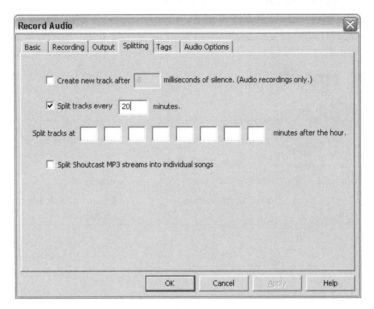

9

Replay A/V may seem a bit pricey at $49.95, but keep in mind that it can do a lot more than convert Audible recordings into MP3s. It can also capture streaming audio and video from just about any online source, meaning you can record music from Internet radio stations, MySpace pages, and the like, as well as video clips from Internet TV stations, music video sites, and so on. In other words, you can use the program to capture a boatload of content for your Zune without having to worry about annoying DRM restrictions. I highly recommend Replay A/V.

Rip Audiobooks from CDs and Tapes

If you've got some audiobooks on CD or cassette, you can turn the contents into Zune-compatible MP3 files. We already covered this process in Chapter 5, though the focus there was on music CDs and tapes. Fortunately, the procedure is pretty much identical for audiobooks, so head back to Chapter 5 to learn how to "rip" this media.

 *Your local library may be a great source for audiobooks on CD. Of course, after you've checked them out, ripped them, and played them on your Zune, you should delete the files in accordance with copyright laws.*

Where to Find It

Web Site	Address	What's There
Audible	www.audible.com	Audiobooks you can download
Apple	www.apple.com/itunes	iTunes
Applian Technologies	www.applian.com	Replay music
LibriVox	www.librivox.com	Free-to-download public domain audiobooks

Chapter 10

Share Music and More with Other Zunes

How to...

- Enable wireless communication

- Set your online status

- Find other Zunes

- Send songs to other Zunes

- Receive songs from other Zunes

- Play songs you've received

- Turn song trials into song purchases or downloads

- Synchronize received media with your PC

- Share pictures with other Zunes

Suppose I'm having lunch with my buddy Dave, who generally has dramatically different musical tastes than mine. (I like music that sounds pleasant, while he prefers harsh, droning guitar licks and discordant, manic-depressive voices.) I say to Dave: "Have you heard the new Amy Winehouse album?"

"No, who's Amy Winehouse?" Dave replies.

"You'd like her—her lyrics have a manic-depressive edge," I say.

"Okay, but you have to check out Black Rebel Motorcycle Club," he says.

"Deal."

Then we whip out our Zunes (mine is black; Dave carries a pink one for some reason) and wirelessly exchange albums. Within two minutes, Dave is able to experience the soulful bliss that is Amy Winehouse, while I'm looking for gauze to stuff in my now-bleeding ears after listening to Black Rebel Motorcycle Club (kidding!).

That, dear readers, is the joy of Zune-to-Zune music sharing—the ability to receive new music from friends (or even newly met strangers) and share music you think others will enjoy. In this chapter you'll learn how to leverage your Zune's wireless capabilities for sharing songs and even photos.

NOTE   *As noted in Chapter 1, the Zune's wireless capabilities don't extend beyond trading songs and photos—yet. As of this writing, there are rumors that Microsoft will soon make it possible to download new music from Zune Marketplace right to your Zune—no PC required. Check my blog (http:// zunebook.wordpress.com) to see if any such update has been released.*

Enable Wireless Communication

To share media with another Zune user, you must first enable your Zune's wireless radio. (The other Zune user must do the same.) Here's how:

1. From the main menu, click Settings.

2. The very first item in the Settings menu is Wireless. Click the OK/Select button to toggle it from "off" to "on." (This assumes, of course, that wireless was turned off to begin with. As you'll learn in Chapter 13, in between bouts of sharing, you should leave wireless communication off to conserve battery life.)

3. While still in the Settings menu, scroll down to Online Status, and choose either Basic or Detailed. Find out more about these two options in the next section.

   I should mention here that simply enabling your Zune's wireless radio doesn't enable other Zune users to rummage around your device, or even to connect to it. It simply broadcasts your presence; any actual sharing of media is up to you to initiate. Find out more in the upcoming section "Share Songs and Pictures."

 *See Chapter 3 if you need a refresher on navigating the Zune's Settings menu.*

10

Set Your Online Status

While in the Zune Settings menu, you can choose between two online status options. This isn't a crucial setting, but here's the scoop on the two choices:

- **Basic**   When your Zune is set to Basic, other Zune users will see a generic message about your status, such as "online."

- **Detailed**   When your Zune is set to Detailed, other Zune users will see more detailed information about your status, such as the name of the song you're currently playing, the name of the radio station you're listening to, "viewing pictures" if you're, well, viewing pictures, and so on.

Which status setting should you choose? Unless you leave your Zune's wireless radio on all the time, it hardly matters. And even then it hardly matters; it's really just a question of how much information you want to share with other Zune users.

Find Other Zunes

To locate other Zunes in your immediate vicinity (within about 30 feet), head to the Community menu, and scroll left or right until you see the Nearby option. Assuming there's a Zune in range that has its wireless radio enabled, in a few seconds, you should see its name and status. This is a one-way operation: Your Zune simply detects the presence of other Zunes; it doesn't broadcast its own existence.

As discussed in Chapter 3, the Community menu includes two other options: Inbox, which displays any media you've received on your Zune, and Me, which displays the name and status of your Zune.

This step is, in fact, optional. If you're getting ready to share media with a friend and you know his or her Zune is ready to receive (meaning its wireless radio has been turned on), you can skip searching for nearby Zunes and head straight to the media you want to share (see the next section). Searching for Zunes is more of a way to connect with strangers—if you're into that sort of thing. Given the relatively limited number of Zunes that are "in the wild" right now, it's pretty unlikely that you'll find one nearby for "anonymous" sharing.

Suppose you see a stranger on the subway listening to his or her Zune. Without so much as saying a word, you could attempt to send that person a song, album, playlist, or photo. The person would see your request on the screen and have the option of accepting your media, refusing your media, or blocking your device altogether (how rude!).

Share Songs and Pictures

Sharing media with your Zune is admirably easy. Before we get to the actual process, however, let's look at what media can be shared:

- A song
- An album
- A playlist
- A picture
- A group of pictures

Now let's stick with my earlier example of having lunch (or, heck, any meal) with a Zune-owning friend who has already enabled his or her Zune's wireless radio. I'm going to share an album with this friend, though the process is pretty much identical for sharing any of the aforementioned media types. Here's how:

1. Make sure you've enabled your Zune's wireless radio, as described in the previous section "Enable Wireless Communication."

2. Using the Zune menus, navigate to the album you want to share, and click OK/Select to choose it.

3. In the album menu that appears, click Send.

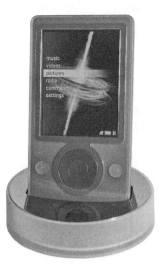

4. Your Zune will then search for nearby devices (in much the same way as described in the previous section). When it finds your friend's Zune, press OK/Select to begin the transmission.

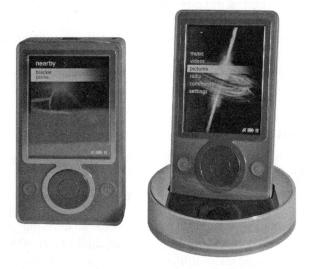

5. Wait a minute or two while the album is sent to the other Zune. Your Zune will be otherwise inoperable during this process (though you can press OK/Select to stop the transmission, if necessary).

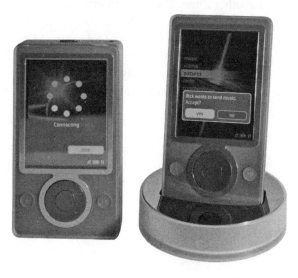

How long does it take to transmit an entire album? In my experience, usually one to two minutes, though it can vary, depending on the number, length, and file size of the tracks. Individual songs can be sent in a matter of seconds, while a single photo transfers almost instantaneously.

No changes are made to your media during the sharing process. In other words, the receiver will get the entire track (not some 30-second abridgement) at its originally recorded bit rate. You're literally transmitting an exact copy.

Sharing Limitations

There are a few restrictions on what media you can share from your Zune. Any unprotected MP3s on your device are fair game, as are unprotected WMA and AAC files (see Chapter 5 if you need a refresher on file types). As for songs downloaded from Zune Marketplace (either as purchases or subscription tracks), you can share many of them, but not all. That's because some music labels are still skittish about losing control of their music and required Microsoft to disable the "send rights" for their songs. Unfortunately, there's no way to know which songs have send rights and which ones don't until you try to send them.

A writer at the Zune fan site Zunerama conducted an interesting test. He downloaded Zune Marketplace's "top 50" songs into a playlist and then attempted to send that playlist to another Zune. The result: Only 29 of the songs were actually transferred. The others couldn't be shared due to "rights restrictions."

I had an even worse result with my own test: Only three of 24 downloaded songs would transfer. Sadly, there's nothing to be done about this. Some songs simply can't be shared, end of story. Hopefully this will change over time as music labels stop being so overprotective of their material.

How to ...   **Share More Than Just Songs and Pictures**

It doesn't seem fair that the Zune limits you to sharing songs and pictures. What if you want to share a video, for example? Or perhaps even some other files that you've loaded onto your Zune (using the "hack" described in Chapter 12)? It's possible, though not exactly easy. Here's how:

1. Modify your Zune so it can function as an external hard drive. This is fairly easy procedure; it's described in Chapter 12.

2. On your hard drive, locate the file you want to share, and change its extension to ".jpg." The idea here is to fool the Zune into thinking the file is a picture. If you're not sure how to do this (by default, Windows doesn't even display file extensions), do a Google search for "windows change file extension."

3. Using Windows Explorer or your preferred file manager, copy the new file.jpg to the Zune's Received Pictures folder. Note that the folder must also include at least one actual photo.

4. Now, using the sharing instructions described in "Share Songs and Pictures," send the entire Received Pictures folder to your fellow Zune user.

5. The next time that user synchronizes his or her Zune, the "picture" will be copied from Zune to PC. All that's left is to change the file extension back to whatever it's supposed to be.

Yes, this is a complete waste of time. I mean, there might be some practical uses for it, but I think if you want to share a file with someone, it's a lot easier to just e-mail it or, if it's too large, send it using a service like GigaSize (www.gigasize.com) or YouSendIt (www.yousendit.com). At any rate, you can find more Zune "hacks" like this one (many of which are actually useful!) in Chapter 12.

10

Receive and Play Songs and Photos

I know, I know—it's better to give than to receive, right? Well, where Zune media sharing is concerned, receiving is a *lot* more fun. It's easier, too. All you do is click Yes when your Zune alerts you that someone is trying to send media your way, and then wait for the media to arrive. When the transmission is complete, you'll immediately land at your Zune's Inbox (which is normally accessible within the Community menu), where you can play the song(s) or view the picture(s) you just received.

However, the Zune handles received songs and pictures a bit differently. The latter are accessible from within the standard Pictures menu, where you'll find a new category called Received Pictures (clever, no?). Those pictures can be viewed—and even sent to other Zune users—just like the pictures you loaded from your own library.

Music is a different story. For one thing, you won't find any received songs, albums, or playlists in your Zune's Music menus. They remain in the Community menu's Inbox, where you can play them just like you would if they were in your regular library. However, these songs are saddled with a critical (but understandable) restriction: They can be played only three times and will expire in three days (whether you play them three times or not).

A "play" is counted once the song reaches one minute or the halfway mark, whichever comes first.

In other words, the album you just received from your Zune-carrying friend isn't yours to keep. Microsoft refers to these tracks as "samples," the idea being that you're getting a chance to sample the music and see if you like it. Specifically, you can play each received song in its entirety three times within three days of its receipt. At the end of three days, whether you've played the song three times or not, the song will no longer play (though you'll still see the song in the Community menu, and it'll still appear in your Zune Marketplace Inbox after you synchronize). By the way, don't bother asking your friend to send "expired" songs again—the Zune keeps track of songs you've received and won't let you receive them a second time.

All songs carry this restriction, even if they're unprotected MP3s. However, received photos are not limited in any way.

TIP *To see how many plays and/or days a song has left, just select it. The details screen will say something like, "2 plays remaining in 3 days."*

So what happens if you really like the songs you received and want to keep them? Simple: You can buy them from Zune Marketplace (or download them, if you're a Zune Pass subscriber). Of course, you could also buy the CD, shop at other online music stores, or get the music from any number of other sources (see Chapter 5). But as you'll see in the next section, turning received songs into Zune Marketplace downloads is the most expedient method.

Synchronize Received Media with Your PC

When you receive shared media on your Zune, everything lands in the Inbox. And when you synchronize your Zune with your PC, everything gets copied to the Zune software's Inbox—sort of. Music and pictures are each handled a bit differently during the synchronization process:

■ **Received pictures**   These are automatically copied from your Zune to your PC's hard drive (specifically, to your default pictures folder, which is probably My Pictures on Windows XP systems and Pictures on Windows Vista systems). Naturally, you'll also find them in the Zune software's Recently Added section in the Pictures library. Now you can manage the received pictures like you would any others (see Chapter 7). The following illustration shows how a received picture is represented in the Zune software Inbox.

■ **Received songs**   The Zune doesn't copy received songs to your PC the way it does pictures. However, it does send *information* about the songs to the Zune software's Inbox, as shown in Figure 10-1. Remember, received songs are samples—they're not yours to keep indefinitely. That's why they stay put on your Zune (three plays, three days—see the previous section). However, by leveraging the information that appears in the Zune software Inbox, you can easily download received songs or search for them in Zune Marketplace. Find out more in the next section.

FIGURE 10-1   The Zune software's Inbox lists all media received on your Zune. Pictures are automatically copied to your PC, while songs can be searched or downloaded.

What You Can Do with Received Songs

The Zune software Inbox shows all the songs that you received on your Zune. The songs themselves, however, remain on your Zune (until you've used up your three plays or three days, that is), meaning you can't play them on your PC or add them to your library—yet. So what exactly *can* you do with the information that appears in the Zune software Inbox? As you can see in Figure 10-1, there are two options:

■ **Download/Buy**   If a song you received was originally obtained via Zune Marketplace, you'll see a Download or Buy button in the Action column. Assuming you have an active Zune Pass subscription, one click is all it takes to download that song (or buy it, if you're not a subscriber) and make it part of your library. From there, you can give it a permanent home on your Zune.

■ **Search**   If a song you received is an MP3 file or another track that wasn't obtained via Zune Marketplace, you'll see a Search button in the Action column. Clicking it searches both your local library and Zune Marketplace. Assuming the song isn't found in your library (if it was already there, why would you have bothered to receive it on your Zune?) but is available from Zune Marketplace, you'll see the same download option described in the preceding paragraph. If it's not available from Zune Marketplace, the Zune software gives you the opportunity to search the Web for it.

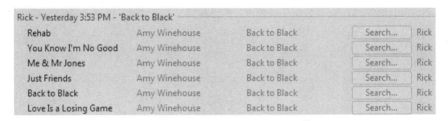

   *If you see an In Library button for any song, it means the Zune software did detect it in your library. Click the button to jump directly to that song.*

Want to learn more about Zune-to-Zune file sharing? Microsoft's Zune.net site offers a wealth of information: http://tinyurl.com/2baslq.

10

Chapter 11

Zune Accessories

How to...

- Choose a case
- Apply a skin
- Protect the Zune screen
- Use your Zune in your car
- Connect the Zune to your stereo or TV
- Choose Zune speakers
- Choose replacement headphones
- Watch video on a virtual screen
- Recharge your Zune while traveling

Your Zune is not an island. To really make the most of the device, you need to accessorize it: dress it up, protect it, give it some speakers, and so on. This chapter is all about cool and practical accessories for your Zune—everything from cases and car kits to skins and speaker docks. We'll also talk about portable charging options, which are imperative for keeping the music (and video) playing while you're on the road.

As you go out into the world in search of these and other accessories, keep in mind that many products designed for iPods will work just fine with the Zune. A good example is the Hammacher Schlemmer iPod Digital Drumsticks (http://tinyurl.com/2s664u), which, even though it has iPod in its name, can easily plug into a Zune. That's because the Zune (like the iPod) employs an industry-standard headphone jack, so pretty much any product that's designed to plug into one should work with the Zune.

Choose a Case

You don't plan to let your Zune run around naked, do you? Give some serious consideration to a case, which can be both practical and stylish. For example, if you spend a lot of time jogging or working out at the gym, you might want a case that keeps your Zune strapped to your arm. If you're more of a walker, a belt-clip case might be more suitable. And if you frequently find yourself tossing your Zune into a bag, backpack, glove compartment, or other cluttered space, you'll definitely want a case that offers protection from dings and scratches.

Although the Zune hasn't been around all that long, there are dozens of cases designed specifically for the device. I'm going to spotlight a few of them and then give you a list of case manufacturers (see Table 11-1) so that you can do some additional research on your own. After all, choosing a case is a personal decision, what with all the colors, styles, and options. Ultimately, it's up to you to pick the perfect case for your Zune. Heck, you might even end up picking two:

- **Armband case**   If you're into exercise, you'll no doubt want to keep your Zune secure and accessible while you run, bike, or whatever. For that, you'll want an armband case, which attaches the Zune to your upper arm while keeping its controls readily accessible. One of my favorite armband options is the DLO Action Jacket, a soft-neoprene case that protects both the screen and the shell. It comes with a removable, pivoting belt clip that, when turned sideways, props your Zune at the perfect angle for movies and photos (so it's equally useful when you're *not* exercising). This handy case retails for $29.99.

11

- **Belt-clip case**   When you're just walking around, you might want something a little less obtrusive than an armband case. Consider a belt-clip model that keeps your Zune holstered at your waist. One interesting option is the Incipio Zune Micro-Suede Slip Case, which comes in several bright colors and includes a removable belt clip. The Zune slides in and out of the case with ease, and gets the added benefit of screen protection while inside. Plus, it's something of a bargain at $14.99.

■ **Kickstand case**   If you plan to watch a lot of videos on your Zune, you may want a case that doubles as a kickstand, able to prop up the screen at a good viewing angle so you don't have to hold the Zune for hours at a time. Belkin makes an attractive, executive-minded case called the Folio Kickstand Case ($29.99). However, in my tests, it frequently pushed on the Zune's controls, making the unit turn on after I turned it off. You can (and should) work around this by locking the controls; otherwise, you could end up with a dead battery.

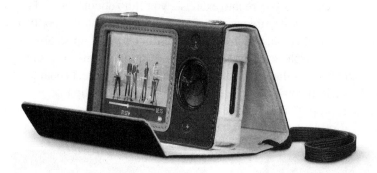

■ **Leather case**   Sometimes you just want to keep up appearances, and that means a stylish, business-friendly leather case. Most Zune case-makers offer at least one leather option, but I've yet to find anything more sumptuous-looking than the Speck Executive. Available in black or brown, the case features a play-through design (meaning you can access all controls and ports while the Zune is holstered), screen protection, a belt clip, and a magnetic front flap that includes a slot for business cards. All this luxury comes at a price though: the Executive will set you back $44.95.

■ **Protective case**   I don't know about you, but I'm pretty clumsy. In fact, I dropped my Zune at least twice while working on this book, and it's a dread-filled couple of moments as you hear the device hit the ground and then inspect it for damage. All the more reason to consider some kind of protective case, which can help reduce the risk of impact damage while keeping the Zune free of scratches, dings, and other wear-and-tear marks. I'm not wild about the form-fitting silicone cases offered by a number of different vendors—to me, they're ugly and offer little in the way of drop protection. If you really want to keep your Zune safe, consider something thicker, like the aforementioned leather and kickstand cases. On the other hand, you could also try Speck's military-looking ToughSkin, which sells for $34.95 and looks like this:

Company	URL	Products
Belkin	www.belkin.com	Acrylic, holster, and kickstand cases
DLO	www.dlo.com	Armband, rubberized, and leather cases
Incipio	www.myincipio.com	Leather, silicone, slip, and sport cases
Proporta	www.proporta.com	Aluminum, leather, silicone, and waterproof cases
Speck	www.speckproducts.com	The Executive leather case
Vaja	www.vajacases.com	Various high-end leather cases, including a custom case with your choice of colors

TABLE 11-1   Zune Cases

11

Apply a Skin

Sure, the Zune comes in a handful of nifty colors, but if you really want to dress up your device, you need to "skin it." The Web site www.decalgirl.com carries several dozen decorative decals that adhere to both the front and back of your Zune. They won't fade or smudge, according to the vendor, nor will they leave behind any glue residue if you decide to take them off. They're reasonably priced, at just $6.99 apiece, and as for the designs, well, you need to browse the site and see them for yourself. Some samples are included in the following illustrations.

As an added bonus, the skins will keep your Zune free of scratches and smudges (well, the front and back, anyway). Honestly, I love these things. They're crazy-cool, and they add much-needed bursts of style and color to the Zune.

TIP *Want to design your own skin? The DecalGirl.com Web site offers a Photoshop template that you can use to create custom artwork. Send the finished product to the site, and they'll create the skin for you. You could make a skin with a photo of your pet or family, or maybe the logo of your favorite sports team. The sky's the limit. Fun!*

11

Give Your Zune a Custom Paint Job

Bored with brown? Rethinking the pink? www.colorwarepc.com offers custom paint jobs for computers and can give your Zune a fresh look. The service offers a choice of 28 automotive-style colors and lets you select a different one for the front, back, navigation pad, and OK/Select button. Now that's customization! Colorware also applies a scratch-resistant coating to keep your Zune looking pretty. The price for a single-color mod job is $74; additional colors cost $20-30 extra. You"ll have to part with your Zune for a few days while Colorware performs the makeover.

Protect the Zune Screen

Your Zune's screen is where all the action happens, so it stands to reason that you'd want to protect it. After all, one scratch or scrape, and suddenly your movies and photos aren't going to look their best. Fortunately, it's not difficult to protect your screen. All you need is a clear plastic overlay, like the BoxWave ClearTouch Anti-Glare, which, true to its name, has the added benefit of reducing glare (always welcome when you're trying to watch a video in a brightly lit environment). The ClearTouch comes with a soft cloth to buff your screen clean before applying the plastic sheet, as well as a plastic applicator card designed to help apply the sheet without any air bubbles appearing underneath.

In the past, I've used the ClearTouch on my personal digital assistants (PDAs) and can definitely recommend the product. The Zune version sells for $12.95. If you want something a little less expensive, try the Zune Clear Screen Overlay Protector (http://tinyurl.com/2otklc), which also protects the screen from scratches (though not glare). It sells for $4.99.

Use Your Zune in Your Car

If you're like most people on this planet, you spend a considerable amount of time in your car. Wouldn't it be great if your Zune could connect to your car stereo and play music, podcasts, audiobooks, and more right through its speakers? You can do exactly that, though you'll need a bit of hardware to help out.

Don't even think about listening to your Zune through earphones while driving. It's not only against the law in some states, but also quite unsafe and rude to your passengers.

Use Car Mounts for Zunes

First, you need a way to mount your Zune, preferably so it's at eye level and arm's reach. If you leave the Zune on the seat beside you or in the center console, you'll have to take your eyes off the road while you reach for it and fiddle with the controls. You also run the risk of it flopping onto the floor, and if your car is anything like mine, you do *not* want your Zune touching the floor. There are all sorts of icky stuff down there!

 *For absolute safety, you should never, ever interact with your Zune while driving. Ask your passenger to select your desired song, or just wait until you come to a stop light.*

There are several products that can give your Zune a secure, practical home in your car. My two favorites are the following:

- **Belkin TuneBase FM for Zune**   Priced at $79.99, the TuneBase kills numerous birds with one stone. It combines a Zune dock with a cigarette-lighter mount; a flexible steel neck bridges the gap between the two. That means you can position the Zune to your liking (assuming there's sufficient clearance around your cigarette lighter), even turning it horizontally so that your passenger(s) can watch videos. (If you try to do that while driving, it means almost certain death—for you and one or more other drivers. Please don't.) The TuneBase also charges the Zune and, best of all, transmits audio via FM to your car stereo.

- **ProClip**   The ProClip combines a dashboard mount that's custom-designed for your car, with a pivoting holster that's specially built for the Zune. This swivel version costs $34.95, and it's one of the sturdiest mounts available. I'd argue that it's the safest option for mounting your Zune, as it keeps the device almost at eye level (though depending on the location of your cigarette lighter, the TuneBase might be just as good). That said, the ProClip is only a mount; it doesn't bridge the gap between your Zune and your stereo. For that, see the products in the next section.

Connect the Zune to Your Stereo

In an ideal universe, your car stereo would have Wi-Fi, and your Zune could wirelessly beam tunes to it. Unfortunately, we're stuck with various other solutions that aren't quite so high-tech. There are three basic ways to feed music from your Zune to your stereo:

- A stereo cable that plugs into your Zune's headphone jack and your stereo's line-in jack. This is the most attractive option, as you can pick up such a cable for around $5 at Radio Shack, and it delivers the best possible audio fidelity. However, few car stereos have a line-in jack, so you're probably going to be stuck with one of the next two options.

- A cassette adapter that plugs into your Zune's headphone jack and your stereo's tape player. These work pretty well, and you can pick one up at any electronics store for around $20. However, fewer and fewer car stereos have cassette players (it's all CDs nowadays), so this might not be an option, either.

- An FM transmitter that plugs into your Zune and wirelessly broadcasts audio from the Zune to an unused frequency on your car stereo. The aforementioned Belkin TuneBase FM is one such option; others include the DLO TransDock Micro (see Figure 11-1), Microsoft Zune Car Pack with FM Transmitter (which also includes a cigarette-lighter charger), and Monster CarPlay Wireless Plus. All four products sell for $70 to 80, but I recommend the Belkin, because it also provides a secure mount for your Zune. That said, you can use just about any third-party FM transmitter with the Zune, so long as it's designed to plug into a headphone jack (as many of them are) and not a specific device port (like, say, the bottom of an iPod).

FIGURE 11-1   The DLO TransDock Micro is one of several Zune accessories that will
charge your Zune and transmit audio through your car's speakers.

11

NOTE   *The big downside to using an FM transmitter is that it's often difficult
to find an unused frequency, especially if you live in or near a big
city. Even if you do find one, it's not uncommon to encounter static or
"broadcast bleed" while driving around, which forces you to search out
another unused frequency—not exactly fun. Unfortunately, there's no real
solution to this problem; it's just something you should be aware of before
spending any money on an FM transmitter. You can also try Radio Locator
(www.radio-locator.com) to look for unused frequencies.*

Connect the Zune to Your TV

Say, that's a mighty nice home theater you've got there in the living room. Wouldn't
it be great if you could play your music library through those fancy speakers and
navigate the Zune's menus on your TV? You can: All you need is the right gear

to connect your Zune to your equipment. Let's take a look at some of the options available:

- **DLO HomeDock** True to its name, the DLO HomeDock consists of a dock for your Zune—a small box that holds your Zune upright and provides audio-visual (A/V) connectivity. In other words, you can connect it to your TV and/or stereo and then operate your Zune via an included wireless remote (which serves up a full complement of controls). It also charges the Zune and comes with a Universal Serial Bus (USB) port, so you can connect it to your PC for Zune synchronization. The HomeDock sells for $99.99.

- **Microsoft Zune Home A/V Pack**   Like the HomeDock, Microsoft's kit consists of a dock/charger, A/V cables, and wireless remote—all for $99.99. On the plus side, Microsoft includes a spare sync cable for connecting the dock to your PC. On the downside, the remote offers fewer buttons than the HomeDock's, so you may actually have to leave the couch on occasion.

- **Microsoft Zune A/V Output Cable**   If you just want to connect your Zune to your TV/stereo and don't need a dock, remote, and all the rest, the Zune A/V Output Cable gets the job done on the cheap. It sells for just $19.99. You can get a third-party cable for even less at a site called HandHelditems (http://tinyurl.com/34dqdh), where the nearly identical Zune A/V cable costs $14.99. Search Google and/or eBay, and you may find an even better deal.

Now for a big caveat: Although the Zune makes a fine jukebox for your stereo, it's not a great video source for your TV. That's because Zune videos are formatted for the device's 320×240-pixel screen. High definition TVs (HDTVs), and even regular TVs, operate at a much higher resolution than that, meaning your videos will probably look less-than-stellar (by which I mean grainy and washed-out). I wouldn't say the video quality is terrible, but you probably wouldn't want to watch a movie this way.

But listening to your entire music collection? That's awesome, and reason enough to spring for a dock or cable to connect your Zune to your stereo.

11

Create Your Own TV Output Cable

If you're a do-it-yourselfer (meaning you're fairly handy with a wire cutter and soldering iron), you can build your own cable to output audio and video from your Zune to your TV. You'll need to cannibalize (or order online) a couple of cables, but overall, it's a fairly easy project. The steps are clearly outlined in this online tutorial: http://tinyurl.com/3295ru.

Choose Zune Speakers

If you don't have a stereo, or if you want to enjoy your Zune in different rooms, consider picking up a set of external speakers or, better yet, a speaker dock. I've got one of the latter in my master bathroom, of all places, because I like to listen to music while I shower—and it's the greatest. Here are some speaker options worth considering:

- **Altec Lansing M604 Portable Speaker System for Zune**   Far and away my favorite Zune-speaker solution, the M604 offers room-filling power, deep bass, and a wireless remote. The latter is the only weak point, however, as it offers only the most rudimentary playback controls (you can't even navigate the Zune's menus with it). But the M604 charges the Zune, includes a video output port for connecting the Zune to your TV, and even works with other MP3 players (via a line-in jack). Plus, you can even mount it on a wall! It's a bit on the pricey side at $199.95, but it's an excellent solution for playing music beyond the earphones.

- **Octavio 1**   Quite a bit pricier at $499.99, the Octavio 1 offers many of the same features as the M604 (remote, video out, Zune charging, etc.), but a lot more power: 100 watts versus 60 watts from the M604. Plus, the Octavio 1 comes with three speaker grilles for customization: white, black, and hot pink.

Thus, if you're a power user who doesn't mind spending more on speakers than you did for the Zune itself, this could be the speaker dock for you.

■ **Third-party speakers**   The Zune will work with virtually any portable and/or external speaker system. As long as it can accept connections from a headphone jack (as opposed to requiring a sync-port connection, as some speaker docks do), it'll pump out Zune audio just fine. There are literally hundreds of these kinds of speakers on the market, in all shapes, sizes, and prices. For example, the Logitech X-240 ($49.99) consists of two speakers and a subwoofer, plus a generic "dock" that can hold a Zune, iPod (shown in the following illustration), and other MP3 players.

11

Choose Replacement Headphones

Speakers are all well and good, but you'll probably spend most of your time keeping your music to yourself—that is, listening to your Zune through headphones. The Zune comes with a pair of headphones known as earbuds, which are designed to fit just inside your ears. Although I think they sound pretty good, you may want to consider alternatives. For example, earbuds can get uncomfortable after awhile, which might make traditional, over-the-ear headphones more appealing. Alternately, if you fly a lot, you may want something that can help block out that deafening engine noise.

Because the Zune has a traditional 3.5-mm headphone jack, you can use just about any third-party headphones on the market. I wouldn't presume to pick a pair for you, not with so many varieties and prices out there. But I will recommend a couple of products I like:

- **JAVOeBuds**   The problem with most headphones is their long, easily tangled cords. The JAVOeBuds keep the cord wound in a spring-loaded spindle—just pull the two ends when you want to listen to your tunes, and then pull them again to retract the cord. Pretty cool, except that the hard plastic earbuds can get a little uncomfortable. But you can't beat the $18.95 price tag. I find them great for the gym, where the spindle keeps extra cord from getting in the way while I exercise.

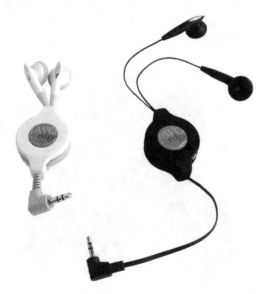

■ **Microsoft Zune Premium Earphones**   The first of two in-ear headphones I'm going to recommend, Microsoft's offering is attractive on many levels. First, they actually look attractive: dark and rounded. Second, they're attractively priced—$39.99—quite a bit less than the next product on my list. Third, they sound great. Because they fit snugly in your ear canal, they help isolate outside noise (thus saving you from having to crank the volume—your ears will thank you for that). Microsoft supplies three earpiece sizes and a hard plastic carrying case. I really, really like these.

■ **V-Moda Vibe**   Like Microsoft's in-ear headphones, the Vibe slips snugly into your ear canal, blocking outside noise and delivering truly outstanding audio. In fact, the bass response from these earphones greatly exceeds that of pricier sets I've tried, including the Etymotic 6i Isolator and Shure E3c (also good products, by the way). They're also way cooler-looking, with a choice of four metallic colors and a sleek, almost industrial design. The Vibe comes with silicon fittings in three different sizes, a slick little carrying case, and a rubber cord-management clip that keeps the earphones from getting tangled. Now for the sticker shock: $101, though you can find it for a little less if you shop online. Trust me, you'll love these.

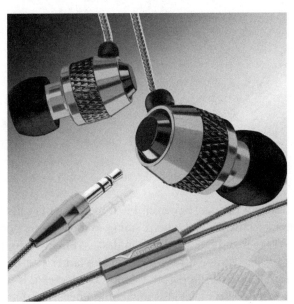

11

The Zune earbuds have one nifty feature that makes them worth keeping: a sliding plastic nub that can help keep the cord from getting tangled. When you're done listening to your Zune, slide the nub all the way up until it meets the earbuds. Then put the earbuds back to back—they're magnetic! Finally, wrap the cord around the Zune. Make this a habit, and you'll rarely have to spend time de-tangling the cord—and trust me when I say that's a chore you don't want.

Watch Video on a Virtual Screen

One of the more interesting accessories I tested while writing this book was the ZuneVG, a set of virtual-display glasses you wear on head while watching videos. Instead of squinting at the Zune's relatively small screen, you see the video on the equivalent of a 37-inch TV (as seen from about two meters away). It's a nice option for those times when you're on a long flight and want to watch something other than the in-flight movie.

There are a couple of caveats, however. First, the ZuneVG sells for $250, so it's not exactly an impulse buy. Second, you're going to look a little goofy wearing the glasses, which are bigger and bulkier than sunglasses. Finally, I found that videos looked noticeably grainy, a trade-off for viewing at a larger size. The overall quality was okay, but definitely not as sharp as the Zune's own screen. If you want to learn more about the product, there's a lengthy and comprehensive review at the Zune fan site Zunerama: http://tinyurl.com/3cs9z6.

Recharge Your Zune While Traveling

Is there anything worse than a dead battery? Not when you're in the middle of, say, a mini-marathon of *The Office* (British version or American version, your choice) or Amy Winehouse's awesome album, *Back to Black*. Alas, your Zune doesn't have the world's best battery life, so traveling with extra power is essential.

There are numerous ways to power and recharge your Zune while you're on the road. For example, the various car kits mentioned earlier in this chapter will keep the juice flowing, so if you're planning to buy one, you're all set (for the car, anyway). Let's take a look at some other portable-power options:

■ **Belkin TunePower**   A power pack for power users, the $60 TunePower features its own rechargeable battery that promises 6 to 12 hours of extra play time for your Zune (depending on whether you're watching movies or listening to music). What's more, it includes a fold-out kickstand for hands-free video viewing—just set it on a flat surface, and it props the Zune at a perfect viewing angle. This is definitely one of my favorite Zune accessories; it's a must-have if you travel a lot (and like to watch movies while doing so).

11

■ **DLO Power Pack** The $39.99 Power Pack covers all the bases. It provides an AC adapter for wall charging and a cigarette-lighter adapter for car charging. The included USB cable bridges the gap between the two chargers and your Zune, and also provides a spare synchronization cable.

■ **EZGear PowerStick** Sometimes, nothing beats regular old double-A batteries—the kind you can buy just about anywhere. The PowerStick employs either disposable or rechargeable ones to power and recharge your Zune. According to the company, the PowerStick extends your Zune's operation by three to four times—not a bad deal for five bucks' worth of batteries. The PowerStick sells for $29.98.

■ **Microsoft Zune Travel Pack**   The ultimate road kit, Microsoft's $99.99 Zune Travel Pack comes with a cornucopia of excellent accessories: an AC adapter, a synchronization cable, the Zune Premium Earphones mentioned earlier in this chapter, and a hard-shell carrying case with cutout slots for the Zune, earphones, and other gear. You also get the Zune Dual Connect Remote, which offers two headphone jacks and independent volume controls for each one. That means you can share your music and videos with a friend, but you can each set your own volume. Great stuff.

■ **Replacement battery**   It's actually possible to replace the Zune's battery with one that lasts longer between charges. Find out more in Chapter 12.

Where to Find It

Web Site	Address	What's There
22Moo	www.22moo.com.au	ZuneVG
Altec Lansing	www.alteclansing.com	Altec Lansing M604 Portable Speaker System
Belkin	www.belkin.com	TuneBase FM, TunePower, and other accessories
Colorware	www.colorwarepc.com	Custom paint jobs for your Zune
DecalGirl.com	www.decalgirl.com	Zune skins
DLO	www.dlo.com	HomeDock, Jam Jacket, Power Pack, TransDock Micro, and other accessories
EZGear	www.ezgear4u.com	PowerStick
JAVOedge	www.javoedge.com	JAVOeBuds
ProClip	www.proclipusa.com	ProClip car mount
V-Moda	www.v-moda.com	Vibe
VAF Research	www.vaf.com.au	Octavio 1
Zune.net	www.zune.net	Various Microsoft accessories

Chapter 12

Hack and Upgrade Your Zune

How to...

- Read books and magazines on your Zune

- Replace your Zune's battery

- Install a larger hard drive

- Use your Zune as an external hard drive

- Convert recorded TV shows for Zune viewing

- Watch Divx videos on your Zune

- Find other Zune hacks

To paraphrase the old saying, when life gives you Zune, make Zune-ade! Okay, that's stretching it a bit, but it makes the point about this chapter: If the Zune won't do what you want it to do, hack it!

The word "hack" gets a lot of bad press these days, as most people think of hackers as criminals out to steal your identity or, worse, credit card number. However, a hack can be a positive thing when it describes tweaking or modifying something to make it better. (Look no further than the mega-popular Web blog Lifehacker.com, which serves up a daily helping of hacks designed to help you work, live, and compute better.)

Thus, when we talk about hacking your Zune, it has nothing to do with stealing its identity or Visa number. Instead, it's about making the device better, either by adding capabilities it didn't have before or tweaking the capabilities it does have. This chapter offers a wide assortment of Zune hacks, from tricking the picture viewer into displaying e-book pages to upgrading the hard drive. This is definitely the chapter that separates the power users from the novices, though you don't necessarily need to be tech-savvy to use these hacks. You just need to keep reading.

Read Books and Magazines on Your Zune

Wouldn't it be cool if you could read a book or magazine on your Zune—and listen to music at the same time? Although the Zune itself offers no such options, there are software and services that can leverage the Zune's capabilities—specifically, its photo-viewing capabilities—for on-the-go reading.

Read Magazines with Perooz

Want to read *Car & Driver* on your Zune? How about *Maxim*? Perooz offers these and other magazines, all specially formatted for the Zune's screen.

Music Interviews: **Fat Joe**

From feuding with 50 Cent to calling out Remy Ma, Fat Joe's mouth does more than just eat. FHM catches up with the hip-hop mogul as he weighs in on his latest round of controversy.

Is it true that you're feuding with Remy Ma?
Not really. She's just not down with the crew anymore. She wants to be released, so we're giving her a release. It's really weird when you give everybody an opportunity and they love you.

© 2006, EMAP Metro, LLC. All Rights Reserved   2006 Perooz.com

Instead of requiring you to install special software or perform lots of annoying scrolling, Perooz delivers the content in photo form, reformatted to fit your Zune's screen and with enlarged text for easy reading. You don't get the full content of each magazine, but rather select articles and photos. The site also stocks movie trailers and streaming music videos, though the latter can't be copied to your portable player.

For the moment, the Perooz catalog definitely skews toward the young male (*Maxim, FHM, Stuff Magazine*, etc.), but it's a slickly designed site with a decidedly smart method of content distribution. Oh, and it's all free.

NOTE   *As of this writing, Perooz was undergoing some changes, so the site and its content may be a little different than what's depicted in this section.*

12

Read E-books

An electronic book (or *e-book*) is exactly that: a book that's been converted to electronic form. I've long been a fan of reading e-books on my Palm PDA. Because it's always in my pocket, I always have something to read when I'm waiting at the dentist's office, stuck in line at the DMV, or sitting on an airplane. Ah, if only I could read e-books on my Zune, I'd have one less device to carry around!

Although the Zune itself doesn't support e-books directly (another item for Microsoft's to-do list, I hope), it's possible to load them onto the device thanks to a freeware program called Jpegbook. The program converts text files into pictures, and, of course, the Zune has no problem displaying those. It's kind of like taking a photograph of each page of a book and then loading those photos in sequential order into your Zune. Jpegbook converts e-book files into JPEG image files, which you then load onto your Zune as you do photos.

Before getting started with Jpegbook, you'll need to score some actual e-books. Find out how in the next section.

Where to Find Public-Domain Books

In an ideal world, you'd be able to download *The Kite Runner, The March*, and other great novels and shoot them right over to your Zune. Unfortunately, for the moment, you're limited to public-domain titles—works that have expired copyrights and, therefore, can be copied and distributed free of charge. Commercial e-books are available for other devices (mostly personal digital assistants [PDAs] and smartphones), but not yet for the Zune.

If you want to check out the wonderful world of commercial e-books, I recommend eReader.com and Fictionwise.com. Both offer great selection and discount prices.

Yes, for now, you're stuck with public-domain titles—specifically, those that are available as raw text files (the only kind Jpegbook supports). The good news is that there are over 20,000 e-books available in the public domain, and you can find them all at Project Gutenberg (www.gutenberg.org). This site (see Figure 12-1) was created expressly to distribute books online, and you'll be surprised by some of the free titles available there. A small sampling includes the following:

- *The Adventures of Huckleberry Finn*, Mark Twain

- *Pride and Prejudice*, Jane Austen

- *The War of the Worlds*, H.G. Wells

- *The Last of the Mohicans*, James Fenimore Cooper

- *2 B R O 2 B*, Kurt Vonnegut, Jr.

- Virtually all of Shakespeare's plays and sonnets

Needless to say, there's some pretty good reading in the public domain. All you do is find a book you want (you can browse the Project Gutenberg catalog or search for a particular title or author), and then download the "plain text" version (some books have multiple formats available for download). Make sure to take note of where you save the file on your hard drive, as you'll need it when you run Jpegbook.

| FIGURE 12-1 | Project Gutenberg is home to thousands of free e-books, any of which can be downloaded and converted for viewing on your Zune. |

Use Jpegbook to Convert E-book Files

To convert an e-book text file to JPEG images for viewing on your Zune, you'll need Jpegbook. The site that houses this small program is written in Japanese (though the program itself is in English), so here's a direct link to the download: http://tinyurl.com/3yv8gy. Extract the contents of this Zip file to any folder on your hard drive, run the Jpegbook program, and follow these steps:

1. Click File | Open Textfile and then navigate to the folder on your hard drive containing the e-book you downloaded.

2. Choose an output folder, which is where Jpegbook will deposit the JPEG files it creates. I highly recommend creating a unique folder for these files, as you're going to end up with a lot of them (you'll have to do this using Windows Explorer or your preferred file manager—Jpegbook can't create new folders on its own). Click the little yellow folder icon next to the Output Folder field, and then select the desired folder.

3. Click Edit | Full Config and choose QVGA (320 × 240). That's the resolution of your Zune's screen. Enter a one-word book title in the JPEG File Prefix field—just something simple so you can recognize the book on your Zune. Click OK to exit the settings dialog box.

4. Click the Start button, and wait while the program turns the book into JPEG files.

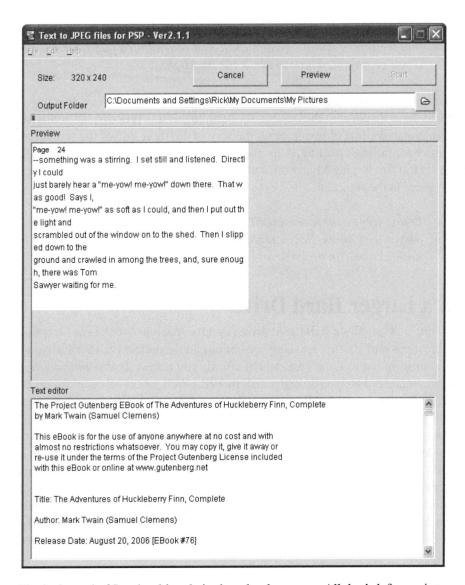

That's the end of Jpegbook's role in the e-book process. All that's left now is to copy the new JPEGs to your Zune, which you can do easily. Just follow the same steps you'd use to add any photos to your Zune (see Chapter 7 if you need a refresher).

Now head to your Zune's Pictures menu, find the book, and open the first "page" (huck001.jpg, for instance). When you're done with that page, press the navigation pad to the right to "turn the page" (that is, load the next image—in this case, huck002.jpg).

You should probably raise the Zune's backlight setting to 30 seconds so that the screen doesn't go dim while you're reading a page. See Chapter 3 if you've forgotten how to tweak the backlight.

Although e-books look bright and readable on the Zune's screen, by now you may have discovered the one big shortcoming to this process: the weird line breaks. Not every line of text goes all the way to the right side of the screen, which can make for difficult reading. Alas, there's no easy way to get around this. All the more reason I'm hoping Microsoft will add some kind of e-book viewer capability to the Zune in the future.

I must give credit where credit is due: The idea for this process came from a user on the Instructables Web site. If you want to read his original tutorial, you can find it here: http://tinyurl.com/yr34eb.

Install a Larger Hard Drive

The Zune's 30-gigabyte (GB) hard drive is pretty spacious—until you start filling it with videos and your increasingly mammoth music collection. (Seriously, an active subscription to Zune Pass, which affords you access to over *three million* songs, can make that 30 GB seem small indeed.) Well, not much you can do about it, right? Maybe someday Microsoft will unveil a Zune with more storage space, but for now, you'll just have to pick and choose what to carry around.

Not necessarily. The Zune incorporates a fairly common kind of hard drive, and at least one enterprising service (Rapid Repair) has figured out how to swap out the 30-GB drive for more capacious models. In fact, believe it or not, your upgrade choices include 40-GB, 60-GB, 80-GB, and even 100-GB drives. Installing one of them will require a little warranty-voiding Zune surgery, but the Rapid Repair site offers detailed instructions if you want to do it yourself. Alternately, you can ship your Zune to Rapid Repair (www.rapidrepair.com) and let them perform the upgrade.

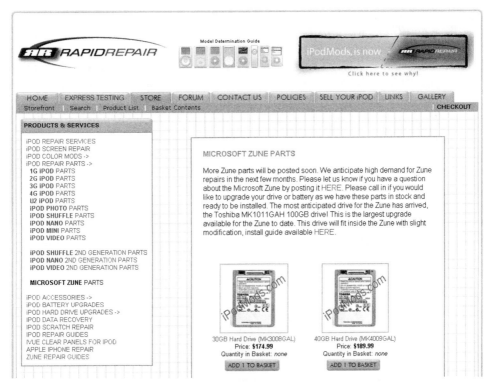

As of this writing, the service was selling these Zune-compatible drives (I've listed the model numbers for reasons you'll see shortly) for the following prices:

- **Toshiba 40GB MK4009GAL** $159.99

- **Toshiba 60GB MK6008GAH** $189.99

- **Toshiba 80GB MK8009GAH** $209.99

- **Toshiba 100GB MK1011GAH** $279.99

Needless to say, upgrading to even a 60-GB drive represents a fairly substantial investment—in the ballpark of what you paid for the Zune itself! The good news is that there's no extra charge if you want Rapid Repair to perform the labor, though you'll have to pay to ship your Zune.

Shop around, and you may be able to find a better deal on the drive you want. That's why I listed the model numbers above. Do a Google and/or eBay search for Toshiba MK6008GAH, for example, and see if you can't locate a better price. I found one eBay vendor selling the 80-GB drives for just $138.99 (with free shipping to boot)—a huge savings. You don't get the drive removal/installation instructions or support of any kind (though the instructions, at least, are freely available on Rapid Repair's site). It's up to you to decide if those things are worth an extra $700.

The actual upgrade process isn't terribly difficult; the only tricky part is opening the Zune case without marring it in some way. Super-tiny flat-head screwdrivers can be helpful, though you may want to pick up a "case open" kit from Rapid Repair or another online store (any kit designed for iPods should also work with your Zune). These come with plastic tools that are less likely to mar your case than metal screwdrivers.

Opening your Zune's case voids the warranty. It doesn't matter if the work is done by you, Rapid Repair, or another service. Is that a major deal? Given that the most likely trauma to befall your Zune is a cracked screen resulting from a fall to the pavement, probably not. That kind of damage isn't covered under your warranty anyway. Even so, you may want to think twice before spilling your Zune's guts.

Replace Your Zune's Battery

While you've got your Zune open for its hard-drive upgrade, why not swap in a new battery at the same time? There are several reasons for doing so:

- **Age**   If you've owned your Zune for more than 6 months, chances are good the battery is already starting to wear out, meaning it's not holding a charge for as long as it used to. This will get worse over time. Expect to need a new battery within 18 to 24 months.

- **Longevity**   Most Zune replacement batteries have a capacity of 850 milli-amp-hours (mAh)—slightly higher than the Zune's stock battery. That means your Zune will run a bit longer between charges—upwards of an hour, by some estimates.

FIGURE 12-2   An inexpensive Zune replacement battery will give you a bit more play
time and refresh an old, worn-out battery.

■ **Price**   The aforementioned Rapid Repair service sells a Zune replacement
battery for $19.99 (see Figure 12-2). However, a cursory peek at eBay
shows many vendors selling virtually identical kits for around $10. As an
added bonus, you get the plastic tools you need to open your Zune case
(which, as a reminder, voids the warranty)—useful if you're also planning
a hard-drive upgrade.

Many thanks to Rapid Repair for providing me with a replacement-battery kit
so I could see for myself how easy it is to perform the upgrade.

Use Your Zune as an External Hard Drive

In another demerit-earning move (I think that's four so far), Microsoft decided not
to allow the Zune to function as an external hard drive. In an ideal world, you'd be
able to connect it to your PC—or any PC—and use it as removable storage, able to

12

ferry large files from one computer to another, or even make on-the-fly backups of important data. iPods and many other hard drive–based media players can do that, so why not the Zune?

Perhaps a future firmware update will add this capability. In the meantime, you'll need to rely on a method developed by a group of crafty Zune users. It's not pretty, but it works. Before I give you the details, however, a few caveats:

- ■ This requires making a few small changes to the Windows registry, which, though fairly easy, is not for the faint of heart. Modifying the registry can cause problems with your PC, so I really don't recommend this for anyone who's not reasonably computer-literate.

- ■ The advantages to performing this operation are fairly minor. For example, it's not like you'll be able to plug your Zune into any PC and immediately use it as an external hard drive. The Zune software must be installed, and the registry must be modified as described previously. What's more, the process of actually copying files to your Zune could best be described as "messy." To me, it's almost not worth the trouble.

So why bother with this at all? For some users, it's like climbing Mount Everest: You do it because it's there. But, as stated previously, there are a few practical reasons, like transporting files and backing up important data. If you want your Zune to gain at least some external hard drive functionality, here's how:

I tested this process on a computer running Windows XP. If you have a different operating system, your mileage may vary.

1. Disconnect your Zune from your PC, and close the Zune software.

2. Click Start | Run, and then type **regedit**. This will run Windows' Registry Editor utility.

3. First things first: Let's make a backup of the registry before we tinker with it. Click File | Export, choose the All option under Export Range, and then provide a name for the backup file (such as *regbackup*). Click Save to create the registry backup.

4. Click Edit | Find and type **portabledevicenamespace**. Click Next, and wait while this item is located. (It may take a minute or two.) When the search is done, you'll see a list of entries, as shown in the following illustration.

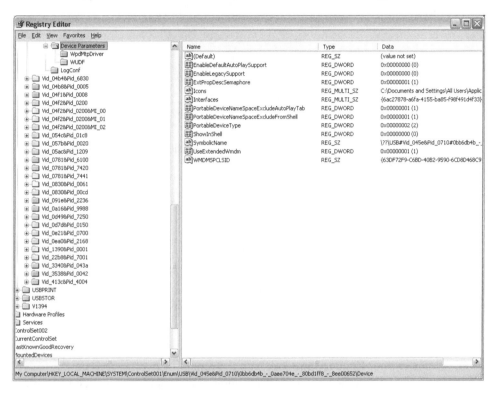

5. Double-click the EnableLegacySupport entry, change the Value Data field from 0 to 1, and then click OK.

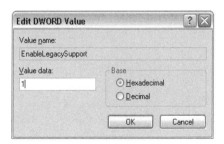

12

6. Double-click the PortableDeviceNameSpaceExcludeFromShell entry, change the Value Data field from 1 to 0, and then click OK.

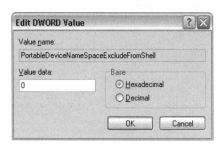

7. Double-click the ShowInShell entry, change the Value Data field from 0 to 1, and then click OK.

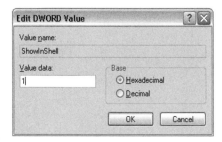

8. Exit Registry Editor.

9. Connect your Zune to your PC, wait a moment or two for it to be recognized, and then open My Computer. You should see two icons (don't ask me why) with your Zune's name. Double-click either one, and presto: You've got access to all the folders and files on your device.

The good news is that you can now copy just about any files you want from your Zune to your PC. The bad news is that if you want to copy files *to* your Zune, there are hoops through which you must jump. Sigh…always with the hoops.

In a nutshell, the only time you can successfully create new folders on your Zune or copy files to it is while the Zune software is in the process of synchronizing the Zune. In other words, you need to click Start Sync and then go to Windows Explorer or your preferred file manager and perform whatever file-copying/folder-creation activities you want to get done.

 *This is not an ideal method for adding music, photos, and other media to your Zune that you actually want to play on it. Although it does work (assuming you copy the right stuff to the right folders), it's almost always better to use the Zune software.*

If your Zune syncs too quickly to make this practical, there's another solution, though it's pretty "out there." After starting the synchronization, press CTRL-ALT-DEL on your keyboard, click the Zune software entry, and then click End Task. This should leave the Zune in "sync mode" until you unplug it, thus allowing you to create folders, copy files to it, and so on.

Like I said earlier, turning your Zune into an external hard drive isn't pretty. If you're having any trouble with the process, or if you want to read more about this hack's development, head to the Zune Boards message thread that covers it: http://tinyurl.com/2ejwru.

Copy Files from Your Zune to Your PC

Although it can't readily function as an external hard drive, the Zune does let you retrieve media files with relative ease. Why would you want to do this? I can think of a few reasons:

- If you've installed the Zune software on a second PC, you can use this method to copy all your media to it.

- You're visiting a friend's house and want to share some of your songs, photos, or videos. By connecting your Zune to his or her PC (which must have the Zune software installed) and selecting Guest Sync (see Chapter 2), you can copy whatever media you want (keep in mind, however, that Zune Marketplace purchases and downloads won't copy, as they're protected).

- If your hard drive ever suffers a catastrophe and you don't have a backup of your media files, guess what: your Zune is a backup. You can easily copy some or all of your media back to your PC. That could be a lifesaver indeed, especially if you have irreplaceable music, photos, and the like stored on your Zune.

Traditionally, synchronizing copies files from your PC to your Zune. What we're talking about here is a "reverse" synchronization—copying files from your Zune to your PC. Here's how:

1. Connect your Zune to your PC, and run the Zune software.

2. Wait for the initial synchronization to complete.

3. If it's not already highlighted, click the Sync icon above the list pane.

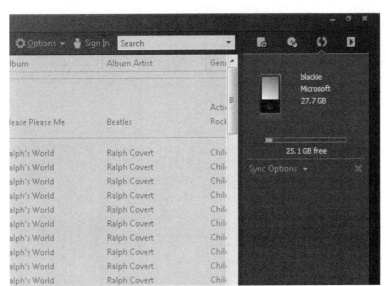

4. Click your Zune's name in the navigation pane, and then locate the content you want to copy to your PC. You might have to click Artist, Album, Songs, or another category to find exactly what you want. (Click the Video or Pictures icon at the top of the navigation pane to choose from those categories.)

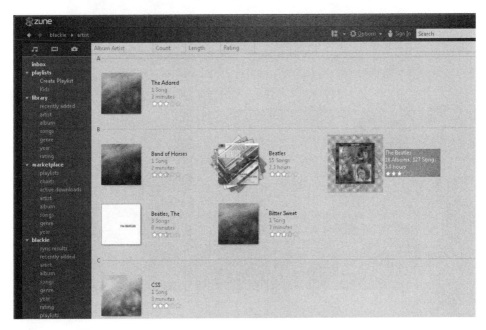

5. Once you've found the media you want to copy, select it in the details pane, and drag it to the list pane. Notice that the Start Sync button at the bottom changes to a Copy From Device button. Click it to begin the copy process.

By default, the Zune software will copy music to your My Music folder, videos to your My Videos folder, and pictures to your My Pictures folder (which are called Music, Videos, and Pictures, respectively, in Windows Vista).

If you receive an error message in the Zune software, it's likely because the content is copy-protected and, therefore, can't be copied. If you get an "already in library" message, it's because the Zune software has detected matching files on your hard drive and doesn't want to overwrite them.

Convert Recorded TV Shows for Zune Viewing

As you know from reading Chapter 6, I'm a huge fan of using Windows Media Center to record TV shows to my PC. I'm an even bigger fan of copying those shows to my Zune for on-the-go viewing. However, the Zune software doesn't make this easy, which is why you need to hack your way through it.

Chapter 6 offers a few options, but my favorite can be found in the Spotlight section of this book (those colorful pages in the middle). If you have even the slightest interest in watching TV shows on your Zune, you'll definitely want to check it out.

Watch Divx Videos on Your Zune

If you're an active downloader of Internet videos, chances are you've got some Divx files you might like to watch on your Zune. Unfortunately, the Zune software doesn't natively support Divx (see Chapter 6 for more information on this), even though it is actually capable of converting Divx files to a Zune-compatible format. What you need is way to trick the Zune software into recognizing Divx files so it can work its magic.

The answer lies in a simple registry hack. Unlike the one described earlier in "Use Your Zune as an External Hard Drive," this hack requires no manual editing of the registry. You just open a small file and you're done.

The file—*zuneavi.reg*—can be found at the Zune Scene Web site (www .zunescene.com/zune-divx/), along with a message thread devoted to working with Divx files. Just download it, double-click it, and restart the Zune software. Next, press F3 to access the program's monitored-folders list, and then add the one(s) containing your Divx files. You won't be able to play these videos in the Zune software, but you will be able to add them to the synchronization queue and, ultimately, copy them to your Zune (after the software converts them).

12

 *If you're planning to use the process described in this book's Spotlight section, which accomplishes the same thing for DVR-MS files (the kind used for Windows Media Center–recorded TV shows), you can skip this entire hack. That's because that registry hack also adds support for Divx files, rendering this one unnecessary.*

Find Other Zune Hacks

If this chapter has whetted your appetite for Zune hacking, you don't have to stop here. The Web is home to loads of other nifty hacks and upgrades; you just have to know where to look:

■ **Zune Boards' Hacks & Mods forum (http://tinyurl.com/23copq)**   Zune Boards offers message forums for a variety of Zune-related topics, and the Hacks & Mods area is specifically for, well, hacks and mods (short for "modifications"). In fact, some of the hacks in this chapter were originally posted to Zune Boards, so it's a great place to start your search for new and exciting hacks.

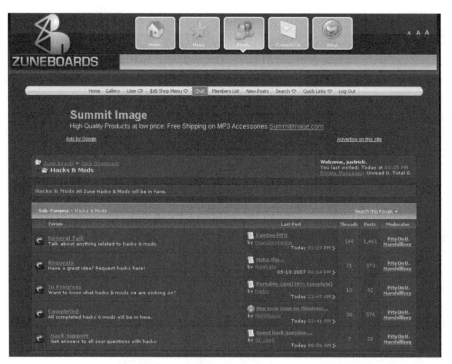

- **Make Magazine (http://tinyurl.com/3cd9cb)**   This cool magazine for do-it-yourselfers offers a handful of interesting Zune hacks, including specific information on the Zune's USB protocols (for the really tech-savvy users out there who know what to do with such data).

- **Improve the quality of album art (http://tinyurl.com/2lp3kl)**   If you've noticed that album art looks grainy or otherwise unsatisfactory on the Zune's screen, this tutorial can help you improve its appearance. This really isn't a hack, per se, but it's definitely a project that only hardcore Zune users will want to undertake. (Personally, I don't mind album art that looks a little fuzzy.) See Chapter 13 to learn how to deal with the problem of *missing* album art.

- **This book's blog (http://zunebook.wordpress.com)**   As I encounter new and interesting hacks, I'll post information about them on the blog that accompanies this book. It's also the place to find book updates and corrections (not that I've made any mistakes, mind you—every word is perfect!).

Where to Find It

Web Site	Address	What's There
Project Gutenberg	www.gutenberg.org	A huge library of public-domain e-books
Rapid Repair	www.rapidrepair.com	Replacement batteries, hard drives, and other parts
Zune Boards	www.zuneboards.com	Lively message boards, including one devoted expressly to Zune hacks

Chapter 13

Zune Problems and Solutions

How to...

- Get help online

- Reset your Zune

- Update the Zune's firmware

- Maximize battery life

- Repair a broken Zune

- "Normalize" song volume

- Fix metadata

- Add missing album art

- Replace lost downloads

- Make room for new media on a Zune that's "full"

Zunes aren't perfect. Like any other electronic gizmo, they can suffer from a myriad of problems—especially when you factor in the often-flaky Zune software, the inherently troublesome nature of Digital Rights Management (or DRM, the technology used to copy-protect Zune Marketplace downloads), and the fact that it's a Microsoft product (ouch! Cheap shot!).

This chapter is all about solving Zune problems. You'll learn what to do if your Zune meets the pavement in an unfriendly way, how to establish consistent volume levels for all your music, how to squeeze every last ounce of play time from the Zune's battery, and much more. Let's kick things off with arguably the largest problem-solving dilemma: Where to find help.

Get Help Online

Having trouble copying a DVD to your Zune? Can't get your Zune to synchronize properly? Need opinions on which case to buy? The answers to these and countless other questions can be found in one convenient place: the Internet. For example, if you head to Microsoft's Zune.net site (see Figure 13-1) and venture into the Troubleshooting section, you'll find a Frequently Asked Questions (FAQ) page devoted expressly to common Zune problems. In fact, here's a handy batch of links that will take you directly to Microsoft's various help pages:

- **Zune troubleshooting**   http://tinyurl.com/2ndaby

- **Zune Marketplace troubleshooting**   http://tinyurl.com/355tvj

| **FIGURE 13-1** | Microsoft's Zune.net support section offers a wealth of handy troubleshooting info. |

- **Zune software troubleshooting**   http://tinyurl.com/2vtxeg
- **Zune instruction manual downloads**   http://tinyurl.com/25vqow
- **Zune Frequently Asked Questions**   http://tinyurl.com/35o4ow

Microsoft's site is always a good place to start, as it's the most likely to contain current and/or updated information. However, it doesn't connect you with the very *best* resource for Zune help: other users.

You see, the Zune has a small but devoted fan base that populates various homegrown Zune sites (see Figure 13-2). These users are as knowledgeable as they come (way smarter than me), and they're usually more than willing to help out fellow users in need. Thus, by registering with one or more of these sites (don't worry, they're free) and posting your question on their message boards, chances are quite good you'll get a helpful answer.

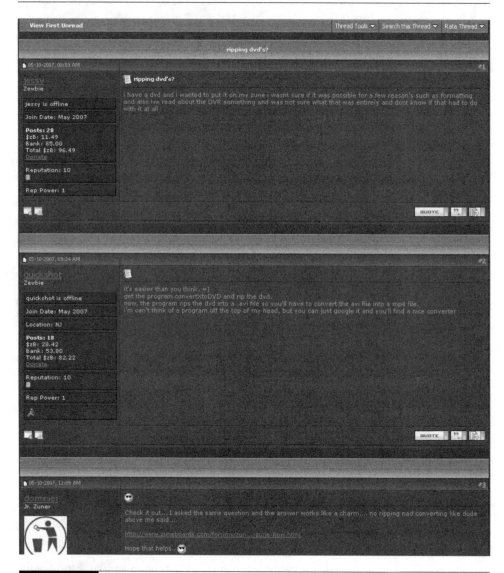

FIGURE 13-2 Sites like Zune Boards are home to Zune-savvy users who can often provide answers to tricky questions.

NOTE *Take any advice you get with a grain of salt. Remember, these aren't paid support professionals; they're just other users like you.*

While you're at it, you can search or browse the message boards to see if someone else has already asked—or answered—a similar question.

Of course, your best bet for finding user help is to hit the sites that attract the most users. As of this writing, the following sites offered some of the Web's most active Zune-related message forums:

- **Zune Boards**   www.zuneboards.com

- **Zunerama**   www.zunerama.com

- **Zune Thoughts**   www.zunethoughts.com

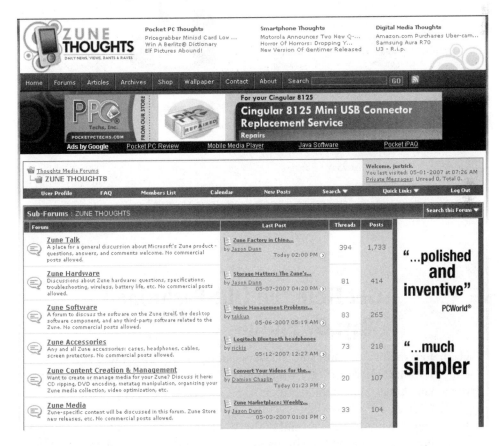

Register with all three sites and post your question on every one of them. That increases your chances of getting a useful answer.

Many of these sites also feature user-authored tutorials covering a huge range of topics. One of my favorites is "How To: Convert DVDs to play on your Zune – using Super" (http://tinyurl.com/2ufvth). Of course, you learned all about DVD conversion in Chapter 6, but this guide gives you a slightly different way of doing it—this time, using the awesome freeware utility Super.

Back to main How-Tos page

Zune How-Tos

How To: Convert DVDs to play on your Zune – using *Super*

This tutorial shows how to convert your DVDs into a file that is readable by Zune, using free software. This tutorial is noob friendly, so just follow the steps exactly and you should be okay. Feel free to ask questions using the comments link at the bottom.

Note: Click on any graphic to see a full-size view of it.

Overview

Here's what you'll be doing:

Short version: Taking your DVD and getting the data onto your computer, then putting it into a file format playable by your Zune.

How to ... Get Help the Old-Fashioned Way: By Phone

Need help right away? Can't find answers among your fellow Zune users? Believe it or not, Microsoft offers that most old-fashioned of support options: live human beings. Here's the number:

877-GET-ZUNE (438-9863)

Hearing-impaired users can call 800-801-1189.

The hours of operation for Microsoft's live support department are 9 a.m. to 1 a.m., Eastern Time. The department is open seven days a week. Impressive!

Reset Your Zune

Is your Zune non-responsive? Has the screen gone blank, the controls dead? It might have locked up (not an unfamiliar scenario for anyone who's ever used a computer). Fortunately, you can usually resurrect a locked-up Zune by resetting it.

> **TIP** *Before you do so, check the hold switch. Sometimes, it gets activated by accident, resulting in lockup-like symptoms. (Remember, the whole point of the hold switch is to render the Zune's controls temporarily inoperable. See Chapter 1 if you need a refresher.) Heck, I'll even cop to this: On a few occasions, I enabled the hold switch and then forgot about it, only to freak out later because my Zune was suddenly "broken."*

To reset your Zune, hold down the Back button and the Up button simultaneously for several seconds. In a moment, you'll see the Zune logo and, soon after, the Zune menu. If that doesn't do the trick, you may have a more serious problem (like a failing hard drive), in which case, a call to Microsoft may be in order (see "Get Help the Old-Fashioned Way: By Phone").

Update Your Zune's Firmware

Throughout this book, I've repeatedly used the phrase, "hopefully, Microsoft will address this in a firmware update." Firmware, of course, is the operating system that runs your Zune. When you first install the Zune software and connect the Zune to your PC, it should check the latter's firmware version and download any available updates. (As of this writing, the current firmware is version 1.4.)

Having the latest firmware is essential. For example, version 1.3 (which was released while I wrote this book) corrected a problem that some users had with Zune Marketplace downloads—namely, songs would "skip" during playback. Future firmware updates will likely fix other issues, as well as add podcast support, enhanced wireless capabilities, and other features.

In theory, the Zune software should automatically detect any firmware updates released by Microsoft, download them to your PC, and install them on your Zune (you'll see notifications that this is happening and instructions for proceeding). However, when Microsoft released the version 1.3 update, I had to retrieve it manually.

Here's how to check for—and retrieve—firmware updates, something you should do periodically:

1. Connect the Zune to your PC, and run the Zune software.

2. Right-click your Zune's name in the navigation pane, and select Check for Zune Device Updates.

3. If the Zune software finds any updates, it will notify you. Follow the prompts to retrieve and install the updates.

Maximize Battery Life

A Zune with a dead battery is about as useful as [insert your own joke here—I was going to say "Congress," but thought my editors might object]. Fortunately, there are steps you can take to wring every last ounce of power from your Zune before it needs recharging:

- **Turn off the wireless radio**   The only time wireless should be turned on is when you want to share files with other Zune users (see Chapter 10). Otherwise, leave this battery-draining feature off. Just head to the Settings menu: Wireless is the first option in the list.

- **Set screen brightness to low** While you're in the Settings menu, head to Display, and set Brightness to low. Unless you're watching a video, there's really no need for the brightness setting to be any higher.

- **Reduce backlight duration** And while you're in the Display menu, set the backlight as low as you can tolerate it (probably 5 or 15 seconds).

- **Avoid skipping songs** The less your Zune has to access its hard drive, the longer its battery will last. Skipping songs requires extra hard-drive activity and, therefore, slightly diminished battery life. Obviously, there are times when you just don't want to hear the current song, in which case, you should skip it. I'm just pointing out that frequent song-skipping can reduce battery life. Do what you will with the information.

- **Don't use the equalizer** There's only anecdotal evidence to support this, but some users have reported that using any equalizer setting (see Chapter 3) other than "none" can reduce battery life.

- **Turn the Zune all the way off** As you learned in Chapter 1, holding down the Play/Pause button for a few seconds turns the Zune off. Except that it really doesn't: It puts the Zune into a low-power standby mode. (If there's no activity for a day, *then* the Zune shuts down all the way.) That's how it's able to perk right up again the moment you press a button. But it also consumes precious power. To force the Zune to turn off (and save the battery), hold down the Back and Down buttons simultaneously for a few seconds. The only downside to this approach is that when you turn your Zune on again, you'll have to wait several seconds while it boots up. But if it nets you an extra hour or two of power, isn't it worth it?

Of course, all these tips will get you only so far. To really maximize battery life, you should pack a portable charger. See Chapter 11 for all kinds of batteries, car kits, and other on-the-go power solutions. And see Chapter 12 for information on replacing a Zune battery that's old, worn out, and no longer holding its charge like it used to.

Repair a Broken Zune

Cracked screen? Dead hard drive? These and other physical ailments may sound like the end of the road for your Zune, but repairs are possible. See Chapter 11 for information on replacement hard drives, batteries, and the like. Or just head straight to the Zune parts store at Rapid Repair (www.rapidrepair.com/shop/microsoft-zune-parts.html).

Of course, a video is worth a thousand pictures. If you want to see firsthand how to take your Zune apart (so you can replace the screen, battery, hard drive, etc.), there's a video that demonstrates it: http://tinyurl.com/ytxr6t.

Fix Your Songs

It's not uncommon to have a music collection that derives from a variety of sources. For instance, you might have MP3s you downloaded from Napster during its music-swapping heyday, songs you ripped from CDs, music from Zune Marketplace or another online service, and perhaps even some tracks a friend gave you. Perhaps you've even created digital audio files from your old albums or cassettes (see Chapter 5).

Such an eclectic library is likely to have some problems. For example, it's quite likely that the volume levels aren't consistent across all your songs. If you frequently find yourself having to raise or lower your Zune's volume with each new song that plays, it's precisely because your music came from different sources.

Likewise, the ID3 tags—or *metadata*—attached to each song might not be accurate. This is especially true of songs downloaded from file-sharing services or songs ripped from CDs back in the old days, before online music databases were readily available. Thus, you might have some songs with the correct title and artist, for example, but the wrong album name. Little glitches like that can make library navigation both challenging and frustrating.

Finally, there's the issue of album art. Whenever you play a song on your Zune, you should see the appropriate album cover on the screen. If you don't, it's because the artwork is missing. Or perhaps you're seeing the wrong artwork for a particular song. Whatever the case, it certainly can be annoying.

Good news: It's possible to correct all of these problems. Let's start with volume level.

All these wrinkles represent another point in favor of a Zune Pass subscription. If you get all your music from the same place, it should have consistent volume levels, accurate metadata, and album art. In fact, if you do subscribe to Zune Pass, I recommend using it to rebuild your library, just for consistency's sake. Ditch your old collection (that is, move it to a DVD or external hard drive), and then re-download all your songs from Zune Marketplace. It might take some time, but in the end, you'll have a pristine, perfect library.

Fix Volume Levels

Also known as *normalizing*, volume leveling is the process of scanning your music library and raising or lowering the volume of each track so that it's consistent.

The tracks themselves don't undergo any changes; thus, it's completely safe to perform this process. I've done it myself, and with excellent results.

My volume-leveling tool of choice is called MP3Gain, which is widely regarded as one of the best utilities for normalizing audio files. It's easy to use, effective, and, best of all, free. Here's how to level your library:

NOTE *One important caveat here: MP3Gain normalizes only MP3 files, not the tracks you purchase or download from Zune Marketplace. If you want to normalize those kinds of songs as well, I recommend a program called Media Monkey (www.mediamonkey.com). It's a freebie as well.*

1. Download and install MP3Gain from the Web (http://mp3gain .sourceforge.net).

2. Click Add Folder and then select the folder containing your MP3s.

3. Choose a method of volume analysis: album or track. When you analyze by album, MP3Gain focuses on all the songs in any given album, relative to each other. When you analyze by track, it's like your entire library is one big album: MP3Gain calculates the volume level for each individual song. I recommend the latter option, as our goal here is to achieve consistent levels for your entire library.

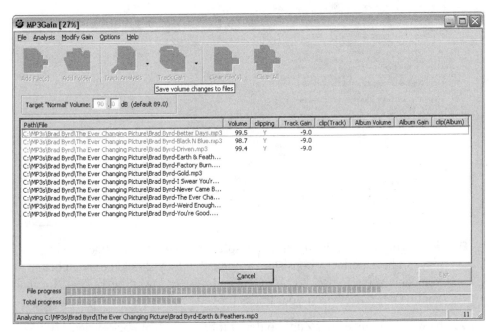

4. By default, MP3Gain strives for a volume level of 89 decibels (dB), but you can change this value if you like in the Target "Normal" Volume box provided. After that, click the Track Analysis button, and then be prepared to wait while the program analyzes your library. It's worth noting at this point that MP3Gain makes no changes to the encoding of the MP3 files themselves, meaning song quality won't be affected. What's more, the program stores analysis and undo information inside each file's metadata, so you can reverse the process or make additional changes later on. In other words, the volume adjustments are only semi-permanent.

5. Once MP3Gain completes the analysis, you can review the results (see the included Help file for detailed descriptions of what everything means), or just go ahead and start the leveling procedure by clicking Track Gain. (Again, you have the option of adjusting the volume by album instead, but for our purposes, stick with track.) This will take even longer than the analysis, so be prepared to wait awhile.

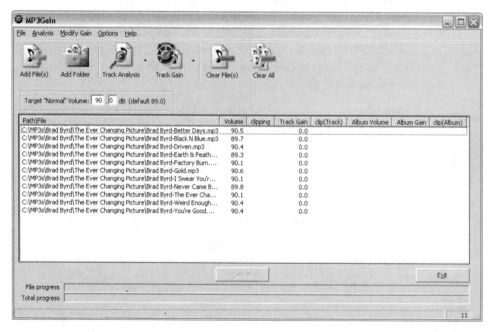

6. When you're done, fire up the Zune software, and test your tracks. They may not have perfectly consistent volume, but they should be much better. You can always go back to MP3Gain and raise or lower the Target "Normal" Volume a few decibels if your tracks prove to be too soft or too loud.

7. Now synchronize your Zune so that it inherits the volume-leveled MP3s.

Fix Metadata

Your songs' ID3 tags, also known as metadata, are arguably their most important asset, as they're the key to identification and organization. Think of metadata as a little database associated with each song. Within that database are "tags" that identify the song name, artist, album, music genre, release year, and more. Obviously, those tags tell more about the file than a file name ever could; you could have an MP3 called *JQ7b$.mp3*, but as long as it has accurate tags, your Zune will identify it as "Feel Like Myself" by Brendan Benson off the *Alternative to Love* album.

> **NOTE** *The Zune Help files refer to metadata as "media data."*

As noted earlier, songs obtained from peer-to-peer software and other questionable sources are notorious for having messed-up tags. Even CD rips can produce incomplete tags if the software wasn't configured to fetch album data from the Internet. In short, there's every chance that at least some of the songs in your library have missing or inaccurate metadata.

> **NOTE** *Every song you purchase or download from Zune Marketplace should have accurate metadata, so there's no need to worry about those tracks. The idea here is to fix the ones you imported into the Zune software from your existing library.*

Fortunately, the Zune software can fix metadata, either manually or automatically. The latter method is best, though it may not always work. That's because it relies on an Internet database to supply the information, and you may have some albums that aren't in the database. In that case, you'll need to fix the metadata manually—but let's come back to that in a bit.

For starters, let's answer a key question: How can you tell if a song in your library has messed-up metadata? Looking at the Expanded Tile or Details view in the details pane might reveal some clues, like if a song shows no album title or something else really obvious. More likely is that you'll hear a song on your Zune and notice an inaccurate name, artist, or album.

> **NOTE** *Album art is, technically speaking, also part of a song's or album's metadata, but there's a somewhat different process to fixing it. See the next section "Fix Album Art."*

When that happens, you can't fix the metadata right on your Zune—but you can flag the song (see Chapter 3) so that you'll remember to attend to it the next time you run the Zune software. As you may recall, items flagged on your Zune appear in the Zune software "inbox."

13

So how do you actually repair or update a song's metadata? Let's start with the semi-automated method:

1. Right-click any song in your library, and choose Change Album Info.

2. The Zune Software will search for the song in an online database. In most cases, it should find a match, though if the metadata was heavily inaccurate or incomplete, the search may come up empty. In that case, you can try using the Refine Your Search option.

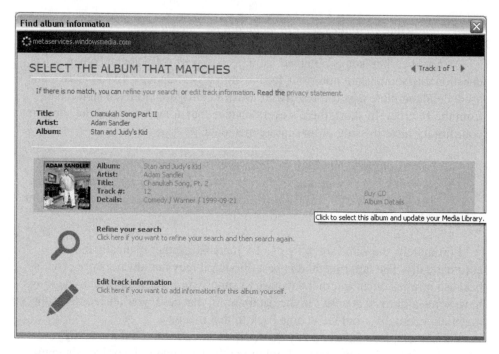

3. If it does find a match and the corresponding album/artist/track info looks correct, click to apply the metadata. As an added bonus, this will also retrieve and apply the corresponding album art.

That's all there is to it. However, there may be times when you want to modify the metadata yourself. It's a snap:

1. Right-click any song in your library, and choose Edit Track Info.

2. You'll see fields for all kinds of metadata (some of it is quite superfluous, in my humble opinion, but you could theoretically use it to create hyper-specific auto-playlists). Fill in one or more fields with whatever information you want. Click the Artist Info tab for even more metadata choices.

3. When you've filled everything in to your liking, click OK, and you're done.

For manual and automatic metadata editing alike, you can hold down the CTRL key to select more than one song at a time. Then right-click any one of them, and choose the desired option.

13

The Zune software's Help files cover metadata editing in even more detail, so I'll refer you there if you want to learn more about this subject. Just press F1, click the Search tab, and then type **edit media information** in the Search field.

Fix Album Art

It's easy to see which albums in your library have artwork attached and which don't. Under the Library heading in the navigation pane, click Album. You should see thumbnail representations of each album; if not, click the Change Layout icon above the details pane, and choose either Icon or Tile. Ultimately, your album collection should look something like this:

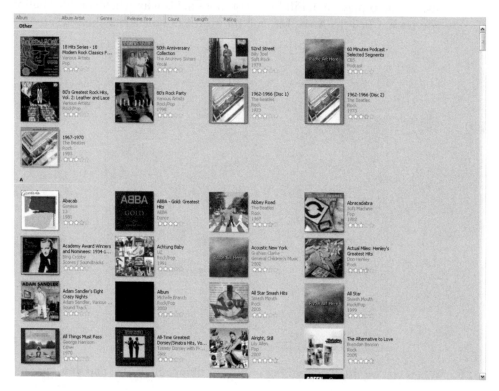

Notice that in my library, most albums have artwork, but a few don't. For those, there's a colorful bit of generic art and the words "Paste Art Here." It's an easy matter to supply the missing artwork for these albums. All you need to do is dig up the appropriate artwork on the Internet, copy it, and then paste it. Here's how:

1. Pick an album that's missing artwork. In my example, I've chosen *Essential Bob Dylan*. You don't actually need to click the album or anything at this point; just zero in on the album title.

2. Open your Web browser and head to Amazon.com. There are other online sources for album art, but to me, this is one of the best.

3. Search for the album in question, and then click the resulting link to visit the product page for the album. You should see a nice big image of the album art.

4. Right-click the image and choose Copy (or Copy Image if you're using the Firefox Web browser).

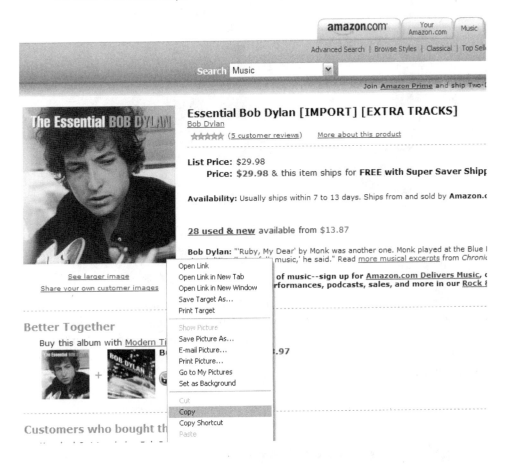

5. Return to the Zune software, right-click the image that says "Paste Art Here," and choose Paste Album Art.

6. Presto! You've just added the artwork for every track in that album. Synchronize your Zune, and you should see the art the next time you play those songs.

Repeat this as necessary for other albums in your library. It's worth noting, too, that when you use the Zune software's Change Album Info auto-update feature to modify the metadata for any songs or albums (as described in the previous section), you'll likely obtain the album art as well—thus rendering this process unnecessary.

 *If you can't find a particular album at Amazon.com, try www.albumart.org.*

Frequently Asked Questions

As noted earlier, Microsoft maintains its own Frequently Asked Questions (FAQ) page for the Zune (http://tinyurl.com/35o4ow). I've got a few questions and answers of my own to add:

■ **My computer died and took my Zune Marketplace purchases/ downloads with it. How do I replace them?** This is one area where Microsoft and Zune Marketplace beat Apple and iTunes hands down.

After you've fixed your PC and reinstalled the Zune software, sign in to your Zune account. Then click Account Management, and choose Restore Library. Follow the instructions from there to retrieve any and all songs you've purchased from Zune Marketplace or downloaded via Zune Pass.

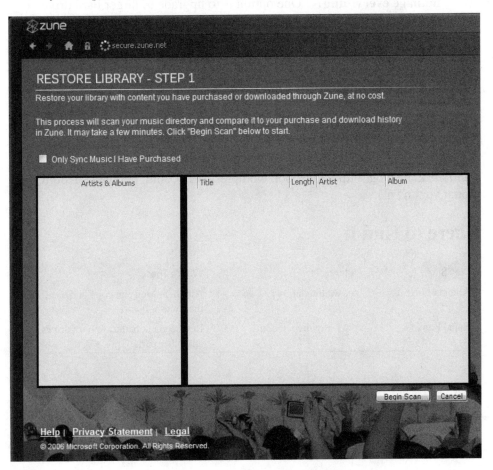

■ **Why doesn't the Zune Software show the media I just added?**   When you add new media to one or more of your monitored folders, don't be surprised if the Zune software doesn't immediately display it. Sometimes, it takes a few minutes for the program to detect the presence of new stuff.

■ **The songs I downloaded from Zune Marketplace won't play anymore. What happened?**   Most likely, your Zune Pass trial subscription expired. You have to maintain an active subscription; otherwise, your songs will "deactivate" after 30 days. See Chapter 2 for more details.

■ **Can I use my Zune Pass on more than one computer?**   Yep, you can use it on up to three.

■ **I have more media than will fit on my Zune's hard drive. How can I manage everything?**   One option is to upgrade to larger hard drive (see Chapter 11). Another is to take advantage of the Zune software's Random Sync Priority option. In the navigation pane, right-click your Zune, and then click Set Up Sync. Assuming you've configured your Zune to synchronize automatically, you'll see a Random Sync Priority check box below the playlist list. Enabling it shuffles your playlists; those that aren't already present on your Zune are synced first. The playlists at the bottom of the list are automatically removed to make room for the new stuff.

I'll answer more frequently asked questions on the *How to Do Everything with Your Zune* blog (http://zunebook.wordpress.com). And, of course, feel free to submit your own.

Where to Find It

Web Site	Address	What's There
Albumart.org	www.albumart.org	Album art you can copy and paste into the Zune software
Rapid Repair	www.rapidrepair.com	Replacement batteries, hard drives, and other parts

Index

22Moo, 266

A

AAC (*See* Advanced Audio Coding)
About menu, 84
AC adapters, 22, 24
Accessories, 245–266
    battery chargers, 263–265
    for car, 252–255
    car mounts, 253
    cases, 246–249
    headphones, replacement, 260–262
    paint, custom, 251
    resource Web sites for, 266
    screen protection, 252
    skins, 250–251
    speakers, 258–259
    stereo connections, 254–255
    TV connections, 255–257
    virtual display, 262
Action Jacket, 247
Active Downloads option, 94
Actors listing, 100
Add To Now Playing, 89
Advanced Audio Coding (AAC), 7, 40, 144–145, 238
Album art, 9, 166
    display of, 73
    fixing, 303–306
    and metadata repair, 298
    quality of, 288
Album name, 73
Albumart.org, 303–306, 308
Albums:
    downloading, 136–137
    Marketplace listing of, 96
    Marketplace playing of, 120
    order of, 64
    playing single, 118
    purchasing, 47–48, 51–52
    rating of, 123
    selecting, 66–67
    sharing (*see* Media sharing)
    vinyl, 156
    Your Zune listing of, 99
Albums menu, 66–67
All Pictures option, 102
All Songs Considered (from NPR), 145
All Video option, 100
Alphabetic organization, 66, 67
"Already in library" message, 285
Altec Lansing, 266
Altec Lansing M604 Portable Speaker System for Zune, 258
Amazon Marketplace, 143
Antenna, radio, 27, 180, 207
AntennaWeb.org, 180
Apple, 143, 192, 214, 230
Applian Technologies, 230
Apply As Background option, 78, 202
Armband cases, 247
Articles in titles, 66, 67
Artist(s), 65, 67
    favorite "new," 138
    Marketplace listing by, 94–95
    Marketplace playing of, 120
    name of, 73
    Your Zune listing by, 99
Artwork, custom, 251
Aspect ratio, 170, 171
Audacity (program), 157
Audible.com, 13, 223–224, 226–228, 230
Audio format, 149–151
Audio player, default, 214
Audiobooks, 13, 223–230
    from CDs/cassette tapes, 230
    downloading, 226–229
    resources for, 223–226, 230
AudioBooksForFree.com, 225
Auto playlists, 161–164
Automatic synchronization, 53–55
AV jack, 25

B

Back button:
    illustration of, 24
    operation of, 25
    return to Main menu with, 29, 61
    return to now-playing screen with, 62, 73
    return to previous screen with, 27, 77
Background, 29–32
    creating unique, 32
    custom, 31–32
    themes for, 83
Backlight:
    and battery life, 83
    duration of, 297
    and e-books, 274
    and inactivity, 62
Backward button, 25
Basic online status, 84, 234
Batteries:
    charging, 21–24, 57
    replacement of, 276–277
Battery chargers, 263–265, 297
Battery gauge, 74
Battery life:
    and backlight, 83
    maximizing, 296–297
    and wireless option, 81

Belkin, 20, 23, 248, 249, 253, 263, 266
Belt-clip cases, 247
Billboard Chart, 93
Bit rate, 114, 151–152
Blog(s):
    author's, xii, 56, 102, 288
    Zunester, 32
Bookmarks, 76
Books on tape, 158
BoxWave ClearTouch Anti-Glare, 252
Brightness, screen, 83, 297
Broadcast bleed, 255
Burning disks:
    CDs, 112, 125–128
    MP3 CDs, 128

C

Cables:
    A/V output, 257
    stereo, 254
    TV output, 257
Car accessories, 252–255
Car kits, 22
Car mounts, 253
Car stereos, 210
Cases, 246–249
    armband, 247
    belt-clip, 247
    kickstand, 248
    leather, 248
    protective, 249
    resource Web sites for, 249
Cassette adapters, 254
Cassette players, 5, 156
Cassette tapes:
    of audiobooks, 230
    books on, 224
    ripping from, 155–158
Caulton, David, 32
CD players, 5
CD ripping, 147–155
    and audio format, 149–151
    of audiobooks, 230
    automation options, 154
    and bit rate, 151–152
    and copy protection, 153
    process of, 152–154
    storing music from, 147–149
CD-R media, 126
CD-RW drive, 126

CDs (compact discs):
    books on, 224
    burning, 112, 125–128
    digital downloads vs., 154–155
    and history of portable music players, 5
    MP3, 128
    music from, 9
    playing, 128
    resource Web sites for, 143
    and sound quality, 144, 152
    See also CD ripping
Channel Frederator, 185
Chargers, battery, 263–265, 297
Charging batteries, 21–24, 57
Charts, Marketplace, 93
Child accounts, 45
Clearing:
    of expired song tracks, 137
    of now-playing screen, 114
    of search bar, 111
Coding Workshop, The, 192
Colorware, 251, 266
Community menu, 80, 234, 235, 240
Compact discs (See CDs)
Connecting Zune to your PC, 53–57
    automatic synchronization, 53–55
    "guest" synchronization, 56–57
    manual synchronization, 55
Content Scrambling System (CSS), 171
Control pad, 25–27
    community, 80
    menu navigation, 26
    music, 26, 71, 117–118
    photo, 27
    picture, 77–78, 201
    radio, 27, 207
    rotation of, 30
    video, 27, 75
Copy protection, 41, 50, 153, 285
Crucial.com, 18, 19
CSS (Content Scrambling System), 171
Custom artwork, 251
Custom backgrounds, 31–32

D

Date(s):
    playlists created by, 163–164
    view photos by, 75, 200
Date Taken, 102
DecalGirl, 250, 251, 266
Decals, 250–251
DeepDiscount.com, 143
Deleting:
    of playlists, 89, 166
    of songs, 89
Detailed online status, 84, 234
Details pane, 103–107
    layout selector, 104–107
    resizing, 116–117, 136
Details view, 106
Diamond Multimedia PMP300, 6
Digital audio players, 6–7
Digital Rights Management (DRM) technology, 50, 290
Disconnecting Zune, 57
Display menu, 82–83
DivX video format, 285–286
DLO, 247, 249, 254–256, 264, 266
Double-click, 89, 92, 101
Downloading:
    of albums, 136–137
    of audiobooks, 226–229
    defined, 46
    of podcasts, 216–217
    of received songs, 242
    of songs, 133–136
    of TV shows, 178
    of YouTube videos, 190–191
    with Zune Pass, 49
    of Zune software/updates, 36
Downloads:
    active, 94
    CDs vs. digital, 154–155
Drag-and-drop synchronization, 55
DRM technology (See Digital Rights Management technology)
DRM-free alternatives, 145–147
DVD Decrypter, 175
DVD ripping, 169–177
    free software for, 174–177
    legal issues, 171
    M2Convert for Zune software, 170, 171

Pocket DVD Wizard, 171–172
PQ DVD to Zune Converter, 172–173
Xilisoft DVD to Zune Converter, 173–174
DVD to Zune Converter, 173–174
DVD±RW drive, 126
DVDs:
  converting, 294
  renting, 178
  video from, 10
DVD-WMV converter, 174–177, 192
DVR-MS format, 168, 181, 286

E

Earbud headphones, 27
E-books, 269–274
  and backlight setting, 274
  converting, 271–273
  public-domain, 270–271
  reading, 273
Edit In List Pane, 89
E-mail, author's, xii
EMI (music label), 41, 143, 144
EMusic, 145–147
End Slideshow option, 78–79, 202
Equalizer setting, 82, 297
EReader.com, 270
ERightSoft, 192
Etymotic 6i Isolator, 261
Executive, Speck, 248
Expansion cards, 20
External hard drive, 239
External hard drives, 19, 20
EZGear, 264, 266

F

FairPlay, 50
Family settings, 45
FAQs (*See* Frequently Asked Questions)
Favorites:
  artists, 138
  podcasts, 222
  TV shows, 177
FeedYourZune, 186–187, 192
Fictionwise.com, 270

File extensions, 239
File formats:
  music, 40, 149–151
  photo, 55
  video, 55, 168–169
File sharing, 239, 243
File storage, 13–14
Files:
  copying, 281–285
  location of, 89
Firmware:
  defined, 52
  updating, 37–38, 295–296
  version of, 84
Flag option:
  music, 72, 88, 89, 133
  picture, 79, 202
Flash memory, 6, 7, 17
FLV format, 168
FM radio, Zune, 205–210
  advantages of, 206
  car stereo and, 210
  headphones as antenna for, 207
  NPR on, 145
  playback controls for, 209
  and RBDS, 209
  station presets, 208
  tuning, 207–208
  uniqueness of, 16
FM transmitter, 210, 254–255
Folder monitoring, 43–44
  for audio podcasts, 218
  for music, 148–149
  for video podcasts, 190
Folders:
  adding media, 42–44
  creating, 281–282
  media, 42–44
  monitoring, 43–44
  pictures sorted by, 102
  view photos by, 75, 200
Folio Kickstand Case, 248
Formats, file (*see* File formats)
Forward button, 25
Free converters, 174–177
Frequently Asked Questions (FAQs), 291, 306–308

G

Games, 16, 17
GB (gigabyte), 149

Genre(s), 67–69
  Marketplace listing by, 98
  videos listed by, 100
  Your Zune listing by, 99
Genre tags, 221
Gigabyte (GB), 149
GigaSize, 239
Glare, 252
Google Video, 10, 191
Graphic equalizer, 114
"Guest" synchronization, 56–57

H

H.264 format, 168–169
Hack(s):
  for copying files, 282–285
  defined, 268
  for Divx videos, 285–286
  for external-hard-drive use, 277–282
  finding other, 286–287
  for reading books/magazines on Zune, 268–274
  resources for, 288
  for TV-show conversion, 285
Hammacher Schlemmer iPod Digital Drumsticks, 246
HandHelditems, 257
Hard drives:
  description of, 19
  for file storage, 13–14
  illustration of, 20
  installing larger, 274–276
  Zune used as external, 239, 277–282
Hauppauge, 180
HBO Documentary Films, 185
HD antenna, 180
HDTV (high-definition TV), 179
Headphone jack, 25
Headphones:
  as antenna, 27, 207
  and driving, 252
  and pause function, 62
  replacement, 260–262
  tangle prevention for, 262
Help:
  online, 290–294
  by phone, 294
High-definition TV (HDTV), 179

Hi-Speed USB 2.0 five-port PCI card, 20
Hi-Speed USB 2.0 PC card, 20
Hold switch:
  illustration of, 24
  as inoperable controls, 295
  for locking radio controls, 209
  operation of, 24–25
Home movies, 10
HomeDock, 256

I

Icon view, 105
ID3 tags, 166, 218 (*See also* Metadata)
iFilm, 10
In Library button, 243
Inactivity defaults, 62, 73
Inbox option, 80, 235, 240, 242
Incipio, 247, 249
Installation, Zune software (*see* Zune software installation)
Instructables Web site, 274
Instruction manual downloads, 291
Internet, downloading TV shows from, 178
iPod, 7, 8, 16–17, 150
IrfanView, 194, 202
iTunes:
  and AAC format, 145
  audio podcasts from, 213–218
  copy protection on, 144
  and DRM, 50
  format from, 168
  installing, 214–216
  music from, 40–41
  running, 216–217
  system requirements for, 215
  video podcasts from, 188–189

J

Jacks, headphone/AV, 25
JAVOeBuds, 260
JAVOedge, 266
JPEG format, 194
Jpegbook, 269–273

K

Keywords, 102
Kickstand cases, 248
Kingston.com, 18

L

Lala, 143
LAME MP3 encoder, 157
Layout selector, 104–107
Leather cases, 248
Left button:
  music, 71
  video, 75
Legal information, 84
Legal issues (with DVD ripping), 171
Library:
  music, 90–92, 219–221
  photo, 199–200
  pictures, 102
  public, 225, 230
  search of, 110
  video, 100
  view layout selector, 104–107
LibriVox.com, 225, 230
List pane, 111–114
  burn files to disc in, 112
  create/edit playlists in, 112
  edit in, 89
  Now Playing display in, 114
  resizing, 114–116
  sync content in, 112
Local music, 118
Locking controls, 24–25, 295
Logitech X-240, 259
Lossless format, 150

M

M2Convert for Zune, 170, 171
M2Solutions, Inc., 192
M4V format, 186
M604 Portable Speaker System for Zune, 258
Magazines, 269
Make Magazine, 288
Manual synchronization, 55
Manuals, instruction, 291
Marketplace (*see* Zune Marketplace)

MB (megabyte), 149
Me option, 80, 235
Media:
  adding, 38–44, 307
  displaying, 307
  folders for, 42–44
  managing, 308
  music, 39–42
  sharing, with Xbox 360, 42
  and syncing, 40
Media Center PCs (*see* Windows Media Center PCs)
Media sharing, 14–15, 231–243
  and downloading/buying music, 242
  enabling wireless communication for, 233
  of files, 239
  limitations on, 238
  receive feature of, 240–241
  and searching for music, 243
  and searching for Zunes, 234–235
  send feature of, 236–238
  setting online status for, 234
  synchronizing, 241–242
Megabyte (MB), 149
Menu navigation, 26
Message boards, 32, 293
Message forums, 286
Metadata, 68, 166, 298, 301–303
Microsoft:
  phone number for, 294
  products from, 254, 257, 261, 265
  troubleshooting Zune through, 291
Microsoft points (*see* Zune Points)
Microsoft support, 43, 45
Modifying interface, 114–117
Monster CarPlay Wireless Plus, 254
MOV format, 186
Movies, downloading, 17
Moving Picture Experts Group (MPEG), 7
MP3(s):
  as audio format, 40, 149–151
  converting audible files into, 228–229
  defined, 7
  and DRM, 145

podcasts as, 12
sharing, 238
sources for, 10
MP3 CDs, 128
MP3Gain, 299–300
MP4 format, 168
MPEG4 format, 168–169
MSN account, 45
MTV News, 185
Music, 39–42, 131–166
    capabilities for, 8–10
    from cassette tapes, 155–158
    from CDs, 143, 147–155
    control pad for, 26
    controls, 61–63
    from eMusic, 145–147
    formats for, 40
    from non-Zune sources,
        40–42
    from NPR, 145
    from online services,
        143–147
    order of, 64
    during photo slideshows, 202
    playlists of, 158–166
    and podcasts, 219–221
    rating, 26
    sharing (see Media sharing)
    and slideshow, 79, 202
    and song tags/album art,
        158–166
    streaming from PC to Xbox
        360, 123–125
    from Zune Marketplace, 47,
        132–143
Music, playing, on your PC,
    117–123
    local music, 118
    rating songs, 121–123
    Zune Marketplace music,
        119–121
Music menu, 63–74
    albums, 66–67
    alphabetizing articles, 66, 67
    artists, 67
    categories of organization,
        63–64
    genres, 67–69
    hierarchy of, 60
    and ID3 tags/metadata, 65
    and left/right selection, 66
    now-playing screen displays,
        73–74

playback options, 71–73
and playlists, 69–70
and Quick List, 70
and Shuffle All option, 65
songs, 65–66
Music navigation, 88–99
    library, 90–92
    marketplace, 92–98
    playlists, 88–89
    your Zune, 98
Music option, 81–82
Music subscription, 16
Music-download services, 9
Mute button, 209
MyTV ToGo, 181

N

Napster, 41, 50
National Geographic Video
    Shorts, 185
"Native" H.264 format, 169
"Native" MPEG4 format, 169
Navigation, 26
Navigation pane, 88–102
    music (see music navigation)
    pictures, 101–102
    resizing, 116
    videos, 99–101
NBC Nightly News, 185
Nearby option, 80, 234
Non-Zune sources, 40–42
Normalizing volume, 298–300
Now-playing screen, 62,
    73–74, 114
NPR, 145, 212
NTSC (TV system), 83

O

Octavio 1, 258–259
Okoker DVD to Zune
    Converter, 171
OK/Select button:
    illustration of, 24
    photo, 78
    variable function of, 26, 27
    video, 75
Online help, 290–294
Online music services, 10,
    143–147
    and AAC files, 144–145
    and copy protection, 50

music from, 41
and sound quality, 144
Online status, 84, 234
Open File Location, 89
Opening Zune case, 276
Operating systems, 18
Orientation, screen, 75, 77, 201
OTA (over-the-air)
    broadcasts, 179
Outlook synchronization, 16
Over-the-air (OTA)
    broadcasts, 179

P

Paint, custom, 251
PAL (TV system), 83
Pausing music, 62
PC(s) (personal computers):
    charging from, 21–22
    connecting Zune to your,
        53–57
    disconnecting Zune from
        your, 57
    hard drive in, 19
    operating system of, 18
    playing music on (see Music
        on PC, playing)
    processor of, 18
    RAM in, 18
    streaming music to Xbox
        360 from, 123–125
    USB port on, 19–20
    Zune requirements for,
        18–21
PCI cards, 20
Perooz, 269
Personal computers (See PC(s))
Phones, help by, 294
Photos (see Pictures)
Pictures, 193–202
    control pad for, 27
    format, 194
    formats for, 55
    and music, 202
    navigating, 101–102
    from non-Zune software,
        197–198
    playback options, 201–202
    received, 241, 242
    resource Web site for, 202
    selecting, 197
    sizes/resolutions of, 198–199

Pictures (*Cont.*)
    syncing, 194–197
    viewing, 200–202
    Zune capabilities for, 11
    Zune Photo Library for,
      199–200
Pictures menu, 75, 77–79
    hierarchy of, 60
    and music, 79
    playback options, 78–79
    reading e-books with, 273
    and received pictures, 240
    sample photos, 77
    screen rotation, 77
Pictures option, 82
Plastic tools, 276, 277
Play option, 89
Play Slideshow, 77
Play time, 73
Playback options:
    music, 71–73
    picture, 78–79, 201–202
    radio, 209
    video, 75
Playback order, 118
Playlists, 158–166
    accessing Zune, 48
    of audio podcasts, 218–221
    auto, 161–164
    creating, 88, 112, 159–164
    by date, 163–164
    defined, 69
    deleting/renaming, 166
    editing, 112
    examples of, 158–159
    importance of, 65
    Marketplace, 92
    Marketplace playing of, 121
    navigating, 88–89
    ordering, 112
    picture, 102
    playing, 118
    by ratings, 161–163
    selecting, 69–70
    syncing, 165
    video, 101
    Your Zune listing by, 99
Play/pause indicator, 74
Play/Pause/Power button:
    illustration of, 24
    for music, 62
    operation of, 25
    for radio mute, 209
    startup with, 28

"Plays," 240–241
PlaysForSure, 50
PMP300, 6
Pocket DVD Wizard, 171–172
Podcasts, 185–190, 212–223
    audiobooks from, 225
    defined, 212
    examples of, 212–213
    favorite, 12, 222
    FeedYourZune program,
      186–187
    folder monitoring for, 44
    folders for, 190
    format, 186
    from iTunes, 213–218
    iTunes software, 188–189
    Juice/MyPodder software,
      189–190
    lack of support for, 38
    and music library, 219–221
    organizing playlists of,
      218–221
    playing, 222–223
    playlists of, 159
    sources for, 145
    support for, 17
    as video sources, 11
Podcatching programs,
    189–190
Portable music players, 5–8
Power Pack, 264
PowerStick, 264
PQ DVD to Zune Converter,
    172–173
PQ DVD to Zune Video Suite,
    181, 183
PQDVD.com, 192
Prepaid cards, 139
Preset stations, 208
Processors, PC, 18
ProClip, 253, 266
Progress meter, 73
Project Gutenberg, 270,
    271, 289
Proporta, 249
Protected WMAs, 40
Protective cases, 249
Proximity limits, 234
Public domain:
    audiobooks in, 225, 226
    e-books in, 270–271
Purchasing from Zune
    Marketplace, 137–143

Q

Quick List, 69–70
Quick-scroll, 63
QVGA, 272

R

Rabbit ears, 180
Radio:
    control pad for, 27
    FM (*see* FM radio)
    settings for, 84
    Zune capabilities for, 11–12
Radio antenna, 27
Radio Broadcast Data System
    (RBDS), 209
Radio Data System, 12
Radio Locator, 255
Radio menu, 79
Random access memory (RAM),
    18, 19
Random Sync Priority
    option, 308
Rapid Repair, 274–277, 289,
    297, 308
Rating(s):
    in list pane, 116
    of music, 26, 53, 56, 71,
      121–123, 162
    pictures listed by, 102
    playlists created by, 161–163
    videos listed by, 100
    Your Zune listing by, 99
RBDS (Radio Broadcast Data
    System), 209
Received Pictures, 240
Receiving media, 240–241
Recently Added media, 90, 99,
    100, 102
Registry, Windows, 278–280
Registry hack, 285, 286
Renaming playlists, 89, 166
Repairing broken Zunes,
    297–298
Repeat indicator, 74
Repeat mode, 72, 82
Replay A/V, 228–229
Resetting Zune, 295
Resizing, 114–117, 136
Resolution, picture, 198–199
Restrictions, music, 240–241
Reverse synchronization,
    282–285

Rhapsody, 41
Right button:
    music, 71
    video, 75
Rights restrictions, 238
Ripping:
    of audiobooks, 230
    from cassette tapes, 155–158
    from CDs (*see* CD ripping)
    from DVDs (*see* DVD
        ripping)
Rocketboom, 185
Rotation, screen, 30, 75, 77, 201
Roxio, 181, 192

S

Samples:
    music, 240
    photo, 77
Sampling songs, 47
Screen:
    brightness of, 297
    illustration of, 24
    rotation of, 30, 75, 77, 201
    size of, 16
Screen protection, 252
Search bar, 107–111
Searching:
    for received songs, 243
    for Zunes in vicinity,
        234–235
Seek mode, 207
Send option:
    music, 72
    picture, 79, 202
Send rights, 238
Sending media, 236–238
Set up, 35–57
    connecting Zune to your PC,
        53–57
    disconnecting Zune, 57
    installing Zune software,
        36–52
Settings menu, 80–84
    About menu, 84
    display, 82–83
    music, 81–82
    online status, 84
    pictures, 82
    radio, 84
    sounds, 83
    wireless, 81

Show song list, 71
Shuffle All option, 65, 219–221
Shuffle indicator, 74
Shuffle mode:
    album, 66
    genre, 67
    music, 82, 92, 118
    photo, 78, 201
    song, 72
Shure E3c, 261
Simply Audiobooks, 226
Skins, 250–251
Skip forward/backward
    buttons, 25
Slideshows:
    ending, 78–79
    launching, 77
    viewing, 102
Software:
    for DVD to Zune, 169–177
    Zune (*see* Zune software)
Software interface (*see* Zune
    software interface)
Song name, 73
Song tags, 158, 164, 166 (*See
    also* Metadata)
Songs:
    battery life and skipping, 297
    deactivated, 307
    downloading, 48, 133–136
    fixing, 298–306
    Marketplace listing of, 97
    Marketplace playing of, 119
    order of, 64
    playing, 118
    purchasing, 47–48, 51–52
    rating of, 121–123
    received, 241, 242
    sampling, 47
    selecting, 65–66
    sharing (*see* Media sharing)
    volume of, 298–300
    Your Zune listing of, 99
Songs menu, 65–66
Sony Walkman, 5
Sound quality, 144, 151–152
Sounds, 83
SourceForge, 192
Speakers, 258–259
Speck, 248, 249
Squirting, 14–15
Standby mode, 62, 297
Static, 255

Station presets, 208
Stereo cables, 254
Stereo connections, 254–255
Stereo patch cords, 156
Storage space, 84, 132
Streaming:
    with Replay A/V, 229
    to Xbox 360, 42
    from Zune Marketplace, 133
    with Zune Pass, 49
SUPER conversion software,
    183–185
Sync cables, 21
Sync Results, 99
Synchronization:
    automatic, 53–55
    and copying files, 281–282
    defined, 53
    and disconnecting Zune, 57
    and folder creation,
        281–282
    "guest," 56–57
    manual, 55
    optimizing, 199
    with PC library, 57
    of pictures, 194–197
    of playlists, 165
    random priority of, 308
    of received media with PC,
        241–242
    reverse, 282–285
    as task, 112–113

T

Tags:
    podcast, 221
    song (*see* Metadata;
        Song tags)
Task selectors, 111–114
Television shows (*see* TV shows)
"The" in titles, 66, 67
Themes option, 83
Third-party power sources, 23
Third-party speakers, 259
Thumbnails, 77, 200
Tile view, 106
Time remaining, 73
Timing out (of music), 15
Tools, plastic, 276, 277
ToughSkin, 249
TransDock Micro, 254, 255
Transition time, 82

Troubleshooting, 289–308
  for album art, 303–306
  battery life, 296–297
  FAQs, 306–308
  for metadata, 301–303
  with online help, 290–294
  by phone, 294
  repairing your broken Zune,
    297–298
  resetting your Zune, 295
  resources for, 308
  for songs, 298–306
  updating firmware, 295–296
  for volume levels, 298–300
TuneBase FM for Zune, 253
TunePower, 23
Tutorials, 294
TV connections, 255–257
TV Out option, 83
TV shows:
  converting, 285
  copying, 180–182
  favorite, 177
  and Media Center PCs,
    178–180
  Media Center PCs as source
    for, 178–182
  sources of, 178
  as video sources, 10
TV System option, 83
TV tuner cards, 178–180
Twist interface:
  advantage of, 16
  and music, 63, 65–67
  and navigation, 28
  and pictures, 75
  and playlists, 70
  and videos, 74

U

Universal Serial Bus (USB)
  ports, 19–20, 24, 53, 256
Unprotected WMAs, 40
Updates:
  downloading, 36
  firmware, 295–296
Up/down buttons:
  music, 71
  video, 75
Upgrade(s):
  of battery, 276–277
  for hard drive installation,
    274–276
USB 1.1 ports, 19, 20

USB 2.0 ports, 19, 20
USB ports (See Universal Serial
  Bus ports)
USB protocols, 288
User-authored tutorials, 294

V

VAF Research, 266
Vaja, 249
Vibe, 261
Vidcasts (see Podcasts)
Video(s), 167–192
  control pad for, 27
  conversion software,
    183–185
  from DVDs, 169–177
  favorite TV shows, 177
  formats for, 55, 168–169
  from Internet/home movies,
    183–185
  legal issues, 171
  navigating, 99–101
  order of, 74
  from podcasts, 185–190
  repair, 298
  resource Web sites for, 192
  resume play of, 190
  sharing, 239
  sources for, 10
  from TV, 178–182
  from YouTube, 190–191
Video files, 11
Video podcasts, 11
Video-conversion software,
  183–185
Videos menu, 74–76
  bookmarks, 76
  hierarchy of, 60
  playback options, 75
Views, layout selector for,
  104–107
Vinyl albums, 156
Virtual display, 262
V-Moda, 261, 266
Vodcasts (see Podcasts)
Volume buttons, 25, 29
Volume levels, 298–300
Vongo, 17

W

Wi-Fi, 16, 17
Windows Live ID, 45

Windows Media Audio (WMA):
  advantage of, 149
  bit rate for, 152
  compatibility of, 149
  as format, 7, 40, 238
  lossless format, 150
Windows Media Center PCs,
  168, 178–182
  copying TV shows from,
    180–182
  defined, 178–180
  for TV shows, 178–182
Windows Media Encoder 9, 174
Windows Media Player, 181
Windows Media Player 11,
  117, 119
Windows Media Video
  (WMV), 168
Windows Movie Maker, 182
Windows .NET Framework, 175
Windows registry, 278–280
Windows versions, 37
Windows Vista, 18, 182
Windows XP, 18
Windows XP Media Center
  Edition, 18
WinTV-HVR-950, 180
Wireless communication:
  and battery life, 296
  enabling, 233
Wireless option, 81
Wireless radio, 80
WMA (See Windows Media
  Audio)
WMV (Windows Media
  Video), 168

X

Xbox 360:
  charging from, 22, 23
  media sharing with, 15
  sharing media with, 42
  streaming music from PC to,
    123–125
Xilisoft, 173–174, 192

Y

Yahoo music service, 41
Yahoo Music Unlimited, 50
Year:
  Marketplace listing by, 98
  Your Zune listing by, 99

Your Zune, 99
YouSendIt, 239
YouTube, 10, 168, 190–191

Z

Zoom In option, 78, 201
ZPL file extension, 89
Zune:
    About menu, 84
    audiobook feature of, 13
    background image, 29–32
    capacity of, 4
    charging, 21–24
    Community menu, 80
    controls, 24–27, 61–63
    defined, 52
    file-storage feature of, 13–14
    future of, 17
    hierarchy of software, 60–61
    iPod vs., 16–17
    music feature of, 8–10
    Music menu, 63–74
    music-sharing feature of,
        14–15
    and PC requirements, 18–21
    photo feature of, 11
    Pictures menu, 75, 77–79
    podcast feature of, 12
    proximity limits for, 234
    radio feature of, 11–12
    Radio menu, 79
    repairing your broken,
        297–298
    resetting, 295
    resources about, 32–33
    Settings menu, 80–84
    starting, 28–29
    turning off your, 297
    video feature of, 10–11
    Videos menu, 74–76
    warranty and opening case
        of, 276
    Web site for, 140
    Xbox-360-sharing feature
        of, 15
Zune account:
    accessing, 140
    restoring library from,
        306–307
Zune account signup, 44–52
    definitions, 52
    and DRM technology, 50

family settings/child
    accounts, 45
and Zune Marketplace,
    46–49
and Zune Pass, 49–50
and Zune Points, 51–52
Zune A/V Output Cable, 257
Zune Boards, 286, 289, 292, 293
Zune Car Pack with FM
    Transmitter, 254
Zune Clear Screen Overlay
    Protector, 252
Zune controls, 61–63
    Back button, 24, 25, 61
    headphone/AV jack, 25
    and headphones, 62
    Hold switch, 24–25
    inactivity defaults, 62
    OK/Select button, 24, 26, 27
    Play/Pause button, 62
    Play/Pause/Power button,
        24, 25
    Quick-scroll, 63
    See also Control pad
Zune Dual Connect Remote, 265
Zune Home A/V Pack, 257
Zune instruction manual
    downloads, 291
Zune Marketplace, 92–98
    accurate metadata from, 301
    active downloads, 94
    album, 96
    artist, 94–95
    capabilities of, 46–49
    charts, 93
    defined, 52
    genre, 98
    limited media on, 17
    Microsoft Web page for, 121
    music downloads from, 9, 10
    music from, 132–143
    and music sharing, 241
    as music subscription
        service, 16
    playlists, 92
    search of, 110
    sharing music from, 238
    songs, 97
    troubleshooting, 290
    year, 98
Zune Marketplace music,
    132–143
    album downloads, 136–137

album purchases, 141
buying from, 137–143
downloading, 133–137
favorite "new" artists, 1
playing, 119–121
purchasing from, 137–14
song downloads, 133–136
song purchases, 141–143
streaming, 133
subscription, 133–137
and Zune points, 139–140
Zune Micro-Suede Slip
    Case, 247
Zune Movie Video
    Converter, 173
Zune Pass:
    consistency with, 298
    defined, 49, 52
    downloads/streaming/
        copying with, 49–50
    with multiple computers, 308
    and music, 42, 242
    subscription/trial
        subscription to, 133, 307
Zune Photo Library, 199–200
Zune Points:
    adding, 139–140
    buying, 48
    cost of, 139
    defined, 52
    obtaining, 52
    purchasing music with,
        51–52
Zune Premium Earphones, 261
Zune software, 9
    defined, 52
    downloading updates for, 36
    troubleshooting, 291
Zune software installation, 36–52
    downloading software/
        updates, 36
    and firmware, 37–38
    media, 38–44
    signup for Zune account,
        44–52
    and syncing, 40
    and Windows versions, 37
Zune software interface, 85–128
    CD burning, 125–128
    CD playing on PC, 128
    details pane, 103–107
    elements of, 86, 87

–143

88

search bar, 107–111
streaming music from PC to
    Xbox 360, 123–125
Zune Thoughts, 32, 293
Zune Travel Pack, 265
Zune TVWatcher, 182
Zune users, 291, 292
Zune VG, 262

Zune Wallpapers, 31
Zunemytube plug-in, 190–191
Zune.net, 33, 266
Zunerama Web site, 32, 33, 238,
    262, 293
Zune-related information, xii
Zunester, 32
ZuneTVWatcher, 192